Blissful
Marriage
A Practical Islamic Guide

Blissful Marriage

A Practical Islamic Guide

[NEW EDITION]

Drs. Ekram and M. Rida Beshir

amana publications

First Edition
2003 AC/1424 AH

Second Edition
2005 AC/1426 AH
Reprint
2017 AC/1438 AH

© Copyright 2003 AC/1424 AH
amana publications
10710 Tucker Street
Beltsville, MD 20705-2223 USA
Tel. 301-595-5777, 800-660-1777
Fax 301-595-5888, 240-250-3000
Email: amana@amana-corp.com
Website: www.amanapublications.com
1-59008-039-4 (10-digit ISBN) / 978-1-59008-039-9 (13-digit ISBN)
Library of Congress Cataloging-in-Publication Data

Beshir, Ekram.
    Blissful marriage : a practical Islamic guide / Ekram and M. Rida
Beshir. -- New ed.
    p. cm.
    Includes bibliographical references.
    ISBN 1-59008-039-4
    1. Family--Religious aspects--Islam. 2. Family--Religious life.
 3. Family--Koranic teaching. 4. Muslim families--North America
--Social conditions.   I. Beshir, Mohamed Rida. II. Title.
    HQ525.I8B47 2005
    297.5'77--dc22

2005026978

Printed by Mega Printing in Turkey

ACKNOWLEDGMENT

We would like to express our sincere gratitude to our daughter Hoda for the endless hours she spent in front of the computer, the tireless dedication she showed in editing this book, and the gracious patience that she conducted herself with through the entire experience. May Allah keep her always patient and dedicated to the Islamic way of life and reward her with the best rewards.

We also like to express our sincere thanks to our son-in-law Mohamed Haroun for his help in writing the Arabic text of the *ahadeeth* of the prophet *SAAW* and helping in verifying the sources of theses *ahadeeth.*

We would also like to express our sincere gratitude to all our children, Amirah, Hoda, Noha, and Sumaiya, for all their help with this book. We recognize that the time spent writing this book was precious time that we could have spent with our children; however, because of our children's maturity, they themselves encouraged us to embark on this project for the benefit of Muslims everywhere. May Allah reward them and all the dedicated Muslim boys and girls who struggle in the path of truth.

Drs. Ekram and M. Rida Beshir

Contents

Preface

To our parents who taught us the pure Islamic creed (*Aqeedah*) in a very simple yet effective way which with the grace of Allah, ensured our love, loyalty, and adherence to this wonderful *Deen* of Islam.

To our beloved children: Amirah, Hoda, Noha, and Sumaiya, because of whom we hope Allah will have mercy on us and admit us into paradise.

To our dear sons Mohamed and Mohamed, whom we are blessed to have in our family.

To those who know what it is to share their laughter, their tears, and their innermost thoughts, to share their breakfasts, lunches, dinners, and midnight snacks.

To those who look toward the future of their family: the honeymoon years, the childrearing years, and the golden years.

To those who pray together, get up for *Suhur* together, read Qur'an together, or want to start. To those who want to be examples of *Mawadah* and *Rahmah* for their children.

To those who dream into the future, years from now, and see themselves as a unit, rocking on their front porch, reading bedtime stories to their grandchildren.

This book is for you.

Introduction

There is no doubt that the family institution in North America is going through very serious crises. A quick look at the divorce statistics and a glance over the multitude of books in the solving problems in spousal relationships' section in any bookstore would certainly support this claim. Better yet, you can read the preface of Dr Rudolf Dreikurs', M.D., book, "The Challenge of Marriage", where he analyzes the present situation of the American family.

His analysis clearly supports this conclusion:
"Our cultural inability to live with each other as equals, is most painfully felt in our closest relationship, in marriage."[1]

"Without knowledge and skill in coping with each other in a democratic atmosphere, our families become a battleground, torn by tension, antagonisms and hostilities. Husbands and wives find it difficult to get along peacefully."[2]

Our continuous research and counseling involvement in the institution of the family in North America have led us to conclude the following crucial points:

- The family institution in North America is facing a serious dilemma. The statistics in chapter one of this book clearly support this.
- There is a continuous power struggle between the two genders to dictate the social convention of the society. Whichever gender has the opportunity to develop and establish such conventions, does so for its own benefit and liking. In the past, it was men, and, more recently, it is women.
- Equal status for all is the answer for social stability in the society as well as peace and harmony within the family.

---

[1] *The Challenge of Marriage*, page v
[2] Same reference, page viii

- The disintegration of the family is having extremely serious effects on children's behaviors. Of course, these effects are negative. Children now present, in Dr. Dreikers' words, "[a] Considerable social threat." This is evident in popular teen culture which is characterized by individualism, physical indulgence, and complete lack of respect for authority, to say the least.

There is no doubt that environment has a deep and long lasting effect on individuals and groups, as clearly indicated in the following *hadeeth* of the prophet *SAAW*. He said,

"كل مولود يولد على الفطرة ، فأبواه ينصرانه أو يهودانه أو يمجسانه"

"Every new born baby is born in a state of pure innate nature. It is his parents (the first circle of environment) who can influence this nature and convert him to a Jew, a Christian, or a fire worshipper"[3] As such, Muslim families living in North America are not immune from the effect of the environment. We witnessed this during our intense family counseling sessions in various cities in this continent. The detailed statistics in chapter one of this book are proof of this sad situation.

In our view, the only way to protect the Muslim family is to follow Islamic manners and etiquettes regarding family formation as well as family interactions.

It is encouraging to know that the problems identified by Dr. Dreikurs are readily solved in Islam through the following facts:
- Social norms are not left for genders or others to legislate. They are clearly legislated by Allah
- The question of equality between genders is completely resolved, and the relation between genders is well defined and very clear.

---

[3] Agreed upon

- Moral values are well established and equally applicable to both genders, with no room for exceptions or innovations.

In addition, marriage is a very important institution for Muslims because of the following reasons:

1. Marriage is the way/*Sunnah* of prophets as indicated in *Qur'an*. Allah says,

"وَلَقَدْ أَرْسَلْنَا رُسُلاً مِّن قَبْلِكَ وَجَعَلْنَا لَهُمْ أَزْوَاجًا وَذُرِّيَّةً وَمَا كَانَ

لِرَسُولٍ أَن يَأْتِيَ بِآيَةٍ إِلاَّ بِإِذْنِ اللّهِ لِكُلِّ أَجَلٍ كِتَابٌ"

"And indeed We sent messengers before you and made for them wives and offspring. And it was not for a messenger to bring a sign except by Allah's leave. For every matter, there is a decree from Allah"[4]

2. Marriage between men and women is the only lawful and legal way to form a family union. Family is the most important cornerstone in the societal structure. It provides the first circle of environment for children where they learn morals and ethics. A good and happy family atmosphere is one of the most important factors contributing to the formation of an upright, responsible, and confident personality of the children.

3. Procreation and the continuation of human race can only be achieved through the family institution.

4. Marriage is the only sacred and healthy way for both men and women to achieve *Ihssun*, i.e, to satisfy their sexual needs in a clean, regulated, and lawful way.

It is quite encouraging to know that Islamic literature is rich in books on marriage in different languages, particularly in Arabic; however, without exception, the emphasis in these books is mainly on basic legal aspects of Islamic marriage; courting; *Waleemas*;

---

[4] (Q13, V38)

husband's/wife's duties, responsibilities, and rights; etc.; but it often lacks practical implementation techniques and real life examples on how to positively enhance the sacred marital bond.

In addition, most of the available literature is written by scholars who never lived in North America and, in turn, don't have first hand information on the types of pressures that Muslim families go through in this society.

Although these books continue to be great references for Muslim families, Muslim families in North America cannot find in them what they are looking for to help them in their quest for a happy, committed, and strong family that can resist the tremendous pressures from the surrounding environment and continue to live as a happy Muslim family.

That is where the book between your hands fits in. By no means do we claim that this book covers all family matters and aspects of the marital relationship. We tried our best to marry the wonderful Islamic principles provided by *Qur'an* and the teachings of prophet Muhammad *SAAW* with our practical experience in this continent from successfully counseling many Muslim families and come up with concrete practical suggestions. The emphasis of the suggestions in this book is mainly on practical issues that help not only in resolving Muslim family conflicts in North America, but also in providing direction and guidance to ensure happier, more secure, more stable, Muslim families who can effectively carry out their duties and responsibilities.

Before we present you with a summary of the contents of each chapter of this book we would like to emphasize that the purpose of this book is not to address the legal aspects of marriage, the marriage contract, the courting process, the *fiqhi* rules of marriage, etc. Those topics are already covered thoroughly in numerous books of Islamic *Fiqh* that are readily available in the Islamic literature. For more information on some of these subjects, with

emphasis on the North American scene, we request the reader to consult with the following websites:
http://monzer.kahf.com/mcontracts.html
http://www.adamscenter.org/

These websites include material covering the following topics:
Islamic Marriage Contract
Islamic Marriage Certificate
Pre-Nuptial Agreement
Post-Nuptial Agreement
Marriage Application and Profile
Marriage Procedure Form
Matrimonial Profile and Details
Premarital Counseling Questions
Etc.

Because of the variation of laws from one state or province to the other, we recommend also for these matters to consult with your Islamic Center's *Imam* or your community's registered Marriage Officer.

After this introduction, the book contains eleven chapters, which discuss the family crises in North America, objectives of marriage in Islam, the process of spousal selection, tried and proven recipes for successful marriages, family dynamics and family atmosphere, essential spousal obligations, self-purifying and cleansing, common marital problems and their solutions, family stages, and further tips to enhance the marital relationship.

To set the stage for the book, **The First Chapter** discusses family crises in North America. It provides official statistics on the family institution and analyzes the effects of the problems on children. The objective is to make Muslim families living in North America aware of their environment and what kinds of effects it may have on them. As such, a section on the impact of the North American environment on Muslim families is included in this chapter. The chapter concludes with a word of advice and directions to help

Muslim families avoid the devastating effects of this environment on them.

The Second Chapter covers the objectives of Islamic marriage in detail. The vision in this chapter is meant to guide readers and set the stage for all the chapters to come. *Insha'a Allah*, it should help readers put all the knowledge from the coming chapters in the proper context of the objectives of an Islamic marriage and to view this knowledge through the proper perspective. Strengthening the faith of both spouses and enjoining what is good comes at the top of these objectives. It is considered the most important one. Other objectives include realizing and fulfilling the *Sunnah* of creation, procreation, *Ihssun*, fulfilling and satisfying the parenthood instinct in human beings, the progress and advancement of the human race, forming a stronger society, providing a secure family environment, and dwelling in peace and tranquility based on a relationship of love and mercy.

The Third Chapter is completely dedicated to the process of spousal selection with great attention given to the situation of Muslim communities in North America. Communities in North America are scattered all over the continent, and spousal selection represents one of the most serious challenges facing young Muslims, male and female alike. Existing selection methods are summarized with their pros and cons. The recommended method that we feel is very appropriate to Muslims in North America is covered in detail. Two thorough matching questionnaires with several in depth questions addressing particular marital situations and common issues are developed to help young brides- and grooms-to-be to select their future spouses. It is recommended that parents, matchmakers, and matrimonial services personnel should use these questionnaires to facilitate the process of selection and provide a higher possibility of success for the intended marriage. Other techniques complementing the use of questionnaires are also covered. Finally, marriage from the people of the book is discussed in detail.

As for **The Fourth Chapter**, it may be the most important chapter in this book, especially for those who really want to make their marriage a wonderful and successful experience that will last as long as they live together in this life and, with the grace of Allah, when they reunite together after death in *Jannah*. It covers the ingredients of successful marriages represented in essential qualities that both spouses should aspire to acquire and adhere to during their interactions. Among these are qualities such as appreciation, acceptance, accommodation, courtesy, sensitivity, support, respect, sharing, mercy, love, as well as other qualities, and above all commitment to the marriage success. This chapter discusses each quality in detail and suggests practical guidelines on how to practice these qualities. Practicing and adhering to these qualities and principles will, *insha'a Allah,* ensure a very successful marriage. The chapter ends with few relevant recipes for different occasions using various ingredients presented in the chapter.

The Fifth Chapter discusses the family atmosphere that every serious, sincere couple should work hard to create and maintain during their life together. It discusses the factors that help create and sustain such an atmosphere, such as using all the ingredients and recipes provided in Chapter four. It also discusses the factors that threaten this healthy and warm atmosphere such as being blunt, picking on or embarrassing your spouse, and ignoring your spouse's needs and feelings. It recommends avoiding these mannerisms completely.

The Sixth Chapter covers the essential spousal obligations. It divides them into shared or joint obligations that have to be fulfilled by both spouses for each other, essential obligations for wives, and essential obligations for husbands. The chapter draws heavily from the wealth of knowledge available on this subject in various *Fiqh* books. During our counseling sessions, we came across several problems that could have easily been avoided had both husband and wife properly understood the real Islamic standpoint on certain issues related to women as well as the proper concept of *Qawamah*. Because of this, in addition to the traditionally known rights and obligations, these two topics are discussed to help strengthen the marital bond.

To be able to adhere and practice the above qualities, each spouse should exercise self-control and, to do this, needs to embark on a self-searching process for purification and soul cleansing to be a stronger Muslim. This is the subject of **The Seventh Chapter**. It covers the definition of *Tazkeiatu Annafs*, what the *Qur'an* and *Sunnah* say about it, details of the self-search process, Islamic principles and etiquettes of conflict resolution, and how to manage anger and be at peace with yourself.

The Eighth Chapter discusses common cases and typical problems that usually happen between spouses. It describes many case studies for various situations and various stages of the marital relationship, such as early marriage with no children, after few years of marriage with children, interference from in-laws, etc. The readers are asked to analyze these case studies and answer certain questions, thus helping them apply the principles they have learned.

The Ninth Chapter deals with the same case studies presented in chapter eight, but provides detailed explanations, analyses, and solutions. For each case, we explain the cause of the problem, the symptoms for the problem, and a detailed analysis suggesting proper solutions.

The Tenth Chapter deals with various family stages and discusses the husband-wife relationship at these stages: the sweet and critical first two years of marriage; the stage of family formation and having children covering pregnancy, delivery, and how children take over and then the lack of sleep mainly for the mother and how this could contribute to certain conflicts if husbands are not cooperating with their wives. Other problems covered are related to going out with the children, getting them dressed and ready, and how that could lead to battles between spouses because of different expectations. The children's stages of going to school, growing up with peer pressure, and teen years are also covered with emphasis on sources of problems between spouses during these years. Finally, the chapter discusses the stage when children leave home and parents are left alone in the empty nest. A stage which can be very taxing on parents if they have not prepared for it and trained themselves to interact in the proper way and have an open, courteous channel of communication between themselves.

Finally, **The Eleventh Chapter** provides some further tips to help spouses achieve spousal harmony and enjoy their marital relationship, live happily, enhance the quality of their life together, and ensure that, *insha'a Allah*, every minute of their life will be counted as a credit for them in the Hereafter.

A Note about the Writing:
Italicized fonts refer to Arabic names or common Arabic terminology used by Muslims.

The use of (Q j, V i) denotes that this reference is the ith verse from the jth chapter in the *Qur'an*. For example, (Q 2, V 7) denotes the 7th verse in the 2nd chapter of the *Qur'an*

There are six major books referring to the collections of sayings *(hadeeth)* of the prophet PBUH. These books are *Bukhari, Muslim, Abu Dawoud, An-Nisa'ee, At-Termizy,* and *Ibn Majah.* After a *hadeeth,* the names in footnote refer to which book the *hadeeth* was taken from. When the expression Agreed upon appears in the footnote, it means that this *hadeeth* is reported by both *Bukhari* and *Muslim.*

When the abbreviation *SAAW* is used, usually after the name of Prophet Muhammad, it stands for 'may Allah's peace and blessings be upon him.' When the abbreviation *RAA* is used, usually it is after the name of one of the companions of the prophet

SAAW who narrated his sayings, it means 'may Allah be pleased
with him.'

1 - Family Crises in North America And Their Impact on Muslim Families

Introduction

In the preface of his book, _The Challenge of Marriage_, Dr. Rudolf Dreikurs analyzes the present situation of the American family, saying:
"Since the publication of this book, certain trends, suggested then, are now a commonplace in our contemporary scene. The conflicts and tensions that disrupt the harmony and even threaten the survival of individual marriages have increased in frequency and intensity.

However, our American family is not disintegrating despite all its shortcomings. It is true that sexual satisfaction is lacking in many marriages; and they often fail to provide the proper stimulation and guidance for children to grow and mature socially, emotionally, and intellectually. Since these are considered as two crucial functions in marriage, many begin to question the usefulness of this institution. This seems to be unwarranted.

We suggest that the family is not disintegrating, but it rather faced with a serious dilemma. It is the result of the democratic evolution with its concomitant process of equalization. Tradition has not prepared us for it.

Without knowledge and skill in coping with each other in a democratic atmosphere, our families become a battleground, torn by tension, antagonisms and hostilities. Husbands and wives find it difficult to get along peacefully. Under the impact of the ensuing warfare in which the children fully participate, their marital relationship can often be strained to the breaking point. Instead of being an element of unification, children often become an almost unsolvable disrupting influence."

He also emphasized the following: "In the past, men, in exclusive possession of political and social power, established the social conventions to their liking and benefit. The women had to conform and abide . . . .

"Women now have become the arbiters and censors, the custodian of morals and mares, imposing their rules of 'proper conduct' on men and on society as a whole. Today the wives complain that their husbands don't behave properly, in a socially accepted way. They either are too passive, aloof, and withdrawn, or too aggressive and domineering. This desire of women to be perfect, to be right, leaves neither husbands nor children to be good enough. An increasing number of boys grow up with the mistaken conviction that in order to be a real man, one has to be 'bad' or fight.

American women try so hard to be 'good'. One has to define what this goodness means. It is no longer purity, chastity, and virtue, traditionally expected and demanded from women. Women don't want necessarily to be chaste; they want to be proper. Being proper, socially correct, becomes a widely accepted idea for women.

The sexual mares for this country will greatly depend on the attitude and conventions that women will develop and establish. At the present time, they either try to impose on men the demand for fidelity and chastity, previously only required from women; or they arrogate to themselves the same license and sexual freedom that men enjoyed through out the ages.

Another trend that has become more pronounced is the emancipation of children. It is becoming increasingly obvious that adults have lost their power and authority over children, who have gained a sense of freedom and self-determination. However, while children become free to do as they decide, they often don't develop a sense of responsibility. Freedom without responsibility can be a considerable social threat. Many parents become permissive, out of a sincere desire not to be autocratic.

Our cultural inability to live with each other as equals, is most painfully felt in our closest relationship, in marriage. The confusion and vacillation is merely the result of democratic changes, of our grouping for a new relationship, which eventually will be based on equal status for all."

A few crucial points can be deducted from the above analysis:

- The family institution in North America is faced with a serious dilemma.
- There is a continuous power struggle between the two genders to dictate the social convention of the society. Whichever gender group has the opportunity to develop and establish such conventions does so for its own benefit and liking. In the past, it was men, and now, it is women.
- Equal status for all is the answer for social stability, peace, and harmony within the family.
- The disintegration of family is having very serious effects on children's behaviors. Of course, these effects all lead in the wrong direction. To put it in Dr's Dreikurs words, these new behaviors are a "considerable social threat." This is clearly seen in popular teen culture, which is characterized, by individualism, physical indulgence, and complete lack of respect for authority, to mention just a few characteristics.

Shocking Facts

Canadian Statistics

According to the Canadian Press, the latest census numbers from Statistics Canada suggest that the 2001 Canadian census shows that the word traditional no longer describes the universal ideal for families in metropolitan areas or in Canada as a whole.

"The proportion of so-called traditional families - married couples with children - has declined in Halifax over the last five years, according to information from the 2001 census released yesterday. This mirrors the national trend.

The latest census figures show that married couples with children account for 37.6 per cent of the 100,650 families in Halifax, down from 42.3 per cent in the 1996 census. Married couples with no children in 2001 represented 33.4 per cent of total families, while in 1996 it was 31.7 per cent.

Couples in common-law relationships in Halifax make up a higher proportion of families compared to the last census. The number of common-law couples with no children was 8.2 per cent in 2001, compared to 6.8 per cent in the 1996 census. Common-law couples with children represent 4.3 per cent of all families, compared to 3.5 per cent from five years ago. A total of 16.6 per cent of Halifax families were lone-parent families.

The new census data also lists 510 same-sex families in Halifax (0.51 per cent of total families).

On a national level, the census indicates the composition of the Canadian family structure continues to diversify.

The new data shows that married couples with children account for 37.4 per cent of Canadian families, a decrease from 41.3 per cent in 1996. Married couples without children make up 33.1 per cent of the families, up from 32.4 per cent. There is an increase in the number of common-law couples, with or without children (13.8 per cent from 11.7 per cent). The number of lone-parent families accounts for 15.7 per cent while same-sex couples account for 0.41 per cent of all Canadian families.

Statistics Canada says there are several known factors behind the changing numbers: fertility rates are lower, couples are delaying having children and more just aren't having children at all. In addition, Canadians are living longer so couples have more of their lives to spend together as empty-nesters after raising their children. And marital or common-law breakups often create two smaller households.

Nova Scotia and Quebec have the highest proportions of older people in Canada. Nova Scotia's median age rose to 38.8 years from 33.4 between 1996 and 2001.

Nova Scotia has the lowest proportion of couples with kids living at home in the country, which is linked to the older population.

The proportion of couples without children under 25 at home rose to 43 per cent in 2001 from 39 in 1996."[5]

The major newspaper of the nation's capital, The Ottawa Citizen, of October 23rd, 2002 reported the following:

"Canadians appear wedded to relationships even though the institution of marriage continues to slip in popularity, according to the latest census numbers from Statistics Canada, which, for the first time, counted same-sex couples living together.

The agency released data yesterday on Canadian families and households that show the traditional family grouping of mom, pop and the two kids had been overtaken by 2001 by an aging population and a dramatic shift in living arrangements.

Same-sex, common-law partners were only a tiny slice of the shifting scene, accounting for 0.5 per cent of all Canadian couples.

The data say households consisting of four or more people -- what we once thought of as the typical family -- had shrunk to one in four in 2001, as opposed to one in three two decades earlier.

---

[5] The Canadian Press, October 23rd, 2002

This is despite the fact that more young adults -- aged 20 to 29 -- are living with their parents, about 41 per cent in 2001 compared to 27.5 per cent in 1981. The trend was traced to a tendency to put off marriage, the pursuit of higher education and difficulty finding jobs.

The stay-at-home rate was highest in Newfoundland at almost 51 per cent, followed by Ontario at 47 per cent.

Though marriage continued to be the No. 1 choice for most couples at 70 per cent in 2001, down from 83 per cent in 1981, the proportion of common-law families more than doubled from 5.6 per cent to 14 per cent. Common-law relationships were most prevalent in Quebec, running at about 30 per cent of unions.

Same-sex couples accounted for three per cent of all common-law couples in the country, the agency said.

However, analysts and activists cautioned the figure probably represents an 'under reporting' of same-sex liaisons given the stigma still associated with homosexuality and a fear about how the data might be used if gay couples acknowledged their living arrangement.

Nevertheless the percentage of gay couples living together was close to the percentages recorded in New Zealand and the United States during their first counting of same-sex couples, giving analysts comfort the number is within the ballpark.

Of 11 million households surveyed, 34,200 couples said they were living in homosexual relationships, the bulk of them in British Columbia, Ontario and Quebec. Vancouver and the metropolitan area of Ottawa-Hull had the highest proportion of same-sex couples living together, about 0.9 per cent of all couples.

The agency also found about 15 per cent of lesbian couples had children living with them, compared with three per cent for male couples.

Gay activists stressed the data provides an incomplete picture because it does not count gays living outside a long-term relationship, but they called it a good start. 'It sends the message that we do represent a substantial body of the population whose needs cannot be ignored,' said John Fisher, executive director of the gay rights' group EGALE.

Analysts said there is no reason to overreact to what the agency headlined as the continued decline of the 'traditional' family.

Alan Mirabelli, executive director of the Vanier Institute of the Family in Ottawa, says the figures show a population that remains committed to relationships and family despite the gradual disappearance of the so-called traditional family since the 1960s.

'We've been watching this coming for quite some time. I see a portrait of a very dynamic and adaptive family process. People are designing and shaping their way of life to suit their economic circumstances and their aspirations.

From that point of view people are still committed to relationships, they are still committed to relationships over a long term whether they are married or living common law.'

Mr. Mirabelli pointed to the statistics on 'step-parents' as evidence Canadians don't give up on relationships just because of one failed marriage. 'It hasn't tarnished their belief in making a commitment over time,' he said.

Canada had 503,100 step-families in 2001, representing almost 12 per cent of all Canadian couples with children. That was up from 10 per cent in 1995.

Derek Rogusky of Focus on the Family, a pro-family lobby group, also said he was satisfied the figures affirm the prime standing of marriage with Canadians even though he is concerned about the rise in single-parent and common-law families.

He also argued the percentage of same-sex couples is so small that it need not be a preoccupation of governments or society. 'It raises the question as to why we're spending a whole lot of time worrying about things like same sex marriages when really the issues we should be dealing with is just strengthening what the vast majority of Canadians are choosing, that is marriage and families.'

Statistics Canada reported number of households climbed by 6.9 per cent to 11.6 million in 2001 from 10.8 million in 1996. There were as many one-person households in the latest census as there were households with four or more persons.

The agency attributed the decline in household size to lower fertility rates, couples choosing to have fewer children, an increase in childless couples and increases in the number of seniors who are more likely to live alone.

There also has been a sharp increase in 'empty-nesters,' couples who once were part of a traditional family but who no longer have children living at home. The agency also notes the dissolution of marriages and common-law unions also create smaller households."[6]

Here are some more official staggering statistics on Canadian families:
- The family breakdown rate in Canada is about 50%.
- In Canada, a woman is sexually assaulted every 6 minutes. 1 in 3 women in Canada will be sexually assaulted at some time in their lives.

---

[6] *The Ottawa Citizen*, October 23rd, 2002

- 1 in 4 women are at the risk of rape or attempted rape in their lifetimes.
- 1 in 8 women will be sexually assaulted while attending college or university. A study found that 60% of Canadian university-aged males said they would commit sexual assault if they were certain they wouldn't be caught.

United States Statistics

According to the Alabama Department of Archives and History, the divorce rate in the United States of America is 50%. This means that for every 2 marriages, there is one divorce.

The following are more shocking United States statistics on family, according to *Divorce* Magazine:
- The number of divorced adults in 1998 was 19 400 000 which represented 9.8 % of the total population.
- The median duration of marriage in 1997 is 7.2 years.
- 50% of first marriages end in divorce (1997 statistic).
- 60% of remarriages end in divorce (1997 statistic).
- 43% of women whose parents were divorced get divorced within 10 years (1995 statistic).
- 29% of women whose parents stayed together were divorced within 10 years (1995 statistic.)
- 380 000 women are stalked by a husband or an ex-husband every year (1997 statistic).
- 52 000 men are stalked by a wife or an ex-wife every year (1997 statistic).
- One million children experience new divorces each year (1997 statistic).
- 33% of households have 2 parents living with their own children (who are under 18).
- 27% of family households have children with only one parent (1998 statistic).
- 9.2% of all households are run by single moms.
- 2.04 million males are single parents.
- 9.68 Million females are single parents.

- An estimated 1,075,000 children were involved in divorce in 1997 alone.
- 20 million children, which is equivalent to 28% of children, under 18 years of age live with just one parent (1998 statistic).
- The total number of single mothers never married is 4.181 million.
- 32% of births were to unmarried women (1997 statistic).
- 50% of women with kids before marriage divorce within 10 years of getting married (1995 statistic).
- In 1996, children of divorce were 50% more likely to divorce than their counterparts from intact families were.
- Fatherless homes account for 63% of youth suicides, 90% of homeless and runaway children, 85% of children with behavior problems, 71% of high school dropouts, 85% of youths in prison, and well over 50% of teen mothers.
- 80% of divorces in 1997 were due to irreconcilable differences.
- One out of every two marriages today ends in divorce.
- The U.S. Department of Health and Human Services –The Administration on Children, Youth, and Families examined data from each state's Child Protective Services (CPS) system. The sample size included 554 047 "perpetrators" from 21 states. The report said that 61.8% percent of the perpetrators were female and 38.2% percent were male. This means that females were 1.62 times as likely to maltreat children as males were.

Examining the above statistics indicates, without any shade of doubt, that the family institution in North America is in crisis. This crisis is clearly manifested in the shocking divorce rates above. Out of every hundred marriages, fifty end in divorce. This high percentage indicates the disastrous situation of the family in North America. During the last few decades, this situation, no doubt, has had devastating effects on children in this society. These effects are clearly illustrated by childhood poverty, low child morality, and low self-esteem. Many divorcing families include children;

during the difficult period of the divorce process parents, who are the most important people in their children's lives, are usually preoccupied with their own problems. Children are usually frightened, and confused, and feeling very threatened because of their parents' divorce. Divorce can be misinterpreted by children unless parents explain what is happening to them, how they are involved and not involved, and what will happen to them.

In some cases, children believe that they caused the conflict between their mother and father. Many children assume responsibility of bringing their parents back together, sometimes by sacrificing themselves. The traumatic loss of one or both parents through divorce can make children more vulnerable to both physical and mental illnesses.

The stress of divorce can cause young children to become more aggressive, uncooperative, or withdrawn. It can cause older children to feel a deep sadness and loss that may contribute to lower academic achievement as well as behavioral problems. Children of divorce, whether teenagers or adults, often have trouble with their own relationships.

Domestic violence is another important symptom of the family crisis in North America. It is a serious social problem, costing the society between $5-10 billion annually in health care expenses, lost wages, litigation, and imprisonment of batterers.[7] According to U.S. Department of Health and Human Services - The Administration on Children, Youth, and domestic violence is the leading cause of injury to women in the United States, surpassing injuries caused by automobile accidents, muggings, and rape combined. In 2001, New York City's Domestic Violence Hotline received over 190 000 calls, more than double the number of calls received in 1995.

---

[7] Statistical records of Women Worldwide

Impact on Muslim Families

In his valuable research about divorce among Muslim families in North America, Dr *Ilyas Ba-Yunus,* professor of Sociology,[8] State University of New York presents the these important findings:

"It is evident from our research that California has the highest divorce rate among Muslims, just shy of 37%; and Georgia has the lowest divorce rate with almost 29% while the overall divorce rate is hovering around 31%. This is a far cry from two highest divorce rates in the Muslim world (Turkey and Egypt with 10% each). Although this divorce rate is much smaller than the combined rate of U.S. and Canada (48.6 or close to 50%), yet it is much closer to 33.2%, the second highest divorce rate in the world – that of the United Kingdom."

This divorce rate for Muslims is, without a doubt, alarming. It is clear that Muslim families living in North America are affected by the mainstream trend, which, in our view, is very serious. This indicates that Muslim families are not immune to the effect of their environment. Sadly, we have to accept this alarming fact, but at the same time, we have to increase the level of awareness among our Muslim communities, especially among the younger generations, of how to follow the proper process of selection and work hard to keep the family unit intact. This is particularly important because of the lack of reference points for second generation and younger families. They are facing a different environment; therefore, the traditional roles may not be applicable to their situation.

What To Do: A Word of Advice

The Muslim family, whether it is already formed, or still in the process of being formed, can be protected from these negative influences only through the following principles:

---

[8] Unpublished, private communication with the author

1- The proper understanding of Islamic teachings regarding family formation, dynamics, maintenance, and the husband/wife relationship in Islam

2- In depth knowledge of the personality and life style of each spouse by the opposite spouse before the marriage is completed

3- A high level of commitment on the part of both spouses to make the marriage successful and live their life according to the principles of Islam that are clearly described in the verses of *Qur'an* and the *Ahadeeth* of the prophet *SAAW* and are also illustrated by him in his daily life with his family

It is normal for a couple to have conflicts and clashes of interests. It happens even among the most understanding and loving of couples. What really matters is to resolve the conflicts in the spirit of mutual respect. This could be achieved best by following the Islamic teachings and the *Sunnah* of the Prophet *SAAW*.

There are two pitfalls every Muslim family must avoid in order to attain success:

- Following tradition blindly, (the only traditions to be followed are those that don't contradict the Islamic teachings and its spirit.)
- Misconceptions about men/women relationships

To pursue our quest for proper understanding of Islamic teachings regarding all family matters, let us start with the Islamic objectives of marriage in our next chapter, then, continue with other family issues in the chapters to follow.

2 - Objectives of Marriage

Introduction

In Islam, all systems, social; economic; political; and any other systems or institutions should contribute to the ultimate goal of the life of humans on this planet, which is to serve Allah *SWT* completely, to be His vicegerent on earth, and to establish justice and peace on earth. Allah *SWT* says,

"وَمَا خَلَقْتُ الْجِنَّ وَالْإِنسَ إِلَّا لِيَعْبُدُونِ"

" I have only created Jinn and Humans to worship Me." [9]

Allah *SWT* also says,

"وَإِذْ قَالَ رَبُّكَ لِلْمَلَائِكَةِ إِنِّي جَاعِلٌ فِي الأَرْضِ خَلِيفَةً قَالُواْ أَتَجْعَلُ فِيهَا مَن يُفْسِدُ فِيهَا وَيَسْفِكُ الدِّمَاء وَنَحْنُ نُسَبِّحُ بِحَمْدِكَ وَنُقَدِّسُ لَكَ قَالَ إِنِّي أَعْلَمُ مَا لاَ تَعْلَمُونَ"

"Behold, thy Lord said to the angels, 'I will create a vicegerent on earth.' They said, 'Wilt Thou place therein one who will make mischief therein and shed blood? Whilst we do celebrate Thy praises and glorify Thy holy (name)?'

He said, 'I know what ye know not.'"[10]

He also says,

"هُوَ أَنشَأَكُم مِّنَ الأَرْضِ وَاسْتَعْمَرَكُمْ فِيهَا فَاسْتَغْفِرُوهُ ثُمَّ تُوبُواْ إِلَيْهِ إِنَّ رَبِّي قَرِيبٌ مُّجِيبٌ"

"It is He who established you on earth and instructed you to build it accordingly"[11]

---

[9] (Q51, V56)
[10] (Q2, V30)
[11] (Q11, V61)

The institutions of family and marriage are no different. The ultimate objective of the marriage institution is to contribute to these causes and create a conducive environment for the individual to fulfill his/her purpose of being on this earth as Allah's vicegerent and submit to His orders in full obedience. This way the marriage institution will be in full harmony with other Islamic institutions. In Addition, husband and wife will be in harmony with other human beings and all of Allah's creations.

Let us now look at various objectives and benefits of marriage and see how they support the above.

Stronger Faith

Allah says in *Surat At Tawbah*

"وَالْمُؤْمِنُونَ وَالْمُؤْمِنَاتُ بَعْضُهُمْ أَوْلِيَاءُ بَعْضٍ يَأْمُرُونَ بِالْمَعْرُوفِ وَيَنْهَوْنَ عَنِ الْمُنكَرِ وَيُقِيمُونَ الصَّلَاةَ وَيُؤْتُونَ الزَّكَاةَ وَيُطِيعُونَ اللَّهَ وَرَسُولَهُ أُوْلَئِكَ سَيَرْحَمُهُمُ اللَّهُ إِنَّ اللَّهَ عَزِيزٌ حَكِيمٌ"

"The Believers, men and women, are protectors one of another: they enjoin what is just, and forbid what is evil: they observe regular prayers, practice regular charity, and obey Allah and His Messenger. On them will Allah pour His mercy: for Allah is Exalted in power, Wise."[12]

This verse establishes the bigger picture of the relationship between genders in Islam: they are responsible for supporting each other.

Abu Hurairah narrated that the prophet of Allah *SAAW* said,

---

[12] (Q 9, V 71)

25

"رحم الله رجلاً قام من الليل فصلى وأيقظ امرأته، فإن أبت نضح في وجهها
الماء، رحم الله امرأة قامت من الليل فصلت وأيقظت زوجها، فإن أبى نضحت
في وجهه الماء"

"May Allah have mercy on a man who wakes up at night and
prays, and wakes up his wife to pray, and if she resists he would
lightly spray water on her face; and may Allah have mercy on a
woman who wakes up at night and prays, and wakes up her
husband to pray, and if he resists she would lightly spray water on
his face"[13]

Thawban RAA asked the messenger of Allah *SAAW*, "O'
messenger of Allah, what kind of wealth should we keep?"
He replied,

"ليتخذ أحدكم قلبا شاكراً، ولساناً ذاكراً، وزوجة مؤمنة تعينه على أمر
الآخرة"

"Let each one of you keep a heart that is grateful (to Allah), a
tongue that remembers and mentions (Allah), and a believing wife
who assists him with regards to the affairs of the hereafter."[14]

Also *Ali* and *Abu Umamah RAA* reported that the messenger of
Allah *SAAW* said,

"قلب شاكر، ولسان ذاكر، وزوجة صالحة تعينك على أمر دنياك ودينك: خير
ما اكتتز الناس"

"A heart that is grateful (to Allah), a tongue that remembers and
mentions (Allah), and a righteous wife who assists you in the
affairs of your life and religion: those are the best treasures for the
people."[15]

"وَتَعَاوَنُواْ عَلَى الْبِرِّ وَالتَّقْوَى وَلاَ تَعَاوَنُواْ عَلَى الإِثْمِ وَالْعُدْوَانِ"

---

[13] Recorded by Anessae'i and Abu Dawood
[14] Ahmad and at-Tirmizi
[15] at- Termizi and al- Bayhaqi

"Help ye one another in righteousness and piety, but help ye not one another in sin and rancour: fear Allah: for Allah is strict in punishment."[16]

"وَمِنْ آيَاتِهِ أَنْ خَلَقَ لَكُم مِّنْ أَنفُسِكُمْ أَزْوَاجًا لِّتَسْكُنُوا إِلَيْهَا وَجَعَلَ بَيْنَكُم مَّوَدَّةً وَرَحْمَةً إِنَّ فِي ذَلِكَ لَآيَاتٍ لِّقَوْمٍ يَتَفَكَّرُونَ"

"And among His Signs is this, that He created for you mates from among yourselves, that ye may dwell in tranquility with them, and He has put *Mawadah* and *Rahmah* between your (hearts): verily in that are Signs for those who reflect"[17]

(The terminology *Mawadah* and *Rahmah* are explained in detail in chapter four.)

The use of the words لِّتَسْكُنُوا إِلَيْهَا in this verse emphasizes the very special nature of the relationship between husband and wife in this sacred bond of marriage. *Sakan* is the place where one dwells in peace and tranquility. *Sakan* is where one feels comfortable to be herself/himself without fear of being judged by others. It is the place that one resorts to for protection from bad weather or a harsh external environment. It provides shelter, comfort, and a place to rest and rejuvenate after a long, hectic day.

It is also important to notice that the *Qur'an* used لِّتَسْكُنُوا إِلَيْهَا, which means to dwell in tranquility unto them. It didn't use the Arabic word لِّتَسْكُنُوا معها, which means with them. This indicates that the dwelling is not only at the physical level but it is also at the emotional and spiritual level. This means that both husband and wife protect each other. Both of them provide comfort and tranquility to each other and they both seek comfort in each other. They both soothe each others at times of hardships. They both console and calm each other when the need arises. They both

---

[16] (Q5, V2)
[17] (Q 30, V21)

reassure each other that they are committed to the marriage's success and that they will be there for each other when one needs the other.

Examples From the *Seerah*

Abu Addahdah and Um Addahdah

Scholars of *Tafseer* have indicated that the event narrated below took place after the following verse was revealed:

$$\text{"مَّن ذَا الَّذِي يُقْرِضُ اللّهَ قَرْضًا حَسَنًا فَيُضَاعِفَهُ لَهُ أَضْعَافًا كَثِيرَةً وَاللّهُ يَقْبِضُ}$$
$$\text{وَيَبْسُطُ وَإِلَيْهِ تُرْجَعُونَ"}$$

"Who is he that will loan to Allah a beautiful loan, which Allah will double unto his credit and multiply many times? It is Allah that giveth (you) Want or plenty, and to Him shall be your return"[18]

One companion by the name of *Abu Addahdah* said to the prophet *SAAW*, "May my parents be your ransom prophet of Allah. Allah *SWT* is asking us to give Him a loan, even though He is free from all wants and He doesn't need our loan?"

The prophet *SAAW* said, "Allah wants to admit you to paradise."*Abu Addahdah* said, "I'm loaning my Lord a loan with which He would guarantee *Jannah* for me, my children, and my wife *Um Addahdah*." *Abu Addahdah* then asked the prophet *SAAW* to stretch out his hand to make a covenant to that effect, which the prophet *SAAW* did. While holding the blessed hand of the prophet *SAAW*, *Abu Addahdah* said, "I have two gardens, one in the upper part of the city, and the second in the lower part. I have nothing but them, and I'm loaning Allah these gardens." The prophet *SAAW* said, "Loan one to Allah and keep the other as a source of livelihood for yourself and your family." The man said, "I take you as my witness that I loan Allah the better one of the two gardens."

---

[18] (Q2, V245)

28

The prophet *SAAW* said, "Allah would reward you with *Jannah* for this."

Abu Addahdah proceeded to his garden, where *Um Addahdah* was with their children. He chanted the following poem:

إلى سبيل الخير والسداد	هداك ربي سبيل الرشـــاد
قد مضى قرضاً إلى التناد	بيِّني من حائـــــــط الوداد
بالطوع لا منًّا ولا ارتداد	أقرضته الله على اعتمادي
فارتحلي بالنفس والأولاد	إلا رجاء الضعف في المعاد
قدمه المرء إلى المعــــاد	والبر لاشك فخـــــــير زاد

The meaning of these verses is "Allah *SWT* guided us to the right way, the way of goodness and prosperity. Leave this garden, because I have loaned it to Allah willingly in good faith, hoping He will reward me well during the Hereafter. Please leave this garden and take the children with you. Remember, the best provision one can present for the Hereafter is righteousness and good deeds."

Um Addahdah responded, "This certainly is a profitable trade. May Allah bless your act." Then she chanted the following verses:

مثلك أدى ما عليه ونصـــح	بشرك الله بخـــير وفـــــرح
بالعجوة السوداء والزهو البلح	قد متع الله العيال ومنــــح
طول الليالي وعليه ما اجـــترح	والعبد يسعى وله ما قد كدح

The meaning is "May Allah *SWT* give you glad tidings and happiness because you did the right thing and gave us the proper advice. Allah *SWT* is the One who provided my children with this wonderful, delicious variety of dates. Allah's servants should strive hard day and night, for they will only be rewarded according to their deeds." *Um Addahdah* then took the dates from the children and returned them to the garden. Then she took the children to the other garden.

29

The prophet *SAAW* said, "*Abu Addahdah* will have plenty of palm trees with ripe delicious dates and will enjoy a spacious home."

This is a wonderful story vividly illustrating spouses' cooperation in good deeds and how *Um Addahdah* acknowledged her husband's act of charity and helped him fulfill his commitment in loaning Allah *SWT* the best of his two gardens. She also indicated her happiness with her husband's decision, blessed it, and made *dua'a* from him in a very compelling way. This is how spouses should help each other strengthen their faith and promote a higher level of Islamic commitment.

The Evening Visitor
Imam Al Bukhari narrated in his collection of *Hadeeth* that *Abu Hurrairah RAA* said that a man came to the prophet *SAAW* and said, "I'm exhausted and hungry."

The prophet *SAAW* sent to his wives asking for food to feed this man. They all replied that they had no food at all. The prophet *SAAW* asked the companions around him if one of them could host this hungry, tired man. One of the *Ansar* volunteered. He took the hungry man with him to his house. He asked his wife, "Do we have any food to feed the guest of Allah's messenger *SAAW*?"

"The only food we have is the children's food," the wife replied. "Try to put the children to sleep without food and bring their food for the guest," the man said. He also asked her to turn the lamp light off so the guest wouldn't notice that the hosts were not eating with him. She did so and they were able to feed the guest. The next day, the prophet *SAAW* told the man that Allah *SWT* was impressed with him and his wife's actions. Allah *SWT* then revealed the following verse:

"وَالَّذِينَ تَبَوَّؤُوا الدَّارَ وَالْإِيمَانَ مِن قَبْلِهِمْ يُحِبُّونَ مَنْ هَاجَرَ إِلَيْهِمْ وَلَا يَجِدُونَ فِي صُدُورِهِمْ حَاجَةً مِّمَّا أُوتُوا وَيُؤْثِرُونَ عَلَى أَنفُسِهِمْ وَلَوْ كَانَ بِهِمْ خَصَاصَةٌ وَمَن يُوقَ شُحَّ نَفْسِهِ فَأُوْلَئِكَ هُمُ الْمُفْلِحُونَ"

"But those who before them, had homes (in Medina) and had adopted the Faith, show their affection to such as came to them for refuge, and entertain no desire in their hearts for things given to the (latter), **but give them preference over themselves, even though poverty was their (own lot)**. And those saved from the covetousness of their own souls, they are the ones that achieve prosperity."[19]

This is another beautiful example of cooperation in goodness between husband and wife. No doubt, both helped each other with this wonderful act of hospitality and helped each other be closer to Allah and enhance the level of their faith.

When reading these examples in the *Seerah* it may seem obvious that this was the right thing for these couples to do, but when we stop and put ourselves in their shoes, it becomes evident how much they sacrificed with each act. Perhaps this can be roughly compared to a situation in our time: giving charity to the hungry and homeless. This couple sacrificed their children's dinner in order to feed their guest. The wife never protested at her husband's request. This is truly remarkable. By remembering these examples, when our spouses suggest that we donate money to the poor, instead of thinking about the computer we are saving up for or the vacation we would like to take, we may be able to support our spouses and ourselves in strengthening our faith.

These stories offer great lessons for all spouses to provide the best support to our partners when they try to please Allah and be positive influences on them rather than be negative influences as the *Qur'an* describes some spouses:

---

[19] (Q59, V9)

"يَا أَيُّهَا الَّذِينَ آمَنُوا إِنَّ مِنْ أَزْوَاجِكُمْ وَأَوْلَادِكُمْ عَدُوًّا لَّكُمْ فَاحْذَرُوهُمْ وَإِن تَعْفُوا وَتَصْفَحُوا وَتَغْفِرُوا فَإِنَّ اللَّهَ غَفُورٌ رَّحِيمٌ إِنَّمَا أَمْوَالُكُمْ وَأَوْلَادُكُمْ فِتْنَةٌ وَاللَّهُ عِندَهُ أَجْرٌ عَظِيمٌ"

"O ye who believe! Truly, among your wives and your children are (some that are) enemies to yourselves: so beware of them! But if ye forgive and overlook, and cover up (their faults), verily Allah is Oft-Forgiving, Most Merciful. Your riches and your children may be but a trial: but in the Presence of Allah, is the highest, Reward."[20]

Other Objectives of Marriage

In addition to the main objectives we discussed in the previous pages, there are other important objectives discussed in various books of jurisprudence, which the reader can always refer to for details. For the sake of completion we will list these objectives in a brief manner.

Realizing and Fulfilling the *Sunnah* of Creation (Pairing)

The *Sunnah* of creation is pairing. Allah *SWT* created different species in pairs. Allah says,

"وَمِن كُلِّ شَيْءٍ خَلَقْنَا زَوْجَيْنِ لَعَلَّكُمْ تَذَكَّرُونَ"

"And of everything We have created pairs that you may be mindful."[21] Marriage is the normal and legitimate way for those pairs to live together and realize their full potential to fulfill the purpose of their existence.

Procreation

For the human race to continue, the institution of marriage is the only legitimate form of procreation. Through marriage, the human race will continue to fulfill its destiny as Allah decreed.

---

[20] (Q64, V14-15)
[21] (Q51, V49)

Ihssun

Allah *SWT* created human beings with strong sexual urges so that the purpose of procreation would be realized. If this strong and pressing urge is not properly fulfilled, it puts a tremendous burden on people and may even cause physical and psychological problems. *Ihssun* is the process of ensuring that people are protected from resorting to illicit means to fulfill their sexual desires. For Muslims, marriage is the only legitimate way to provide *Ihssun*. It is the clean, pure, and wonderful relationship between genders through which *Ihssun* can be naturally and successfully achieved.

Fulfilling and Satisfying the Parenthood Instinct in Human Beings

Parenthood is another natural instinct that Allah *SWT* created in human beings. Most people love to feel that they have children of their own. Again, this strong feeling helps in fulfilling the purpose of existence and procreation. The marriage institution provides a legitimate, clean, hygienic, and honorable way of satisfying this need.

Progress and Advancement of the Human Race

The marriage institution contributes to the progress and advancement of the human race in two ways: through motivating the family heads to work hard for their families' benefits and through fulfilling the spouses' physical needs and, in turn, allowing them to turn their attention to more important matters.

Carrying the responsibility of marriage motivates people to work hard to satisfy and fulfill the needs of their families. Every family head would work harder and do his best to fulfill his duty and provide the needed physical amenities to his family. The hard work put forth by every family head furthers the knowledge and facilities available to the human race as a whole. In addition, if the physical needs of both spouses are met in a satisfying way through marriage, their effort and energy would be directed to more productive activities rather than being occupied by thoughts of how to fulfill such needs. This, with no doubt, would contribute to the well being of human race in general.

Stronger Society
There is no doubt that a society where the relationships between genders are properly regulated and the family institution is healthy and well established will be much stronger than one without such regulations. Marriage is the only legitimate way for starting a family in Islam. Successful marriages will lead to strong family institutions and consequently to a stronger, more stable society.

Proper Distribution of Tasks and Responsibilities
Human beings have to perform certain tasks for life to continue. Allah *SWT* created each gender to complement the other. This doesn't mean that one gender is superior to the other. There is no doubt that according to the *Hadeeth* of the prophet *SAAW*, both genders are equal. He said,

"إنما النساء شقائق الرجال"

"Women are the twin complements of men"[22]

There are jobs and tasks that are suitable for both genders and other jobs that are more suitable for one gender than the other. For example, Islam considers men the main financial providers of the family and considers women the main caregivers for the children. In a successful marriage, this distribution of tasks and responsibilities is well-defined and the family institution ensures the proper execution and implementation of these tasks.

---

[22] Ahmad

3 - The Process of Selection

Introduction

There are many questions that young people ask themselves regarding love and marriage: How am I going to meet my future spouse? Where will we meet and when? Is it okay to get some help – maybe someone could arrange for us to meet? But what about love? What should I do if the person is good but I am not attracted to her/him? Should I still marry her/him? Would our marriage work? Should I wait until I fall in love and then marry? Isn't that what's supposed to happen in order to have a good marriage?

We all want to have a happy marriage, and a big part of that depends on choosing the right spouse. Many people believe that they must fall "madly in love" with the person they choose. They expect to feel a sudden attraction to the other person, suffer from heartache and sleepless nights, and find it hard to concentrate on their work. If they don't experience these strong emotions, hardships, and excitement, they doubt the validity of their love.

This uncertainty often causes people to question a commitment they may have otherwise made. A young man might choose not to marry someone because he feels that he isn't in love with her enough, when they would otherwise be a good fit. On the other hand, someone who mistakes the emotions and experiences named above as 'true love' might rush into a relationship without examining other factors that are necessary for a successful marriage. This is why it is crucial to understand what love really is and how it relates to marriage.

Love is an emotion, like all other emotions, created by Allah *SWT* for a purpose. We will *insha'a Allah* discuss and examine love as a specific emotion in a later chapter. The lesson we want to derive from this is that those who are looking for a spouse shouldn't make emotions their only selection criteria. They should be more comprehensive in their search for the right match. Again, it is only through following *Qur'anic* advice as well as the prophetic guidelines that we can base our selection on sound and good matching measures that provide a higher chance of success for the intended marriage. Let us now examine some of these guidelines as indicated by the *Qur'an* and the teachings of Prophet Muhammad *SAAW*.

Qur'anic Advice Regarding the Process of Selection

In *Surat Al Qasas*, Allah *SWT* says,

"قَالَتْ إِحْدَاهُمَا يَا أَبَتِ اسْتَأْجِرْهُ إِنَّ خَيْرَ مَنِ اسْتَأْجَرْتَ الْقَوِيُّ الْأَمِينُ"

"Said one of the (damsels): "O my (dear) father! engage him on wages: truly the best of men for thee to employ is the (man) who is strong and trusty"[23].

This verse emphasizes two qualities of the person that a father would seek to marry his daughter: strength and trustworthiness. The daughter observed these two excellent qualities in Prophet *Mosa's* character *SAAW* after he selflessly helped her and her family. She recommended to her father that he hire him to help in the family's affairs. The father asked *Mosa* to marry one of his daughters, and *Mosa* agreed.

The strength observed by the daughter was not only the physical strength, which was very clear in the ability of *Mosa SAAW* to help them physically with watering their flocks, but also the strength in his manners and character, which is depicted in the way he offered to help them. This is an indication that we should be looking for the physical strength as well as other sources of strength relevant and related to the need of the environment we live in.

Trustworthiness is another important quality that fathers should look for in the individuals who want to marry their daughters. After all, after marriage the daughter is entrusted to her husband.

---

[23] (Q28, V26)

She can't go out without his permission. She depends on his financial support. He is the leader of this family union, and, ultimately all decisions related to family issues will be made by him. If the individual is not honest and trustworthy, it is difficult for the wife to live with him on equal footing and to trust that he will treat her with dignity and respect her rights. As such, it is very important for fathers to make sure that the individual seeking the marriage of their daughters possess this very essential quality.

The Prophet's Advice

The teachings of the prophet *SAAW* are full of valuable advice that offers complete guidance for both the bride-to-be and the groom-to-be.

First, the prophet *SAAW* encourages young men to get married as soon as they can afford to, and, for those who can't afford to, he advises them to observe fasting as a practical solution to help curtail their sexual drive. It was reported that the prophet *SAAW* said,

"يا معشر الشباب من استطاع منكم الباءة فليتزوج، فإنه أغض للبصر،

وأحصن للفرج، ومن لم يستطع فعليه بالصوم، فإنه له وجاء"

"Oh young men, those among you who can afford marriage, let them get married, for it helps lower the gaze and guard the private parts (i.e. chastity); and those who can not, let them observe fasting: it is a shield and protection for them."[24]

Uthman RAA reported that Allah's messenger *SAAW* said,

"من كان منكم ذا طول فليتزوج، فإنه أغض للبصر وأحصن للفرج، ومن لا

فالصوم له وجاء"

"Anyone among you who has resources should get married, because it helps lower the (lustful) look and guard chastity; and

---

[24] Al Bukhari, Muslim and others

those who don't have wealth should fast, because fasting restrains the desire"[25]

Second, the prophet *SAAW* advises both spouses to seek the right match and find the proper mate who possesses good moral and religious values. The following *Ahadeeth* illustrate some of his valuable advice to both men and women related to the selection process:

Abu Hurairah RAA narrated that the prophet *SAAW* said,

"إذا أتاكم من ترضون دينه وخلقه فزوجوه، إلا تفعلوه، تكن فتنة في الأرض

وفساد عريض"

"When the one whom you are pleased with his *Deen* (religiousness) and his manners comes to you seeking your daughter in marriage, marry him; otherwise *Fetnah* (harm) and great corruption will become rampant on earth."[26]

We note in this advice of the prophet *SAAW* that he emphasized two qualities; these are the religious practices of the person and his manners. He didn't only mention the *Deen* of the person, but he also specifically mentioned his manners, the way he behaves. The word *Deen* in this *Hadeeth* emphasizes the commitment of the person to meet his pure religious obligations such as praying, fasting, paying charity, etc. Practicing these pure rituals in the proper way mainly benefits the individual himself in terms of elevating his spirituality and making him closer to Allah, but its benefits to others are limited. On the other hand, good manners are key to good relationships and proper interactions between people. As such, the prophet *SAAW* emphasized good manners in his advice to provide a higher chance of success in marriage. Again, this is more so in the case of husbands because they usually have the upper hand in this relationship, and, without being of high moral fiber, they could easily hurt their wives, who are considered

---

[25] An Nesa'i
[26] At-Termezi, Ibn Majah and others

the physically weaker part of this union and should be taken good care of and should never be exploited for their physical weakness.

A'ishah RAA narrated that the prophet *SAAW* said,

" تخيروا لنطفكم فأنكحوا الأكفاء، وانكحوا إليهم "

"Make a good choice of who will bear your children. Marry those who are compatible with you."[27]

This advice to Muslim men shows the importance of the proper selection of those who will carry their offspring. It is recommended to select somebody who is compatible with them, for this would help the proper match and ensure the success of this sacred union of marriage.

Abu Hurairah RAA narrated that the prophet *SAAW* said,

"تنكح المرأة لأربع: لمالها، ولحسبها، ولجمالها، ولدينها، فاظفر بذات الدين

تربت يداك"

"A woman is sought for marriage for four reasons: her wealth, her beauty, her social status, and her *Deen* (religiousness). So select the one who is religious; otherwise, you are at a loss."[28]

Abu Sa'eed Al Khudry, and *Abu Hurairah* narrated also that the prophet of Allah *SAAW* said,

"تنكح المرأة على إحدى خصال ثلاث: تنكح المرأة على مالها، وتنكح المرأة

على دينها وخلقها، فخذ ذات الدين والخلق تربت يمينك"

"A women is married for three qualities: She is married for her wealth; she is married for her beauty; or she is married for her religion. So marry the one of religion and manners, may your right hand then be prosperous"[29]

---

[27] Ibn Maja, Albayhaqy and Al hakem
[28] Agreed upon
[29] Al-Hakim, Ibn Hibban, and Ahmad

The emphasis in these two sayings are mainly the *Deen* and the manners of the lady because both are very important for a good relationship and a strong marital union. However, we shouldn't misunderstand these sayings to mean that the prophet *SAAW* condemns beauty, wealth, and social status. The proper understanding is that these qualities are secondary to the righteousness and religious practices of the woman. First, one should make sure that she is highly committed to her *Deen*. This is the main criterion for selection. After this, one can look at other qualities like beauty, wealth, and social status. They shouldn't be fully disregarded because the prophet *SAAW* also said,

"خير النساء من تسرك إذا أبصرت، وتطيعك إذا أمرت، وتحفظ غيبتك في نفسها ومالك"

" The best of women is the one who pleases you when you look at her, obeys you when you request her, and safeguards you during your absence in regards to herself and your wealth"[30]

Abu Hurairah RAA reported that the messenger of Allah *SAAW* also said,

"خير النساء التي تسره إذا نظر، وتطيعه إذا أمر، ولا تخالفه في نفسها ولا ماله بما يكره".

"The best of women is the one who pleases him (her husband) when he looks at her, obeys him when he requests something from her, and doesn't subject herself or his money to what he dislikes"[31]

Abdullah Ibn Amr RAA narrated that the prophet *SAAW* said,

"الدنيا كلها متاع وخير متاع الدنيا المرأة الصالحة"

"The world is delightful, and its greatest treasure is a righteous wife"[32]

---

[30] At-Tabarany and others
[31] Al-Hakim, Ahmad, and Al-Nesa'y
[32] Muslim, Ahmad and Alnisa'y

Ibn Abbas RAA narrated that the prophet *SAAW* said,

"ألا أخبرك بخير ما يكنز المرء؟ المرأة الصالحة. إذا نظر إليها سرته، وإذا أمرها

أطاعته، وإذا غاب عنها حفظته"

"Shall I tell you the best treasure a man can have? It is a good wife. If he looks at her, she gives him pleasure; if he orders her, she obeys; and if he is away from her, she remains faithful to him."[33]

Annas RAA narrated that the prophet *SAAW* said,

"من رزقه الله امرأة صالحة فقد أعانه على شطر دينه فليتق الله في الشطر الآخر"

"Whoever is granted a good wife, he is helped to follow half his religion, let him obey Allah in the other half."[34]

Among early-generation Muslims, it was said, "When you get your daughter married, let her marry a man of faith; if he loves her, he will treat her nobly, and if he hates her, he will not be unfair."

From all of the above sayings and verses, the selection criteria for men could be summarized as follows:
- Religious practices/Righteousness
- Good manners
- Strength
- Honesty and trustworthiness

A criterion for both of men and women is compatibility.

As for ladies, the main criterion is religious practices, righteousness, and good manners. Secondary is her beauty, wealth, and social status.

The prophet *SAAW* also recommended the following criteria as supplemental:

---

[33] Al Hakim
[34] Al Bayhaqey

- Ability to bear children
- Virginity
- Contentment and loving attitude

These are derived from the prophet's *SAAW* following sayings:

"تزوجوا الودود الولود إني مكاثر بكم الأنبياء يوم القيامة"

"Get married to a woman who is loving and can bear many children, because I'll boast of your numbers (on the Day of Resurrection)."[35]

"عليكم بالأبكار فإنهن أنتق رحما، وأعذب أفواها، وأرضى باليسير"

" Get married to virgins, because they have more fertile wombs, sweeter mouths, less slyness, and are more likely to be satisfied with little."[36]

The North American Situation

Although the number of Muslims in North America is currently increasing at a substantial rate, communities are still scattered all over the continent. With the exception of large communities in big cities, it is not easy for most youth to find a match in the same local community. It may be the case that most marriages taking place in North America are between people from different cities. These marriages are mainly completed in the following ways:

1- Through contacts from parents to their friends in various cities asking about the availability of brides and grooms for their children.

2- Through matrimonial adds in Islamic national magazines and websites, as well as through matrimonial desks during national Islamic conventions and regional conferences. Success rates of good matches using these methods is rare, since the information provided in these adds is very brief and doesn't provide much in-depth knowledge about the personality of either spouse.

---

[35] Ahmad
[36] Ibn Majah

3- Some immigrants resort to contacting people in their country of origin to find a suitable match for their children. The different backgrounds of the bride-to-be and groom-to-be represent an added challenge to the newly formed family. Another disadvantage to this method is the expected imbalance it may create in the male/female ratio of youth at the age of marriage in North America

4- A third group of Muslim youth get married to non Muslims without paying much attention to Islamic marriage rules regarding marrying people of the book. This issue will be discussed in detail later in this chapter.

How Parents and Community Can Help

Parents in North America can do a great deal to help their children get married and form new Muslim families. Here are a few suggestions:

1. Be reasonable in their expectations. Some families have unrealistic expectations from the bride or groom they are seeking for their young adult child. Some may refuse to marry their daughter to a person who may be still studying to finish his university degree. Others may request a very high dowry from the groom. A third group will only consider marrying their daughter to somebody who is financially well established. A fourth group will never consider the thought that their daughter or son could marry a Muslim from a different ethnic background. More narrow-minded parents, which are not rare in this continent, would only consider marrying their daughters to men of certain professions, such as medical doctors or engineers. These unrealistic expectations complicate the matter further, and make it hard for those young adults to get married. Parents should be reasonable in their expectations and should stick to the criteria given by the *Qur'an* and the teachings of Prophet Muhammad *SAAW* as the main source for the selection process of the spouses they seek for their children.

2. Provide the needed support through the proper understanding of the role and status of women in Islam, and avoid the unnecessary pressures of culture. *Insha'a Allah* we will discuss, the status of women in Islam in detail in a later chapter. As for the unnecessary pressures of culture, we have found that many Muslims living in North America stick to the cultural package that they brought with them from their own countries. Some of them even socialize only with families from the same ethnic background. They are very particular about imposing this culture on their children irrespective of its suitability to the new environment. We know that culture could be Islamic, neutral, or, in some cases, anti-Islamic. We believe that Muslims should regularly check their cultural practices and make sure they don't contradict with Islamic practices. We should stick to whatever is Islamic in our culture. As for the Islamically neutral cultural practices, we should test their validity in the new environment. If they are applicable and suitable, we can use them. If they are not suitable to the environment, then it is better not to use them. As for the anti-Islamic cultural practices, we should avoid them completely, at all costs.

3. Provide the proper environment and healthy atmosphere for youth to meet and find out about each other without violating Islamic rules and away from the western style free mixing. This can be done through some of the following activities:
   a) Islamic camps
   b) Community projects
   c) Team building activities

Without a doubt, this has to be done under adult supervision to ensure the safety of the participants and make sure that Islamic principles and guidelines related to gender relations are observed.

Matching Questionnaires

Back in the good old days, in the countries of origin of most Muslim immigrants, marriage was simple. People lived close to each other; they could visit and talk regularly to the family of the prospective spouse. Now, with Muslim communities in North America scattered all over the continent, completing a questionnaire as an initial step may be the best way to simplify the process and save money and travel time for both prospective spouses.

The companions of the prophet *SAAW* were always very careful when they sought information about anybody. *Omar RAA* always demanded complete and accurate details about those whom he dealt with. It was reported that a man came to him asking for a job. *Omar RAA* told the man to bring him somebody who knew the man personally. The man came back with another individual, *Omar* asked him, "Do you know this man?"

"Yes," the man replied.
Omar then asked him "Did you travel with him?"
"No," the man replied.
Omar then asked, "Perhaps you have dealt with him on a financial level?"
"No," the man replied.
Omar said, "Perhaps you are his neighbor?"
"No," the man replied again.
Omar then told him, "Perhaps you have seen him doing his prayer in the Mosque. Go; you don't know him." *Omar* then turned to the first man and told him, "Bring me somebody who knows you."

That is why this questionnaire may look lengthy. It is meant to give detailed knowledge about each marriage candidate to ensure better matching. Following are two questionnaires, one for male candidates and another for female candidates.

Facilitators helping in the matching process must make sure that the information provided is kept completely confidential and should assure candidates of that. Facilitators should be known in the community as trustworthy and God-fearing individuals. They should remove the name and personal data from the questionnaire before passing it to the suggested match. If there seems to be initial agreement from both sides, facilitators should then ask candidates if they agree to pass the personal data to their prospective match.

Of course, this questionnaire can't replace visits and telephone conversations between the two families; however, it will provide the first step in the process of selection, and then of course, other steps will come later.

While completing the questionnaire candidates are encouraged to elaborate as much as they can; extra paper can be used (candidates should remember to indicate the number of the question being answered.) Finally, candidates may answer in either English or any other language that they are more comfortable expressing themselves in, (assuming that the facilitator can understand this language), e.g. Arabic or Urdu. Please type your answers or write very clearly.

For this questionnaire to be of benefit, the candidate needs to think about and write exactly what s/he would do in most situations (not necessarily what s/he should do).

Male Matching Questionnaire

Personal Data

[37]*Name: ---------------------------- *Date of Birth: ----------------

*Address : --

Education : ---

Citizenship(s) : --

Residency status in North America:------------------------------------

Family Data

City and country where parents live: --------------------------------

*Names of brothers & sisters: ---------------------------------------
(please, list in order & indicate marital status with letter M) --------
----

Have you ever married before?
Yes   No
If your answer is Yes, please provide a summary about the case, indicating your status now, the number of children you have, and the reason for dissolving the marriage

---

[37] All personal data marked with * should be masked by the facilitator before passing the completed questionnaire to the potential match.

Get to know more about me

1- I believe that the purpose of life is-----------------------------------

----

2- The main objectives that I want to reach in my life are to (please number them in order of priority)
a) Achieve financial independence
b) Have a good family life
c) Be rich
d) Secure a successful ---- Job------ Career   ------ Business
e) Be a better person by doing more actions that please Allah
f) Work for the Islamic cause and participate in improving Muslims' situation
g) Others, please specify--

3- This is how I spend my extra time after work and dinner
a) Playing sports   %
b) Watching TV   %
c) Socializing with family   %
d) Socializing with friends   %
e) Reading and studying   %
f) Doing Outdoor activities (camping, walking, etc.)   %
g) Attending Islamic activities/community work   %
h) Taking a nap and staying up late at night   %
i) Others (specify)   %

4- Please write about the different hobbies you have, and indicate which of them you are practicing now
----

5- On a scale of 1 to 5, where 1 is low and 5 is high, this is where I measure in the following aspects:

a) I enjoy meeting new people and socializing with them.
                                        1 2 3 4 5
b) I feel comfortable expressing my opinion in a group (family, friends, or strangers).
                                        1 2 3 4 5
c) I feel comfortable defending my opinion in a group (family, friends, or strangers).
                                        1 2 3 4 5
d) I love children's company.   1 2 3 4 5
e) I get annoyed when others don't accept my views.
                                        1 2 3 4 5

f) I feel insecure and depressed when my plans don't work and can't get over it for a long time.

1 2 3 4 5

g) I lose my temper when I am tired but expected to do more.

1 2 3 4 5

h) I stand up for my rights even if it is hard to do so.

1 2 3 4 5

i) I have a hard time making big decisions; often, I leave it to somebody else.

1 2 3 4 5

j) I usually meet my deadlines and am on time for my appointments.

1 2 3 4 5

k) I can work with others and accommodate them.

1 2 3 4 5

l) I expect my partners to do a perfect job and find it hard to overlook their mistakes.

1 2 3 4 5

m) I give my opinion of others in a direct and blunt way.

1 2 3 4 5

n) I feel I can make a difference, and I try my best to improve situations.

1 2 3 4 5

o) I think before I say a word.

1 2 3 4 5

For questions 6 to 9, you may circle more than one choice. You may also cross out parts of the statement if they don't apply to you.

6- When I'm stressed for a major reason, I
a) Lose my appetite and eat very little
b) Lose my temper, yell, and shout
c) Read *Qur'an* and make *Dua'a*
d) Talk to a close friend
e) Take a walk or read a book
f) Go to sleep
g) Blame others

7- Whenever I have an argument (little fight) with a very close family member, this is how I react
a) I get angry and upset. I start shouting and blaming the other person.
b) I go and complain to other family members about him or her.
c) I become very quiet and withdrawn and stop talking to the person for over three days.
d) I become quiet for a short while, (a few hours,) leaving the door open for further discussion at another time.

8- When making a decision that is of concern to the whole family, which of the following would you do?
a) Make the decision alone
b) Consult with the rest of the family members and reach a mutual agreement
c) Consult but don't consider the others' point(s) of view

9- I would like my wife to dress in public as follows:
a) Loose, covering, and nontransparent clothes for body and a scarf to cover her head (whatever she feels comfortable with)
b) *Gelbab* and scarf
c) *Gelbab* and *Khimar*
d) *Niqab* and gloves
e) Others, please specify

10- Give your opinion about the following incidents and suggest the best way to handle the situation.
a) A friend has a daughter who refuses to wear *Hijab* even after she is told the *hadeeth* about not entering paradise because of that.

----

b) A friend has a 1-year-old baby. The wife has no immediate family in the same town to help her. The wife wants to attend an Islamic *halaqa*. This requires that the husband take care of the baby for 3 hours a week during the *halaqa*. The husband says that he is not used to this; the baby is her responsibility.

----

c) A friend is having problems at work. His wife hears him discuss these problems with his friends over the phone, but he never mentions it to her. When the wife asks him about what is going on, his answer is that there is nothing she can do about it, that he can handle this alone.

----

d) A lady is complaining to her mother that her husband never discloses their financial status to her. Every time she asks him about how much he earns or how much their savings are, his answer is, "Why do you ask about this? Don't you have enough?"

----

e) A friend has a wife who has a personality conflict with his sister. Whenever they visit, there is tension in the air. Usually after the visit, the husband is very upset and always blames his wife. The wife feels that she is trying hard enough, while his sister is not. She also feels that the husband is taking his sister's side all the time and demanding too much of her.

----

f) A friend who wants to get married finds the right match in a university student who is ready for marriage provided that she can continue her education after marriage. He is not sure what to do because this may mean delaying having children for a few years as well as less time spent by his wife on cooking and housekeeping. What would you advise him?

11- List the qualities you would like to have in your future spouse in order of priority. Please categorize them in the following categories:

1) Must have	2) Nice to have

12- Write a few lines on your understanding of the concept of *Qawamah* as derived from the following verse:

"الرِّجَالُ قَوَّامُونَ عَلَى النِّسَاء بِمَا فَضَّلَ اللّهُ بَعْضَهُمْ عَلَى بَعْضٍ وَبِمَا أَنفَقُواْ مِنْ أَمْوَالِهِمْ فَالصَّالِحَاتُ قَانِتَاتٌ حَافِظَاتٌ لِّلْغَيْبِ بِمَا حَفِظَ اللّهُ"

"Men are the protectors and maintainers of women, because Allah has given the one more (strength) than the other, and because they support them from their means. Therefore the righteous women are devoutly obedient, and guard in (the husband's) absence what Allah would have them guard."[38]

13- Write a few lines on your understanding of polygamy in Islam
----

----

[38] (Q4, V34)

14- Please write a few lines on your understanding of the following verses:

"لِلَّهِ مُلْكُ السَّمَاوَاتِ وَالْأَرْضِ يَخْلُقُ مَا يَشَاءُ يَهَبُ لِمَنْ يَشَاءُ إِنَاثًا وَيَهَبُ لِمَن يَشَاءُ الذُّكُورَ أَوْ يُزَوِّجُهُمْ ذُكْرَانًا وَإِنَاثًا وَيَجْعَلُ مَن يَشَاءُ عَقِيمًا إِنَّهُ عَلِيمٌ قَدِيرٌ"

"Unto Allah belongs the Sovereignty of the heavens and the earth. He creates what He wills. He bestows female (offspring) upon whom He wills, and bestows male (offspring) upon whom He wills."[39]

15- Please answer the following with Yes or No. Feel free to cross out any part of the statement that doesn't represent your view

---

[39] (Q42, V49-50)

a) I believe that family decisions should be taken by the husband, while the wife and children should listen and follow
Yes   No

b) I believe that family decisions should be discussed between husband and wife to reach a common understanding of the situation. The couple should then involve the children and allow them to express their opinions. It is then the husband's responsibility to make the final decision taking his family's opinion into consideration.
Yes   No

c) I believe that the man is the head of the family. He doesn't need to consult with his family. His wife should obey all his orders in both major issues, such as moving houses; visiting families overseas; and deciding on the children's schooling, and in minor issues such as visiting friends and deciding how to spend leisure time.
Yes   No

d) I believe that a wife should listen to and obey her husband. The husband should be accommodative and, instead of giving orders, discuss and use the "give and take" approach.
Yes   No

e) I believe that my wife's first and most important duty is to prepare tasty good meals, clean the house, and make sure all my needs and wishes are met.
Yes   No

f) I believe that ensuring a reasonably clean and tidy house, preparing healthy meals for the family, and meeting my needs are among my wife's other responsibilities such as increasing her knowledge and education, taking care of the children, participating in Islamic activities, and taking on responsibilities to fulfill community needs.
Yes   No

g) I believe that a husband should help with the children so his wife can be relieved of being with the children all the time.
Yes   No

h) I believe that the children are the mother's responsibility and the father has enough responsibility earning a living for the family. He should not be bothered in helping the mother.

Yes   No

i) I believe that husband and wife can be friends, supporting each other, learning from one another; and sharing knowledge, experience, and feelings with one another in a relationship founded on mercy, kindness, and compassion.

Yes   No

j) I believe that the marriage relationship can't be a friendship. Only the wife can learn from the husband and these limits should be set.

Yes   No

k) I believe that a Muslim man should try to marry more than one wife in an effort to revive the *Sunnah*.

Yes   No

l) I believe that Islamic law allows Muslim men to marry more than one wife as an answer to certain situations.

Yes   No

Islamic Practices

Circle Yes or No; you may cross out parts of the statements.

a) I pray the 5 daily prayers on time except when I can't find a convenient situation.

Yes   No

b) I pray the 5 daily prayers on time under any circumstances and plan my activities around prayer time so that I won't miss any.

Yes   No

c) I pray *Sunnah*, *Nafl*, and *Taraweeh* in *Ramadan*.

Yes   No

d) I fast *Ramadan* and extra days.

Yes   No

e) I attend an Islamic study circle, seminars, and activities.

Yes   No

f) I take an active role in helping with Islamic activities in any way needed.

Yes   No

g) I read Islamic books, magazines, and I listen to Islamic tapes such as ---
----
----

h) I educate myself about the society that I live in so I can have better judgment.
Yes   No

Financial Data and Future Plans

Current employment ---

Monthly income   ---

Financial obligations ---

City and country you intend to live in for the next 5 years:-----------
----

City and country you plan to settle down in -------------------------
----

Female Matching Questionnaire
Personal Data

[40]*Name:-----------------------------------*Date of Birth:------------

*Address:---

Education:---

Citizenship(s):---

---

[40] All personal data marked with * should be masked by the facilitator before passing the completed questionnaire to the potential match.

Family Data

City and country where parents live:

----

*Names of brothers & sisters:
(please list in order & indicate marital status with letter M)

Have you ever married before?
Yes   No
If your answer is Yes, please provide a summary about the case, indicating your status now, the number of children you have, and the reason for dissolving the marriage.

Get to know more about me

1- I believe that the purpose of life is----------------------------------
----

2- The main objectives that I want to reach in my life are to (please number them in order of priority)
a) Achieve financial independence
b) Have a good family life
c) Be rich
d) Secure a successful ---- Job ------ Career ------ Business
e) Be a better person by doing more actions that please Allah
f) Work for the Islamic cause and participate in improving Muslims' situation
g) Others, please specify--

3- This is how I spend my extra time after work and supper
a) Shopping   %
b) Watching TV   %
c) Socializing with family   %
d) Socializing with friends   %
e) Reading and studying   %
f) Playing sports   %
g) Doing outdoor activities (camping, walking...etc.)   %
h) Attending Islamic activities/community work   %
i) Taking a nap and staying up late at night   %
j) Others (specify)   %

4- Please write about the different hobbies you have and which of them you are practicing now
----

5- On a scale of 1 to 5, where 1 is low and 5 is high, this is where I measure in the following aspects:
a) I enjoy meeting new people and socializing with them.
                                                1 2 3 4 5
b) I feel comfortable expressing my opinion in a group (family, friends, or strangers).
                                                1 2 3 4 5
c) I feel comfortable defending my opinion in a group (family, friends, or strangers).
                                                1 2 3 4 5
d) I love children's company.
                                                1 2 3 4 5
e) I get annoyed when others don't accept my views.
                                                1 2 3 4 5

f) I feel insecure and depressed when my plans don't work and can't get over it for long time.

1 2 3 4 5

g) I lose my temper when I am tired but expected to do more.

1 2 3 4 5

h) I stand up for my rights even if it is hard to do so

1 2 3 4 5

i) I have a hard time making big decisions; often I leave it to somebody else. 1 2 3 4 5

j) I usually meet my deadlines and am on time for my appointments.

1 2 3 4 5

k) I can work with others and accommodate them. 1 2 3 4 5

l) I expect my partners to do a perfect job and find it hard to overlook their mistakes. 1 2 3 4 5

m) I give my opinion of others in a direct and blunt way.

1 2 3 4 5

n) I feel I can make a difference, and I try my best to improve situations.

1 2 3 4 5

o) I think before I say a word. 1 2 3 4 5

For questions 6 to 9, you may circle more than one choice. You may also cross out parts of the statement if they don't apply to you.

6- When I'm stressed for a major reason, I
a) Lose my appetite and eat very little
b) Lose my temper, yell, and shout
c) Read *Qur'an* and make *Dua'a*
d) Talk to a close friend
e) Take a walk or read a book
f) Go to sleep
g) Blame others

7- Whenever I have an argument (little fight) with a very close family member, this is how I react

a) I get angry and upset. I start shouting and blaming the other person.
b) I go and complain to other family members about him or her.
c) I become very quiet and withdrawn and stop talking to the person for over three days.
d) I become quiet for a short while, (a few hours,) leaving the door open for further discussion at another time.

8- When making a decision that is of concern to the whole family, which of the following would you do?
a) Make the decision alone
b) Consult with the rest of the family members and reach a mutual agreement
c) Consult but don't consider the others' point(s) of view

9- This is how I dress in public:
a) Loose, covering, and nontransparent clothes for body and a scarf to cover my head(whatever I feel comfortable with)
b) *Gelbab* and scarf
c) *Gelbab* and *Khimar*
d) *Niqab* and gloves
e) Others, please specify

10- Put yourself in the position of the wife in each of the following situations and suggest the best way to handle the situation.
a) This wife gets satisfaction from talking all the time. As soon as her husband walks through the door after work, she starts complaining to him about her day. Her husband feels that she does not have any valuable interests. He tried to discuss this matter with her, and encouraged her to get involved in some meaningful activities, but she was very hurt and insulted. Her response was, "You don't love me anymore."

---

b) This husband expects his wife to handle all the children's affairs without any of his help. His excuse is that he is working out of the house all day long and that the children are the wife's responsibility.

---

c) This husband is very moody. Occasionally he gets upset and hot tempered. During that time, he shouts and yells at his wife and children. When he cools down, he feels bad about what he did and apologizes in his own way. However, before long he gets hot tempered again. This causes the wife to feel unhappy and very concerned about the children's upbringing.

---

d) This wife is concerned and occasionally unhappy. She always has to budget very carefully since her husband's income is limited. She feels guilty about her unhappy feelings, since her husband has always been gentle and kind, and he cares about her a lot.

---

e) A friend of yours has a personality conflict with her sister-in-law. Whenever they visit, there is tension in the air. The husband feels it is important to be good to his family, so usually after each visit, he is very upset and always blames his wife. The wife feels that she is trying hard enough, while his sister is not. She also feels that the husband is taking his sister's side all the time and demanding too much of her. What would you advise her?

----

f) A wife complains that her husband is working very long hours and that she is lonely and bored. She also complains that the husband is not helping at all in any household chores.

----

g) This wife likes to travel every year to spend the summer break with her family overseas. She leaves her husband alone since his work schedule does not allow him to come. Her husband is not happy with this situation. She insists that she needs to go to be able to bear living away from her family.

----

h) This husband has a three-year-old daughter from a previous marriage. His daughter visits him regularly at his house. The daughter is very spoiled and demanding; however, her dad usually lets it go. The wife feels that it has gone too far and that her life is being disturbed by this behavior. Whenever she tells her husband to take a stand, his answer is, "I don't want to loose her to her mother."

I) This husband takes good care of his family as far as meeting their material needs. However, he never pays attention to his wife's request regarding sharing their feelings together. The wife's complaint is that there must be more to their relationship than just eating together and satisfying each other's physical needs. She is trying to think of ways to change this situation.

---

j) This husband provides his family with a good standard of living from the material point of view. However, his wife is really unhappy. She says he never lets her relax and enjoy events. He is always focused on pointing out her shortcomings and what she isn't able to do. He is just as critical with their children and with all people who are close to him. She wants to be happy, but is not sure what to do to fix the situation.

---

k) This wife complains that her husband is not taking part in the children's upbringing. The husband says that when he comes home from work feeling very tired and drained, his wife expects him to take over with the children right away. The wife is looking for suggestions to help the situation.

---

l) This husband feels very grateful to his parents, but he lives far away from them. To make up for being away, he regularly sends expensive gifts and a monthly allowance to his parents. His wife feels that he is not considerate enough to his own family (herself and the children) because he is not saving up for the children's education. She is thinking about seeking somebody else's help, since her husband never takes her requests seriously.

11- List the qualities you would like to have in your future spouse in order of priority. Please categorize them in the following categories:

1) Must have	2) Nice to have

12- Write a few lines on your understanding of the concept of "Qawamah" as derived from the following verse:

"الرِّجَالُ قَوَّامُونَ عَلَى النِّسَاءِ بِمَا فَضَّلَ اللّهُ بَعْضَهُمْ عَلَى بَعْضٍ وَبِمَا أَنفَقُواْ مِنْ أَمْوَالِهِمْ فَالصَّالِحَاتُ قَانِتَاتٌ حَافِظَاتٌ لِّلْغَيْبِ بِمَا حَفِظَ اللّهُ"

"Men are the protectors and maintainers of women, because Allah has given the one more (strength) than the other, and because they support them from their means. Therefore the righteous women are devoutly obedient, and guard in (the husband's) absence what Allah would have them guard."[41]

13- Write a few lines on your understanding of polygamy in Islam
----

----

[41] (Q4, V34)

14- Please write a few lines on your understanding of the following verses:

"لِلَّهِ مُلْكُ السَّمَاوَاتِ وَالْأَرْضِ يَخْلُقُ مَا يَشَاءُ يَهَبُ لِمَنْ يَشَاءُ إِنَاثًا وَيَهَبُ لِمَن يَشَاءُ الذُّكُورَ أَوْ يُزَوِّجُهُمْ ذُكْرَانًا وَإِنَاثًا وَيَجْعَلُ مَن يَشَاءُ عَقِيمًا إِنَّهُ عَلِيمٌ قَدِيرٌ"

"Unto Allah belongs the Sovereignty of the heavens and the earth. He creates what He wills. He bestows female (offspring) upon whom He wills, and bestows male (offspring) upon whom He wills."[42]

15- Please answer the following with Yes or No. Feel free to cross out any part of the statement that doesn't represent your view

a) I believe that family decisions should be taken by the husband, while the wife and children should listen and follow.
Yes   No
b) I believe that family decisions should be discussed between husband and wife to reach a common understanding of the situation. The couple should then involve the children and allow them to express their opinions. It is then the husband's

---

[42] (Q42, V49-50)

responsibility to make the final decision, taking his family's opinions into consideration.

Yes   No

c) I believe that the man is the head of the family. He doesn't need to consult with them. His wife should obey all his orders in both major issues, such as moving houses; visiting families overseas; and deciding on the children's schooling, and in minor issues such as visiting friends and deciding how to spend leisure time.

Yes   No

d) I believe that a wife should listen and obey her husband. The husband should be accommodative and, instead of giving orders, discuss and use the "give and take" approach.

Yes   No

e) I believe that a wife's first and most important duty is to prepare tasty good meals, clean the house, and make sure all her husband's needs and wishes are met.

Yes   No

f) I believe that ensuring a reasonably clean and tidy house, preparing healthy meals for the family, and meeting her husband's needs are among a wife's other responsibilities such as increasing her knowledge and education, taking care of the children, participating in Islamic activities, and taking on responsibilities to fulfill community needs.

Yes   No

g) I believe that a husband should help with the children so his wife can be relieved of being with the children all the time.

Yes   No

h) I believe that children are the mother's responsibility and the father has enough responsibility earning a living for the family. He should not be bothered in helping the mother.

Yes   No

i) I believe that a husband and wife can be friends, supporting each other; learning from one another; sharing knowledge, experience, and feelings with one another in a relationship founded on mercy, kindness, and compassion.

Yes   No

j) I believe that a marriage relationship can't be a friendship. Only the wife can learn from the husband and these limits should be set.
Yes   No

k) I believe that a Muslim man should try to marry more than one wife in an effort to revive the Sunnah.
Yes   No

l) I believe that Islamic law allows Muslim men to marry more than one wife as an answer to certain situations.
Yes   No

Islamic Practices

Circle Yes or No; you may cross out parts of the statements.

a) I pray the 5 daily prayers on time except when I can't find a convenient situation.
Yes   No

b) I pray the 5 daily prayers on time under any circumstances and plan my activities around prayer time so that I won't miss any.
Yes   No

c) I pray *Sunnah*, *Nafl*, and *Taraweeh* in *Ramadan*.
Yes   No

d) I fast *Ramadan* and extra days.
Yes   No

e) I attend an Islamic study circle, seminars, and activities.
Yes   No

f) I take an active role in helping with Islamic activities in any way needed.
Yes   No

g) I read Islamic books and magazines and listen to Islamic tapes such as --
----

----

h) I educate myself about the society that I live in so I can have better judgment
Yes   No

Financial Data and Future Plans

Current employment --

Monthly income   --

Financial obligations ---

City and country you intend to live in for the next 5 years:-----------

City and country you plan to settle down in ---------------------------
----
Are you willing to relocate to another city, if your future husband's work requires?

Yes   Conditional Yes   No
If your answer is conditional Yes, what are these conditions?

How to Make the Best Use of This Questionnaire

1- Take your time to read, understand, and answer all the questions in detail. This is your ambassador to those who read your response.
2- While completing the questionnaire, be very careful not to write what you think you should do, but take a moment to think of what you would actually do and write it, even if you don't like it.

3- When you receive a completed questionnaire, read in between the lines. After reading it once or twice, leave it for a couple of days, then read it again several times.

4- Do *Istekhara* prayer several times. At the same time, try to think objectively about the matter.

5- If you think that it is a good match, you need to do two things:
   a) Arrange a way for you and the candidate to continue communicating with the help of the facilitator or parents. Meetings and telephone conversations are good methods.
   b) Verify the impression you formed through the questionnaire about the person by talking to trustworthy individuals in his community after seeking his permission.

You can start with either a or b.

Final Word Concerning Questionnaires

Finally, we would like to share with you these words of wisdom. Marriage is not a simple relationship. As such preparing yourself for marriage is a wise thing to do. *Insha'a Allah*, it will increase your chances of a successful and happy marriage.

During our counseling for couples with marital problems, we found that the lack of preparation for marriage by one or both spouses is a common reason for problems in most cases. To avoid this, we suggest the following:

1- Prepare yourself for marriage through acquiring authentic Islamic knowledge about the subject.

2- Select a spouse who has the same goals in life and the same value system as you.

3- Work hard at improving your living habits and your social and communication skills.

4- Be realistic regarding your expectations from your spouse, and remember that it is natural for spouses to have different habits and likings. Committed, understanding couples should be able to work out their differences and have a successful marriage. In a later chapter, we will discuss in detail the Islamic way of conflict resolution.

May Allah help every Muslim find the right match and have a good, successful marriage.

Marriage From the People of the Book

As indicated in *Surat Al Ma'edah*, Islam allows marriage from the people of the book, i.e., Jews and Christians. Allah says,

"الْيَوْمَ أُحِلَّ لَكُمُ الطَّيِّبَاتُ وَطَعَامُ الَّذِينَ أُوتُواْ الْكِتَابَ حِلٌّ لَّكُمْ وَطَعَامُكُمْ حِلٌّ لَّهُمْ وَالْمُحْصَنَاتُ مِنَ الْمُؤْمِنَاتِ وَالْمُحْصَنَاتُ مِنَ الَّذِينَ أُوتُواْ الْكِتَابَ مِن قَبْلِكُمْ إِذَا آتَيْتُمُوهُنَّ أُجُورَهُنَّ مُحْصِنِينَ غَيْرَ مُسَافِحِينَ وَلاَ مُتَّخِذِي أَخْدَانٍ وَمَن يَكْفُرْ بِالإِيمَانِ فَقَدْ حَبِطَ عَمَلُهُ وَهُوَ فِي الآخِرَةِ مِنَ الْخَاسِرِينَ"

"This day are (all) things good and pure made lawful unto you. The food of the People of the Book is lawful unto you and yours is lawful unto them. (Lawful unto you in marriage) are (not only) chaste women who are believers, but chaste women among the People of the Book, revealed before your time,- when ye give them their due dowers, and desire chastity, not lewdness, nor secret intrigues if any one rejects faith, fruitless is his work, and in the Hereafter he will be in the ranks of those who have lost (all spiritual good)."[43]

It is important to note the following:

The Condition Stated in the Verse
This condition of "chaste women" stated in the above verse is nearly impossible to meet in today's North American society considering the following statistics[44]:

---

[43] (Q5, V5)
[44] Monitoring the future study, Institute of Social Research, University of Michigan, 1998

- In the next 24 hours in the U.S. alone, 1439 teens will attempt suicide, 2795 teenage girls will become pregnant, 15 006 teens will use drugs for the first time, and 3506 teens will run away.
- One fourth of all adolescents contract a sexually transmitted disease before they graduate from high school.

The Practice of the Early Muslims

Although this marriage is allowed according to the previous verse, it was never recommended. As a matter of fact, most of the time it was discouraged. The following incidents illustrate this fact:

- It was narrated that *Jabir RAA* said "I witnessed the battle of *Qadessiah* with *Sa'd*, at which we married some of the women of the people of the book. When the battle finished and we returned, some of us divorced them and some stayed married to them."[45]

- When *Omar RAA* learned that some Muslims are marrying from the women of the people of the book, he wrote the following to *Hozaifah RAA*:

"It reached me that you took a woman of the people of the book in marriage; I instruct you to divorce her."

Hozaifah answered him, "I will not do what you tell me until you tell me whether it is allowed or prohibited and you explain the reasoning behind your instruction."

Omar RAA answered, "No, I don't say it is prohibited, but I'm afraid that you may marry of the women who are not chaste"[46].

- In another narration, when *Hozaifah RAA* confronted *Omar RAA* saying, "Do you claim that this practice is prohibited so I should divorce her."

Omar RAA answered, "No, it is allowed, but those women are attractive and may spoil your relationships with your Muslim women."[47]

Muslims in North America are a Minority

When discussing this verse, most Muslim scholars indicate that this marriage is allowed mainly in a society where Muslims are a

---

[45] *History of messengers and kings* by Tabary, 3/588
[46] *AlQurtoby Tafseer*:3/68 and *Ibn Katheer Tafseer*:1/376
[47] Same as above

majority. In this case, the general practices of the Muslim society may affect the lady from the people of the book and she may revert to Islam. Even if she doesn't accept Islam, the children are not in great danger of loosing their Islamic identity because of the Islamic environment surrounding them.

The Reality of the North American Condition
The reality is that, for so many cases of marriage from the people of the book over the last few decades, the marriage ended in divorce. The children ended up with their mothers because the court system often grants custody to mothers over fathers. In most cases, the children grew up as Christians because of their mothers' influence and their fathers' absence. We have witnessed these situations through our involvement in marriage counseling.

The Impact on Muslim Women
Another point that Muslims have to consider before making the decision of whether or not to marry from the people of the book is the impact that their decision will have on Muslim women. If many young Muslim men marry from the people of the book, while young Muslim women are not allowed to marry non-Muslim men, there will be an imbalance in the number of Muslim men and Muslim women at the marriageable age. This will definitely put young Muslim women at a disadvantage. Some of these women may not find a husband and may even live the rest of their life without marriage.

A Word of Caution
Considering all of the above reasons, our recommendation with respect to marriage from the people of the book is as follows:
1. At this point in time, this practice should be completely discouraged among Muslim men in North America.
2. In some extreme cases, it could be practiced provided that the following precautions are taken:
   a) The potential spouse must take medical tests to ensure that she does not have any diseases that may have fatal effects on the family.

b) The spouses must include an article in the marriage contract that indicates that, in the case of a divorce, the father will be granted custody of the children. If this is impossible, at least include an article ensuring that the children will follow the *Deen* of their father, i.e. it will be their fathers' right to teach them Islam and their mother can't take them to church or any other religious institutions outside Muslim institutions.

Now, it is important to clarify that, if the woman accepts Islam before marriage, the condition of being chaste should be disregarded, because Allah forgives all the mistakes and sins that people committed before they accepted Islam. The prophet *SAAW* said,

"الإسلام يجب ما قبله"

What this means is that when a person accepts Islam, any bad deeds s/he previously committed are not held against her/him.[48]

---

[48] Muslim

4 - Tried and Proven Recipes
For a Successful Marriage

Introduction

This chapter may be the most important chapter in this book, especially for those who really want to make their marriage a wonderful and successful experience that will last as long as they live together in this life and, by the grace of Allah, after death when they reunite in *Jannah*. *Insha'a Allah*, we will present the ingredients for a successful marriage as essential qualities that both spouses should aspire to acquire and adhere to during their interactions. Practicing and adhering to these qualities and principles will *insha'a Allah* ensure a very successful marriage. At the end of this chapter, we will present several recipes using these ingredients, each for a different situation.

Ingredients

The ingredients of a successful marriage are a combination of good qualities and attributes, mixed with certain positive skills, accompanied by a deep sense of responsibility and dedication toward the success of the marriage. Both spouses have to practice these qualities and instill them into their own habits and behaviors. They also need to strive hard to learn and implement these skills in their daily interactions with each other. Some of these qualities and skills need to be practiced on a regular basis with special attention to timing and tact in terms of not overdoing them. Others have to be completely avoided. Among the ones to practice and cherish are the seven essential Cs (commitment, courtesy, communication, care, contentment, contribution, and compromise), the seven magical Ss (sensitivity, sincerity, security, support, satisfaction, sharing, and sexual gratification), the five wonderful As (adaptation, accommodation, appreciation, anticipation, and acceptance) as well as other qualities such as *Rahmah, Mawadah*, (whose meanings are explained later in the chapter,) forgiveness, trust and faithfulness, open mindedness and understanding, respect, and patience. The qualities to avoid are the three nasty Bs (blunt, blaming, and belittling) and the three ugly Ps (picking on, particular, and perfectionist), which we will discuss in chapter five.

Let us now speak in detail about these qualities, attributes, and skills.

The Seven Essential 'C's

Commitment

Commitment to the marriage tops this list. Without the commitment of both spouses to work hard for the success of this noble bond, it is impossible for the marriage to succeed against all the odds; the new environment, new partner, new habits, and new routines all represent challenges to the marriage. Both spouses need unyielding commitment to resolve problems and work out any differences that may occur at the beginning of the marriage as well as later on. It is normal for conflicts to occur in the marital relationship; they do happen, no matter how close the spouses are. Even the prophet *SAAW* had conflicts with his wives. A strong commitment to the success of the marriage helps spouses resolve these conflicts and avoid further complications in the marital relationship. Marriage is not about getting what you want; rather it is about wanting what you get. You need the commitment in order to be able to be flexible and accommodate each other and, in turn, get along well with each other. To do that, it takes both spouses, not the wife alone or the husband alone.

The divorce rate among Muslim families in North America is much higher than our parents generation's divorce rate. The main reason, in our view, is the level of commitment to marriage. Our parents' generation understood that marriage is as a sacred bond that should not be broken in the face of the first obstacles. They clearly understood how hard they had to work to ensure the success of their marriage. They understood that they have to do what it takes to keep this institution intact, strong, and functional, even, if that means sacrificing their own wants, whims, and desires. They understood the real meaning of the verse

"وَأَخَذْنَ مِنكُم مِّيثَاقًا غَلِيظًا"

"And they have taken from you a solemn covenant."[49]

Many people from this generation are affected by the individualistic attitude of North American society. The environment can have an unhealthy, even detrimental, impact, on individuals and groups unless they do their best to resist its effects via self-elevation and strengthening their personalities through exercising the highest level of minding Allah's instructions and becoming close to Him. Without such closeness to Allah and self-elevation, spouses tend to choose the easy way out whenever they are faced with a problem that may require making a sacrifice rather than working hard together to try to solve it. In so many cases, divorce takes place for the most trivial reasons because of a lack of commitment and the wrong understanding of what marriage is all about.

Doing your homework before marriage and following the proper process of selection based on the prophet's *SAAW* advice, as explained in detail in chapter three of this book will, without doubt *Insha'a Allah*, contribute tremendously to the development of a stronger commitment to the success of marriage. The prophet's *SAAW* advice helps us look for the qualities in our partners that will contribute to better commitment toward the marriage institution and, consequently, aid in achieving spousal harmony and a successful marriage.

---

[49] (Q 4, V 21)

Commitment is a great asset to the marriage. It requires spouses to practice patience and put the success of their marriage ahead of their own individual wants. They need to look at the family institution as a sacred bond and they should be willing to do what it takes to ensure its success.

Courtesy

Courtesy is another significant ingredient in the marriages main meal. It enhances the quality of the marriage and brings spouses closer to each other. The dictionary defines courtesy as "excellence in manner or behavior, politeness"[50]. It also mentions civility and urbanity. This means that spouses have to treat each other in a civil way that exudes respect and indicates that you always think about your spouse, take her/his interests into consideration, and try to make her/him comfortable through your offerings and observations, even through little things in your conduct.

Here are some practical examples illustrating situations and positions when spouses should exercise courtesy toward each other:

- After a long day of work or after coming back from a visit with family or friends, one of the spouses is very tired and lies down on the couch to rest for a while. Because of the exhaustion, s/he falls asleep. Instead of nagging her/him to wake up to perform the *Isha* prayer, repeatedly saying, "Wake up. Read your *Isha,* and then go upstairs to bed." It is more courteous to bring a blanket, cover your spouse, and let her/him have a short nap. If you still have energy and you will be awake for an hour or so, you can wake your spouse later before you go to bed so s/he can read *Isha* prayer. If you are afraid you may fall asleep yourself, set the alarm clock for an hour or an hour and a half later, and leave it next to your spouse. This way, your spouse would have

---

[50] Random House, *The American College Dictionary*

rested, would wake up to read the prayer, and then go upstairs to bed.

- Change the toilet roll in the dispenser as soon as you notice it needs to be changed. Don't always wait for the other spouse to do it.
- Put the milk carton back in the fridge in the same spot. If you notice something missing, write it down on the shopping list. Don't wait for the other spouse to do it.
- If you are both alternating the use of the same car, try to push the car seat back after using the car. This will make it much easier for your spouse to use the car, particularly if one of the spouses is heavy built and the other is a bit slimmer.
- If you are out, call before you come home, and ask your spouse if s/he needs you to pick anything up on your way home. Try to make it a habit; it shows courtesy to the other spouse.
- For the Wife - Be ready to receive him with a big smile and in a nice outfit, when he arrives back from his work in the evening. This applies especially if he has a fixed arrival time and you know it or if he calls before leaving his business/office to inform you that he is on his way home.

Communication

Communicating effectively is another very essential skill that both spouses should try to acquire and practice regularly. Effective and clear communication reduces the chances of misconceptions and, consequently, minimizes the frequency of marital conflicts and, in some cases, can even help spouses avoid these conflicts completely. Active listening is one of the main components of effective communication between spouses. Both should try their best to exercise it and exemplify it on a regular basis in their daily interactions. To help you do so, here are the components of active listening:

Listen

Listen to verbal messages *and* body language. The actual words of a conversation carry less than 20% of the meaning that we understand. We respond more to the speaker's tone of voice, eye contact, facial expressions, body position, etc. (Taping some family times together, with the permission of everyone involved, and then viewing them while focusing on body language, can be informative.)

Reflect

You should repeat back what you believe your spouse was saying and feeling without judging or trying to solve the problem. Allow your spouse to elaborate.

Clarify

Find out if your understanding is correct or if you have misinterpreted. Are there important details that you have overlooked?

Empathize

Empathize by trying to put yourself in your spouse's position. It may help to try to recall a similar incident that you have experienced. Tell your spouse you understand and care about how s/he feels.

This sort of effective listening will not only ensure that you really hear what your spouse is saying, but it will also signal to her/him that you can accept and understand all the that s/he wants to share. This is the beginning of good, lasting, effective communication between both of you.

When your spouse feels that you're keen to listen to her/him and suspend your judgment, s/he will be more attentive and open to your views and will respect your feelings as you did with hers/his. This will greatly enhance your relationship and create an atmosphere of mutual respect, contributing to the well-being of the marriage. *Insha'a Allah* this atmosphere will undoubtedly increase the level of commitment to the marriage and elevate the intensity of the other qualities and skills needed for a successful marriage such as trust, care, courtesy, contribution, acceptance, and willingness to compromise and accommodate each other.

<u>The Dialogue You Want</u>
Communication in marriage should never be one-way. Dialogue is a must in marriage. Scholars categorize dialogues into three main styles. These are Collaborative Dialogue, Combative Dialogue, and Cut Off Dialogue. Spouses should aspire to always achieve Collaborative dialogue. To help you in this quest, following is a table describing the characteristics of each dialogue style as presented by Suzan Heitler in her valuable book "The power of two, Secrets to a strong loving marriage." It describes each style's goal, format, tone, purpose of listening, toxicity, and attitude toward differences.

Strategy	Collaborative	Combative	Cut off
Goal	Shared understanding	To prove who is right and who is wrong. To win by inflicting the most damage or getting the other to give up.	To avoid conflicts, as conflict means unpleasant fighting.
Format	Consensus building	Debate Hurtful comments	Change the topic away from sensitive areas of difference.
Tone	Positive Friendly Productive	Adamant, attempting to persuade. Can become irritable or angry.	Underlying tension; may have false cheeriness to convey that everything is fine when it isn't.
Purpose of Listening	To hear what is right and useful in what each speaker says.	To defend against incoming information.	Listening does not occur because neither party has expressed true concerns.

| Toxicity | Tact minimizes saying anything that might hurt the other. | Toxic comments are seen as legitimate. | Criticism is avoided by steering clear of controversial topics. |
| Attitude Towards Difference | Differences are treated respectfully, appreciated and enjoyed. | Differences are divisive, leading to argument. | Differences produce disengagement, lest discussion of them evoke conflict. |

Here are some examples about phrases we should use and phrases we should avoid.

Phrases to use: what do you think of such and such, can you please get such and such, would you like to do such and such, and how about if we do such and such.

Phrases not to use: Get up, take this, go there, did you do this, and why don't you bring that.

Care

Being caring toward our spouses is another very important quality that we should all possess and try our best to accomplish. Although the husband is usually the main financial supporter for the family, and the wife is the main caregiver for the children, scholars agree that parenting our children are joint responsibilities and obligations for both spouses. Together they have to decide on the techniques that they will use to bring up their children. No husband should say, "The children are your responsibility. I have nothing to do with them! I go out and earn a living for you and put food on the table. I can't do anything with the children." This extreme from fathers is completely unacceptable in Islam. Another extreme that is not appreciated nor accepted by Islam is when mothers spend all day wasting their time on trivial telephone conversations with friends and neglect their children's care. Even when a child does something wrong, those types of mothers may not do anything to discipline him/her. All they do is say, "Go up to your room and wait for your dad to come home from work. You'll see what he is going to do with you." The right attitude is the moderate attitude, that is for both spouses to work together as a team to make sure that proper care is provided for the whole family.

Another form of care that both spouses need to observe is caring for one another, especially during tough times or, for example, when one of them is going through a difficult time with his/her health conditions. Pregnancy is usually a time of hardships, and mood changes for women. Husbands should do their best to provide the needed care and comfort for their wives during this time. It is encouraging to know that the majority of corporations offer new parents a parental leave of absence. It is recommended to use such provisions to ensure that the family receives the proper care. Such caring actions help enhance the quality of the marital relationship and leave a sweet impression in the heart of your spouse, which contributes to the well-being of the marriage and builds a strong and healthy family environment.

Prophet Muhammad *SAAW* illustrated his affection, understanding, and care to his wives in a vivid way as was narrated by *Aisha RAA* in *Sunnan An-Nisa'ee*. During her monthly period, our beloved kind-hearted prophet used to bring a cup of water for her to drink. After she had drank from it, he would look for the place from which she had sipped the water and then put his lips on it and drink from that same place, a sign of affection, care, and understanding from him *SAAW*.

He was kind and caring all the time, but he *SAAW* showed particular extra care and kindness during such times because usually during a woman's menstrual period, she feels uneasy, and needs some accommodations, such as, for example, the fact that she is not required to pray or fast.

Contentment
Contentment is an important quality that both spouses need to observe, especially the wife. It was narrated by *Jabir Ibn Abdullah RAA* that Allah's messenger *SAAW* said,

"عليكم بالأبكار فإنهن أنتق رحماً، وأعذب أفواهاً، وأرضى باليسير" وفي رواية

"وأقل خبا" أي خداعا

87

"Seek virgins in marriage, because they have more fertile wombs, sweeter mouths, less slyness, and are more easily satisfied with little (wealth)"[51]

Being content with our share of wealth and with what we have is certainly a very positive quality that will have a long-lasting effect on the health of our spousal relationships, bestow blessings on our lives, and ensure a wonderful family atmosphere. Complaining about our share of wealth in this life will only cause resentment between spouses, especially if one spouse tries to blame the situation on the other. This doesn't mean that we shouldn't try to improve our financial situations, but it means we have to go about it the right way and always leave the results to Allah *SWT*. After all *Rizq* (provision and sustenance) in this life has already been decided by Allah *SWT* and no one can change it. We are asked to do our best and be satisfied with what we get. Allah says,

"وَفِي السَّمَاء رِزْقُكُمْ وَمَا تُوعَدُونَ فَوَرَبِّ السَّمَاء وَالْأَرْضِ إِنَّهُ لَحَقٌّ مِّثْلَ مَا أَنَّكُمْ تَنطِقُونَ "

"And in heaven is your Sustenance, as (also) that which ye are promised. Then, by the Lord of heaven and earth, this is the very Truth, as much as the fact that ye can speak intelligently to each other"[52]

Allah also says,

"إِنَّ اللَّهَ هُوَ الرَّزَّاقُ ذُو الْقُوَّةِ الْمَتِينُ"

"Surely Allah is the Bestower of sustenance, the Lord of Power, the Strong"[53]

Here is some advice to help us in our quest for acquiring this wonderful quality of contentment:
- Remember that this life is a test and was not meant to be the final abode. Different people are tested with different

---

[51] Ibn Majah
[52] (Q51, V22-23)
[53] (Q51, V58)

tests. Your test may be the amount of wealth you have. Will you resort to non-ethical ways of collecting wealth? Will you be bitter and ungrateful? Or will you try to manage with what you have and thank Allah for all the other bounties that He gave you?

- Sometimes having less in materialistic wealth is a blessing from Allah *SWT* and makes one closer to Him. Having plenty of wealth, on the other hand, may lead to transgression and forgetting Allah's bounties. Allah *SWT* says,

"كَلَّا إِنَّ الْإِنسَانَ لَيَطْغَى أَن رَّآهُ اسْتَغْنَى"

"Nay, people transgress, when they have more materialistic means and they think that they are free of wants"[54]

- Just remember that the prophet *SAAW,* although he was the head of the state in *Madinah* and had access to all kinds of wealth, died while he was in debt, to the extent that his shield was kept by a Jew as collateral. When he died, he left no material wealth after him. *Amr Ibn Al Harith RAA,* the brother of *Joyreiah,* the mother of the faithful, narrated that,

"ماترك رسول الله صلى الله عليه وسلم عند موته ديناراً ولا درهماً، ولا عبداً ، ولا أمة ، ولا شيئاً إلا بغلته البيضاء التي كان يركبها وسلاحه وأرضاً جعلها لابن السبيل صدقة"

"The messenger of Allah *SAAW,* upon his death, left neither *Dinar* nor *Derham,* nor a slave nor a maid servant, nor anything else except his white riding mule, his shield *(marhoonah),* and his land, which he gave in charity for travelers."[55]

- In the house of the prophet *SAAW,* they used to go for one month after another without kindling any fire to cook food with. It was reported by *Orwah* that *A'ishah RAA* said to him,

---

[54] (Q96, V6-7)
[55] Al Bukhari

89

"والله يا ابن أختي إن كنا لننظر إلى الهلال ثم الهلال ثم الهلال ثلاثة أهلة في

شهرين وما أوقد في أبيات رسول الله صلى الله عليه وسلم نار. قال قلت:

يا خالة! فما كان يعيشكم؟ قالت: الأسودان التمر والماء. إلا أنه قد كان

لرسول الله صلى الله عليه وسلم جيران من الأنصار، وكانت لهم منائح

فكانوا يرسلون إلى رسول الله صلى الله عليه وسلم من ألبانها، فيسقيناه"

> "Nephew, by Allah, I used to see the new moon, then the new moon, then the new moon, three moons in two months, and a fire was not kindled in the house of the messenger of Allah *SAAW*."

> *Orwah* said, "Auntie, what were your means of sustenance?"

> She said, "Dates and water. But the messenger of Allah *SAAW* had some *Ansar* as his neighbors and they had milk animals and they used to send him some milk from their animals and he served that to us."[56]

- It was also reported by *Al Bukhari* that the prophet *SAAW* said,

"انظروا إلى من هو أسفل منكم ولا تنظروا إلى من هو فوقكم فإنه أجدر أن لا

تزدروا نعمة الله عليكم"

"Look to those who are less fortunate than you and do not look to those who are more fortunate than you. This way you will appreciate the bounties of Allah"[57]

- Remember also that the messenger of Allah *SAAW* said,

" من أصبح منكم آمنا في سربه معافى في جسده عنده قوت يومه فكأنما

حيزت له الدنيا"

---

[56] Agreed upon
[57] Al Bukhari

"One who wakes up in the morning safe in his house, healthy in his body, and has his food for the day, it is as if he owns the entire world"[58]

- Remember the response of some of the great companions *RAA* such as *Omar Ibn Al Khattab RAA* when he was afflicted with a calamity. He used to thank Allah *SWT* for four reasons. First, it was not in his *Deen*; second, it was not more severe; third, Allah *SWT* will reward him for this calamity; and finally that it was not as big as the biggest calamity ever when he lost the prophet *SAAW*.

- Practice repeating the *Athkar* of the morning and the evening as the messenger of Allah *SAAW* used to do. Among these wonderful sayings of Allah's remembrance is

"...رضيت بالله ربا ، وبالإسلام ديناً ، ومحمد نبياً..."

"I'm pleased and satisfied with Allah as my Lord, and with Muhammad *SAAW* as my prophet, and with Islam as my *Deen*"[59]

Saying this regularly and thinking and reflecting on its meanings will help the heart becoming satisfied, content, and pleased with anything Allah *SWT* selects for us. We will accept all decisions made for us by Allah *SWT* in this life: the amount of wealth we get, the number of children we have and their gender, our health conditions, etc. Not only will we accept these decisions, but we will also be thankful and happy with Allah's provisions for us in every area of life *insha'a Allah*.

Contribution

In a successful marriage, each spouse contributes his/her best. The continuity of marriage and its prosperity depends on the contribution of both spouses. It depends not only on how much they contribute, but also on the content and the quality of their contribution. Every spouse should ask himself/herself, is my contribution positive or negative? Is my behavior helping the marriage or straining it? What should I do to enhance the quality of

---

[58] At-Termezi
[59] At-Termezi

my marriage? What are the long-term consequences of my actions in this relationship? These are all questions that spouses should ask themselves. Acting based on their answers, spouses should try their best to ensure that their contribution is helping and enhancing the quality of their marriage. For example, if there is a disagreement between yourself and your spouse on a certain issue, do you make sure you discuss this issue objectively and try to find a solution that satisfies both of you, or do you just complain and create an unpleasant atmosphere without providing any useful suggestions for a solution. If you do the former, you are positively contributing to your marriage; however, if you do the latter, you are negatively contributing to the relationship. If your husband's job requires him to spend long hours in the office at certain times, and, because of this, he comes home late regularly for a few weeks until this emergency in the office clears up, do you just complain and increase the level of stress within the family? Or do you try your best to accommodate this temporary urgent situation and actually provide him with the needed help and support until he successfully completes this task and goes back to the regular routine. If you do the former, you are contributing negatively to your marriage; however, if you do the latter, you are positively enhancing this union and contributing to its success.

Compromise

Without compromise, marital life becomes very difficult. Compromise is needed because, in marriage, two different people, the bride and the groom, come together to form a new family. They are usually coming from different backgrounds. Before marriage, they belonged to different families. They may also have different life-styles and habits that they each learned from their own families and their circles of friends. In some cases, the marriage is cross-cultural and the husband and wife may be of different ethnicities. Because of all of this, the two newlyweds should always remember that they are two different people and that they may have different likes and dislikes. Each of them lived for approximately two decades with his/her own family. Keeping this in mind will make it easier for both of them to accept the concept of compromising, especially in minor matters and issues of likes and dislikes that are not related to major or fundamental principles of the allowed and forbidden in Islam. Here are some practical examples to illustrate what we mean and where compromise can create a wonderful, warm, and comfortable atmosphere conducive to achieving spousal harmony:

- The type of food and the dishes cooked should never be a source of conflict between spouses. This is particularly true in the case of cross-cultural marriages. There is nothing wrong with having a Curry dish as the main meal and *baklava* for dessert in a marriage where the wife is Arab and husband is Pakistani, just as there is nothing wrong with having *Kabab* as the main dish and *Golab Jamen* for dessert. Spouses should compromise and alternate these delicious dishes rather than make them an issue and a source of conflict. The same goes for spouses who have the same ethnic background because, when it comes to food, everyone has his/her favorite dish.

- Another example of compromise is if one of the spouses likes playing sports as well as watching sports on TV, and the other spouse doesn't enjoy it. He/she would rather go for a long walk in the woods or along the river. In this case, there has to be compromise, and each of them should respect the interest of the other and allow him/her to enjoy it. In this case, either each of them would learn to enjoy their respective hobby separately, or better yet if they both compromise, they would share the activity with their spouse once in a while, even though he/she may not be enjoying it. It is important that the spouse who doesn't enjoy sports does not express resentment as long as the other spouse is considerate and his/her engagement with the sports activity is at a reasonable level and does not compromise the health of the marital relationship. During the time when one spouse is busy with sports, maybe the other spouse can use the time to visit a friend rather than complaining that his wife/her husband is leaving him/her alone and playing soccer or cricket.

- A third area where compromise may be needed between husband and wife is when one of them is a night person who likes to stay up late working or finishing chores while the other is an early bird who likes to go to bed early and doesn't sleep after *Fajr*. There is no doubt that occasional compromise is needed there. Occasionally, the early morning spouse may have to have a nap during the day so he/she can spend sometime with the other spouse late in the evening. Also the night spouse may occasionally have to go to bed early so he/she wouldn't need to sleep after *Fajr*, and thus he/she can share some activities with his/her spouse like a nature walk while they are repeating the morning remembrance (*Athkar*).

The Seven Magical 'S's

Sensitivity
What we mean by sensitivity, in the marital relationship, is that each spouse should be sensitive toward the feelings of the other spouse. Passing unwanted and hurtful comments in a casual way about the other spouse, whether in public or even in private, is something that both spouses should completely avoid. Remember that each comment made and every phrase you say about your spouse leaves a mark on the marital relationship. This mark could be positive or negative, depending on the nature of the comments. Try always to nourish this union with the positive and constructive dialogue and interaction. Allah *SWT* says,

"وَقُل لِّعِبَادِي يَقُولُواْ الَّتِي هِيَ أَحْسَنُ إِنَّ الشَّيْطَانَ يَنزَغُ بَيْنَهُمْ"

"Say to My servants that they should (only) say those things that are best: for Satan doth sow dissensions among them: For Satan is to man an avowed enemy."[60]

This indicates that one should always try to think and select the good word before s/he speaks. The prophet *SAAW* encouraged

[60] (Q17, V53)

94

us to always use goodly words in our interactions with others. He says, "A goodly word is a charity"[61]

It was also reported by *Adey Ibn Hatem RAA* that the prophet *SAAW* said,

"اتقوا النار ولو بشق تمرة، فإن لم تجدوا فبكلمة طيبة"

"Avoid Hell fire even with a piece of date. If you can't find a piece of date, avoid it with a goodly word."[62]

Even in some matters that are allowed, it is important to speak about them in the proper context and they should not be used to tease either of the spouses. A clear example that comes to mind in this respect is the question of polygamy. Islam allows polygamy for certain legitimate situations, however, it didn't recommend practicing it, or make it a must for every Muslim to marry more than one wife.

A clear sign of being insensitive to the feelings of their wives, some husbands like to tease their wives by talking about getting married to more than one wife repeatedly, although they may not have the intention at all to do it. They just like to mention that it is their right to do so. This is a very insensitive attitude toward the wife and her feelings. Although this matter is allowed, as we mentioned, for a certain wisdom and specific situations, but there is no doubts that wives don't like to hear about it day in and day out. It shouldn't be a matter of continuous nagging and bragging at every opportunity from the husband's side. The following examples are of phrases that should be completely avoided by all husbands: "It is my right to marry more than one wife.", "This is the *Sunnah* of the prophet *SAAW*.", and "I want to practice his *Sunnah*. As soon as I can, I'll get married to a new wife." Every husband should avoid these phrases completely. Remember, that there are so many *Sunnan* of the prophet *SAAW* that you are not currently practicing. First try to practice the

---

[61] Agreed upon
[62] Agreed upon

Sunnan that improve your relationship and strengthen your marriage, rather than making your wife feel inadequate and feel that you are not satisfied with her as a wife because of these unwarranted comments. These comments only create a sour taste and leaves negative marks on the marital relationship. They are not forgotten and could easily be a source of continuous conflict in the marital relationship. Dear husband, please avoid them fully and don't take such matters lightly. They go a long way in spoiling this sacred union of marriage that you should be protecting rather than destroying.

On the other hand, some wives may also use certain comments on certain occasions that indicate insensitivity toward their husbands. These comments should also be avoided. For example, in a get together, a wife asks her husband to bring something from the kitchen. He is involved in a discussion with the men in his house and he doesn't do it. She asks him again, and he says he will do it as soon as he finishes this discussion with his friends. The discussion takes some time. The wife comments jokingly, "If you don't bring it right now, you will spend the night on the couch in the living room!" This comment is insensitive to the husband's feelings and should never be said by the wife in private, let alone in the presence of a group of friends, even if they are very close friends.

Another example that indicates insensitivity of the husband toward his wife is when during the discussion of an issue he always assumes that his view is right and her view should not be taken into consideration. Some insensitive husbands may also indicate this verbally by saying, "I know this very well. You have no idea what you are talking about. We will do exactly as I said, end of discussion." Such a comment is inappropriate, uncalled for, and indicates that the husband doesn't have much respect for his wife's view as well as being insensitive to her feelings.

Being sensitive to your spouse's feelings is a very important quality that every spouse should observe in her/his dealings with the other spouse. It promotes peace, respect, and a loving warm relationship, which should be the goal of every married couple.

Sincerity

Sincerity is a very important characteristic that both spouses should try their best to acquire. After all, we are all ordered as Muslims to be sincere in our dealings and to act with the proper intentions and motives, otherwise we may lose the rewards of our deeds. It was reported by *Omar Ibn Al Khattab RAA* that the prophet *SAAW* said,

"إنما الأعمال بالنيات، وإنما لكل امرئ ما نوى، فمن كانت هجرته إلى الله ورسوله فهجرته إلى الله ورسوله، ومن كانت هجرته لدنيا يصيبها أو امرأة ينكحها فهجرته إلى ما هاجر إليه"

"Actions are judged based on the motives and intentions behind them and everyone will get what he intended. If one migrates for the sake of Allah and His messenger, his migration will be counted as such, but if one migrates for better opportunity in life or to get married, his migration will be counted as such."[63]

Both spouses have to be sincere in everything they do related to their marital relationship. They have to be sincere in doing everything within their ability to protect their marriage and make it successful. They have to be sincere in understanding the real objectives of an Islamic marriage and in working together to fulfill these objectives. They have to be sincere in not sparing any effort to please each other and in providing each other with the *Ihssun* each of them needs. They have to be sincere in making sure that the family they are forming through their marriage is a strong, committed Muslim family. In turn, they have to do their best to create the warmest and most loving family atmosphere for their children to grow up as strong confident Muslims. This can only be done with dedication and sincerity from both spouses.

---

[63] Agreed upon

Security

Every spouse is looking for security in a marriage. Every wife wants to feel secure in her house with her husband, and every husband wants to have the same feelings. No spouse at any time or under any circumstances should behave in a way that compromises the security and safety of the other spouse. Safety and security is one of Allah's favours on human beings. Allah *SWT* says,

"فَلْيَعْبُدُوا رَبَّ هَذَا الْبَيْتِ الَّذِي أَطْعَمَهُم مِّن جُوعٍ وَآمَنَهُم مِّنْ خَوْفٍ"

"Let them worship the Lord of This House Who fed them against hunger and secured them against fear"[64]

As indicated in the verse of *Surat Ar Room* earlier, *Sakan* is an important goal of marriage for both spouses. *Sakan* provides and encompasses safety and security. Here are some examples illustrating behavioral patterns that could compromise this sense of security:

- A wife or husband who speeds when driving and doesn't follow the safety rules
- A husband or wife who doesn't control his/her anger, yells, and shouts when he/she is in a fit of rage
- A husband who may resort to the use of force against his wife or his children when he is in a bad mood
- A husband who keeps talking to his wife about his desire of marrying more than one wife. He repeatedly mentions this and claims that this is the right *Sunnah* and he has to apply it!!

Both spouses should do their best to ensure that their home is safe and secure. Their house should be the safest place for themselves and their children. It should always be a place of rest, comfort, and protection for all the family members where no harm can reach them, be it from the bad behavior of any of the spouses or from an external source of harm.

---

[64] (Q106, V3-4)

Support

Support is another important quality that believers should practice with each other in general and with their spouses in particular. Allah *SWT* says,

"وَالْمُؤْمِنُونَ وَالْمُؤْمِنَاتُ بَعْضُهُمْ أَوْلِيَاءِ بَعْضٍ يَأْمُرُونَ بِالْمَعْرُوفِ وَيَنْهَوْنَ عَنِ الْمُنكَرِ وَيُقِيمُونَ الصَّلَاةَ وَيُؤْتُونَ الزَّكَاةَ وَيُطِيعُونَ اللَّهَ وَرَسُولَهُ أُولَئِكَ سَيَرْحَمُهُمُ اللَّهُ إِنَّ اللَّهَ عَزِيزٌ حَكِيمٌ"

"The Believers, men and women, are protectors one of another: they enjoin what is just, and forbid what is evil: they observe regular prayers, practice regular charity, and obey Allah and His Messenger. On them will Allah pour His mercy: for Allah is Exalted in power, Wise."[65]

In addition to the financial support, which is the husband's duty toward his wife and family, a wife will also need other forms of support and cooperation from her husband during different time periods. She will need his support more during some time periods than others. A wife needs her husband's support, undoubtedly, during the period of pregnancy. A wife also needs her husband's support right after giving birth. She is usually physically weak and tired and needs all the help and support she can get.

A husband needs his wife's support and cooperation when he changes jobs. At the beginning, this usually requires longer working hours, which translate into being away from home for long periods of time and not contributing much as far as the house chores are concerned. Certainly, in these circumstances his wife's understanding and accommodation is highly appreciated by him. This also applies for working wives in the same situation.

They both need each other's support when they move from a familiar place to a new city and deal with all the adjustments that come with such a move. They also need each other's support when

---

[65] (Q 9, V 71)

they are going through rough times at work, or when they have to work late to finish certain assignments or urgent projects.

They both need each other's support in cases of death in either of the extended families. Being close to your spouse and knowing her/him well, helps tremendously in getting over this period of grief quickly and getting back to your normal life and regular routine.

They also need each other's support at difficult economic times, if one of the spouses loses her/his job, which is not uncommon nowadays. They need to remind each other of the other bounties that Allah has bestowed upon them and that this life is a test where Allah *SWT* may test us with various adversities. They need to help each other become closer to Allah, be content with their share in this life, and avoid being displeased with Allah's decisions for them. Contentment is a great asset and a wonderful comfort during such times, as explained earlier, and the support and cooperation of spouses is a must for them to successfully face these kinds of hardships and come out of them stronger and better Muslims.

Satisfaction
Satisfaction means that one has to be satisfied with what he/she has in his/her marriage, and, at the same time, also do his/her best to satisfy his/her spouse. Being satisfied with what we have arises from the firm belief that Allah *SWT* always selects the best for us after we do our share in following His instructions as well as the teachings of His messenger Muhammad *SAAW*. As long as we have followed the prophetic guidance in the process of selection, as explained in chapter three of this book, then we have done our part and we should be satisfied with the final results of the selection process and be happy with it. Of course, there may be room for improvement from both sides to ensure that the marriage is successful. We, both spouses, have to do our best to help each other during this improvement process; however, we should not at any time be dissatisfied with our marriage.

The other side of satisfaction helps immensely to keep the marriage healthy and satisfy both spouses. This is when each spouse is trying to satisfy the needs of the other spouse and be closer to him/her. The satisfaction we mean is the deep kind of satisfaction that comes from within, a satisfaction that covers the physical level as well as the emotional and spiritual levels.

A wife has to satisfy her husband's physical needs such as preparing his meals, washing his clothes, and making sure that the house is presentable. This does not imply that the husband is exempted from helping in the house chores. As discussed in chapter six, the prophet *SAAW* always helped with house chores when he was around. The extent to which the responsibility of house chores falls on each spouse's shoulders should be evaluated by both spouses taking all other commitments into consideration. She must also fulfill his intimate sexual needs. She should beautify herself for him and dress in presentable, clean, and attractive clothing. On the other hand, the husband also has to satisfy his wife's physical needs including her intimate sexual needs. He also has to beautify himself for her as *Ibn Abbas* used to do. He used to quote the following verse from *Surat Al Baqarah*:

$$\text{"وَلَهُنَّ مِثْلُ الَّذِي عَلَيْهِنَّ بِالْمَعْرُوفِ"}$$

"And women have the same right as the duty they have to fulfill"[66]

More details on this subject are given later under the section of sexual gratification in this chapter.

As for the emotional needs, both have to satisfy each other through spending time together, perhaps talking and chatting, or sharing some *Halal* entertainment together. The husband has to make sure that his wife is happy and satisfied, especially after spending a long day outside and leaving her alone. In the North American environment, this is an important matter because of the absence of the extended family. Most Muslim families have no close relatives living in the same continent, let alone the same city. It is important,

---

[66] (Q2, V228)

especially for the husband, to call his wife during the day and have a nice phone visit with her. If your work is not very far, make a point of occasionally coming home in the middle of the day for lunch, especially at the beginning of the marriage. Make sure, though, to tell her that you will be dropping by for lunch so that she prepares her time accordingly and you can take advantage of this time together. This will have a great effect on your wife and it will, *insha'a Allah*, help her be emotionally satisfied. Arranging regular visits to close Muslim friends is also recommended to help the emotional health of both of you. Make sure that the discussions during these visits are not only about the problems and conflicts of the local Muslim community and Muslim *Ummah*, but also include some light-hearted subjects and some humour. Be careful in selecting those friends and make sure that the visit will have a positive impact on both of you. Caution should also be exercised to avoid letting these visits take over you social life.

An outing such as a long walk in the park occasionally before or after dinner is another recommended activity that you can use to spend some time together with your spouse and make sure that your emotional needs are met.

It is important that you should be in control, and you should ensure moderation in any activity you practice. After all moderation is an important characteristic of the *Ummah* of Islam. Allah *SWT* says,

$$\text{"وَكَذَلِكَ جَعَلْنَاكُمْ أُمَّةً وَسَطًا لِّتَكُونُواْ شُهَدَاء عَلَى النَّاسِ وَيَكُونَ الرَّسُولُ عَلَيْكُمْ شَهِيدًا"}$$

"And thus We have made you a moderate *Ummah*, so you may witness over mankind, and the messenger witness over you"[67]

Sharing
Sharing is a wonderful virtue in any relationship. It helps develop a good strong bond between those who share. Spouses who care about their relationship make sure they share all kinds of activities

---

[67] (Q2, V143)

with each other. They invest time and energy; they plan, rearrange things, and manage their time properly to make sure they can share as many activities as possible with each other. The more sharing you have with your spouse, the closer you are to each other and the more understanding you develop of each other's personalities.

Try to share time with your spouse in preparing a nice meal together and use the opportunity to talk about memories and funny, silly things which may have happened at the beginning of your marriage, especially matters related to cooking. For sure, being in the kitchen together will bring back some of those memories and you can have a few laughs over them.

Planning an upcoming community activity or implementing a community project may provide you with a good opportunity to share your time. Grab this opportunity; work together, and share some innovative ideas, and, in the process, strengthen your marital bond.

Having a joint regular schedule of *Qur'anic* memorization or recitation is another wonderful chance for both of you to share and develop a strong lasting bond. Also, reading together in books of the *Seerah* of the prophet *SAAW* and his companions will give you a chance to be together and strengthen your relationship.

Sharing a nice walk on a natural trail together is a very healthy exercise, physically and mentally. It also provides both of you with an opportunity to speak about things you like and discuss various matters of interest. Being close to nature and witnessing the beauty of Allah's creation, no doubt opens your hearts and strengthens your marital bond.

Sexual Gratification
This is a very important aspect of marital life. The best we can say about this subject is to quote part of Dr. *Yousof Al Qaradawy's* answer to a question related to this matter in his valuable book *Contemporary Fatwas* and then make some comments of our own.

In his answer, *Dr. Al Qaradawy* says the following: "The sexual relationship between spouses is a very important matter which has a great impact on the health of the marital relationship. Neglecting this aspect of the marital life or practicing it in an incorrect way can lead to drastic results and serious consequences. Some people mistakenly think that Islam did not pay attention to this aspect of marital life due to their misconceptions that *Deen* should only address lofty ideas and not matters such as sex between spouses. The reality is that Islam doesn't overlook such an important and sensitive aspect of human life due to its great effect on the health of family relationships. Islam provides clear guidelines on how to deal with this subject. Some of these guidelines take the form of recommendations and others come as direct instructions and orders to be followed. Here are some of these guidelines:

1. Islam clearly recognizes the sexual drive of human beings as a natural drive and condemns those who try to completely suppress such urges through surgical operations and those who want to avoid marriage. The prophet *SAAW* told those who suggested avoiding marriage, 'I know Allah and fear him more than any of you, but I stand up for prayer at night, and I sleep. I also fast some days and break my fast other days. I also marry women. Those who abandon my way are not among my followers'[68]

2. Islam recognizes the right of both spouses to enjoy such acts to the extent that it considers it an act of worship that one will be rewarded for. The prophet *SAAW* said, "There is a reward for you when you have intercourse with your spouse."

The companions *RAA* said, "Do we fulfill our sexual desire and get rewarded for it?"

---

[68] Agreed upon

The prophet *SAAW* said, "If you do this in a wrong way, (i.e. with a lady that is not your wife {*Zina*}), would it be counted as a sin against you?" They said, "Yes." He said, "Likewise when you do it properly in a lawful setting with your wife, you get rewarded for it." [69]

Islam also takes into consideration that the sexual urge is much stronger and demanding for men as compared to women. As such, usually men initiate such acts because of this difference in the intensity of the urge. Because of this . . .

a) The prophet *SAAW* instructed wives to respond to their husbands' invitations for this act. He said, 'When the husband calls upon his wife to satisfy his sexual need, she should respond favorably, even if she is working at the outdoor oven.'[70]

b) The prophet *SAAW* warned the wife not to refuse her husband's invitation for this act without a legitimate reason. He said, 'When a husband invites his wife to satisfy his sexual need, and she refuses without a legitimate reason, if he is angry with her response, angels would curse her until the morning (or until he becomes pleased with her)'[71] At the same time, husbands should be reasonable and should take the wife's reason into consideration. She may not be feeling well or may be exhausted after a long working day.

c) The prophet *SAAW* also forbade the wife to engage in voluntary fasting without her husband's permission. He said, 'A lady should not fast (voluntary fasting) while her husband is present without his permission'[72]

---

[69] Muslim, Ahmad and others
[70] At-Termezi
[71] Agreed upon
[72] Ahmad, Al Bukhari, and Muslim

3. Islam also didn't forget women's rights to satisfy their sexual desires. Because of this the prophet *SAAW* said to those who used to make *Qiam* during the night and fast during the day like *Abdullah Ibn Amr*, 'Indeed your body has a right upon you and your wife has a right upon you, so give every one who has a right upon you his rights.'

   Imam Al Ghazaly indicated that a husband should have intimate sexual relations with his wife at least once every four days. If she needs more, then he should try to satisfy her need, because it is his duty to provide her with *Ihssun.*[73]

4. Islam also directs the husband not to concentrate only on satisfying his own sexual needs without paying much attention to the needs of his wife. It is recommended to prepare for sexual acts with romantic words, touches, and kisses. The prophet *SAAW* said, "Let no one of you be like an animal when he is trying to fulfill his sexual needs with his wife. Try to have a messenger between you and her." They said, "Like what?" He said, "Like good words and kisses"[74]

Among the etiquettes of sexual intimacy between husband and wife is to mention the name of Allah at the beginning of this act. *Ibn Abbas* reported that the messenger of Allah *SAAW* said, 'When one of you wants to approach his wife, if he should say *'Bismillah, Allahumma Jannib Nash-shaytan, Wa Jannib Ish-Shaytana Ma Razaqtana'* (which means, 'in the name of Allah. O Allah keep Satan away from us, and keep him away from that which You grant us,') If it is then decreed

---

[73] *Ihyaa' Uloom Al Deen*
[74] Abu Mansour and Dailmy in Alferdaws

that they are blessed with a child (from that action), Satan will never harm (the child).'[75]

Preparation for this act and foreplay is very important *Imam Ibn Al Qayem* said, 'It is important, before the close intimate sexual act, that the husband plays with his wife, fondles her, kisses her, and even sucks her tongue.'
It was reported by *Abu Dawoud* that the messenger of Allah *SAAW* used to kiss *A'ishah RAA* and suck her tongue.[76]"

It is obvious from Dr. *Al Qaradawy's* comments that this act is very important to the marriage. This act should bring spouses closer to each other. The difference of opinion on the frequency of this act or any misconceptions related to the way it should be approached, should in no way cause conflicts between spouses. They should both make satisfying each other's sexual needs their first priority. It should be a gratifying experience and they should both invest time together to find out the best way to go about it. Remember, the only way to satisfy this need in Islam is through the legitimate marriage union. As such, every spouse should try to find out what pleases her/his partner, recognize how important it is, and learn how to do it. This is a mutual and reciprocal act where both have to try to satisfy each other to the best of their abilities.

It is beneficial to point out some practical tips here to make sure that this act is not a source of conflict among spouses:

1. **For the Husband**: To avoid disappointment at the end of the day because your wife is exhausted and can't fulfill your need, try to hint during the day that you expect to engage in an intimate act with her during this night. This way she will make sure to rest for a while so she will not be exhausted at night. A good honorable way to do this is to agree together on certain inconspicuous signs by one of the

---

[75] Al Bukhari, Muslim and others
[76] *Zad Almia'ad*, Part 3, page 309, Alsunnah Al Muhammadeiah edition

spouses that would indicate her/his desire to have this act at the end of the day. For example, the husband can place a flower at his pillow before leaving home, or he can phone his wife during the day and indicate that he misses her a lot. This will give a signal to the wife that it is important to prepare herself physically and mentally for this act. At the same time, as a husband, be willing to put up with delaying some of the house chores because of this. It is even better, if you can help her with the house chores because carrying the chores together helps improve the marital bond between spouses. After all, the prophet *SAAW* used to be seen in the service of his family. This advice is applicable for wives also if needed.

2. **From the wife's side**, it is important not to refuse her husband's request for no legitimate reason. Try always to satisfy his needs. You don't have to be fully (100%) in the mood to perform such actions. In some situations you may be tired, rather than bluntly saying 'No, I'm exhausted. Let us delay it for another time.', and making an issue out of it, it is better to engage in this action with your husband to satisfy his need with your body, even if your mind is not fully there. This would leave a good impact on him that you are trying your best to accommodate his needs, and he will reciprocate by being more considerate and accepting of your reasons in the future.

3. Sometimes it may be a good idea for both of you to try to sit together as husband and wife and discuss your expectations out of this act. In fact, because of this meeting, it becomes clear to each spouse, where on the list of priorities of the other spouse this act falls and how important it is for her/him. This will help each spouse to know what the other spouse is expecting and to try to live up to this expectation. Spouses may also agree on dropping other things from their list of things to do, to make sure that they can satisfy each other's need in this area. Another

possible result of this meeting could be an agreed upon schedule for this act. This would help avoid conflicts due to different expectations.

4. It is also recommended that spouses try to take time off occasionally and go for a vacation. The vacation should not always be to visit family overseas or friends. They should make sure to have part of this vacation just for themselves alone. This will provide them with some quality time together without the routine day-to-day activities and interruptions. These vacations usually rejuvenate their relationship and provide them with better opportunity to fulfill their intimate needs.

5. Another very important piece of advice, particularly for **husbands,** is that preparation for this physical intimate relation should never be ignored. Such preparation is very important to the extent that Allah *SWT* emphasized it in the Qur'an and Prophet Muhammad *SAAW* gave us an example for this preparation as was indicated in the previous pages as part of the comments of Dr. *Al Qaradawy*. As indicated in verse 223 of *Surat Al-Baqarah* "Your women are your tilth; go, then to your tilth as you may desire, but **prepare well for yourselves 'Waqademo Le-Anfosikom'** and fear Allah, and know that you shall meet Him. Give glad tidings to the believers," preparing for yourselves well (or making *taqdeem*) for this act is a clear order from Allah *SWT*. The verse also provides a beautiful shade of a healthy and conducive atmosphere for couples to seek each other's comfort in any manner that will give them the greatest and most fulfilling pleasure.

It is quite common that some husbands more often than not, fail to prepare their wives well for this beautiful act. They fail to do the proper *taqdeem.* Some of them, every time they have a free moment, all that they think of is to go to bed with their wives, particularly in the early years of marriage. As such they ignore the mental preparation, and ignore the spiritual aspects of this relationship. This could result in a cold response from the wife's side and could even lead to feelings of resentment on her part.

For a more fulfilling and stronger intimate spousal relationship, following the *Qur'anic* guidance in this matter is a must. The well preparation *"taqdeem"* does not just refer to the physical sexual foreplay. It is a much more comprehensive than just kisses or romantic words. Whatever puts your wife in the right mood for this intimate physical act could be used as a way of preparation *"taqdeem."* As such, it is the duty of every husband to try to find out the right key to his wife's persona and desire and the best way to prepare and put her in the right mood for this wonderful relation. Here are some examples that may work for you, and you can always come up with your own based on your situation:

- Having a nice long/short walk in the park
- Preparing a fancy meal together
- Chatting lightly over a cup of tea
- Sharing some memories of the past
- Massage
- Bring her flowers
- Take her out for a treat (dinner/coffee & dessert)
- Do the dishes for her
- Etc.

Although you may feel that some of these examples of *taqdeem* are not directly related to the intimate relationship, they are much more related than it appears at first glance. When you take your wife out to dinner or bring her flowers or go out for a walk with her or share memories with her, whatever the thing that she appreciates most, this shows her that you care about her as a person. It shows her that you care about her desires and her feelings and her moods. It shows her that you think she is special and fun to be

around. When she feels this appreciated and loved, she will
be happy to spend intimate time with you. However, if she
feels that you just want to spend intimate time with her to
fulfill your own desires and needs, but she feels that you
don't consider her desires and needs, she will resent the
time that you spend together and be upset by it.

So, in order to enrich your intimate relationship with your
wife, find out what she enjoys, what will make her feel
special and put her in a good mood. Then follow the
Qur'anic advice in doing those things, and insha'a Allah
you will see that, as she feels that you would like to please
her and make her happy, she will want to please you and
make you happy as well.

Of course, the above are only suggestions and guidelines for you to
consider. Spouses may come up with other ways and methods to
ensure that this act is a source of pleasure, gratification, and
closeness between them and to realize the real meaning of Sakan
as discussed in detail in an earlier chapter and as indicated in the
following verse:

"وَمِنْ آيَاتِهِ أَنْ خَلَقَ لَكُم مِّنْ أَنفُسِكُمْ أَزْوَاجًا لِّتَسْكُنُوا إِلَيْهَا وَجَعَلَ بَيْنَكُم مَّوَدَّةً
وَرَحْمَةً إِنَّ فِي ذَلِكَ لَآيَاتٍ لِّقَوْمٍ يَتَفَكَّرُونَ"

"And among His Signs is this, that He created for you mates from
among yourselves, that ye may dwell in tranquility with them, and
He has put Mawadah and Rahmah between your (hearts): verily in
that are Signs for those who reflect."[77] (The terminology Mawadah
and Rahmah are explained in detail later on in this chapter.)

It is of utmost importance that the couple realizes that sexual
gratification is a very important component of marriage, and in
Islam, marriage is the only way to satisfy this urge. As such, it is
important for both spouses to make sure it is practiced properly

---

[77] (Q30, V21)

and its potential is exploited fully for the sake of a closer and more satisfying marital relationship.

The Five Wonderful 'A's

Adaptation

This is a very important and crucial quality for the success of the marriage, especially in the first few years. Both spouses are moving to a completely new environment compared to the environment they have been living in with their families thus far. They were both living as members of bigger families, with parents and siblings. They were living as brothers and sisters to their siblings, and sons and daughters to their parents. Their role within the family is completely different from what is expected from them in their new home. They didn't have full responsibility of managing and running a home on their own. Now, they are fully responsible for this new environment and they have to carry out this responsibility all by themselves. They have to play a completely new role, and this requires adaptation on many different levels: adaptation to the new environment, adaptation to the new role, and adaptation to the new companionship. It may be useful here to reflect on one very important verse in the *Qur'an* describing the nature of the marital relationship where Allah *SWT* describes wives as the garments or clothing of their husbands and vice versa. In *Surat Al Baqarah*, Allah says,

"هُنَّ لِبَاسٌ لَّكُمْ وَأَنتُمْ لِبَاسٌ لَّهُنَّ"

"…They are your garment and you are their garment."[78] If we reflect on the quality or the characteristics of clothing, we will find that a very important quality of a good cloth that is made from high-quality fabric is the ability to adapt to the body shape to provide an attractive appearance and, at the same time, to provide the right fit. Allah *SWT* is emphasizing to us, with this description, the importance of being willing to adapt to new situations and environments. Lack of willingness to adapt

---

[78] (Q2, V187)

on the part of one of the spouses or both of them could be a source of problems, discomfort, and conflicts for the new relationship. Hence the significance of the ability to possess this quality and to train ourselves to acquire it, if we don't already have it, can't be ignored.

Accommodation
Accommodation is another vital attitude that both spouses have to regularly exercise to ensure spousal harmony and a good successful marriage. They are new partners in each other's life and each of them has to accommodate the needs and wishes of the other spouse. Accommodation goes hand in hand with compromise. Spouses, no doubt have different likes and dislikes. Unless they accommodate each other's needs, life will be very complicated and difficult.

When the wife wants to visit her family more often, especially at the beginning of the marriage, and the husband is reluctant, he should remember that he has to accommodate her need. The effect of this will, without doubt, enhance the marital relationship positively.

If the husband wants to go and spend some time with his old friends or play a game of soccer or basketball, particularly at the beginning of marriage, the wife occasionally should accommodate his request rather than always saying, "No, don't go and leave me alone."

A good way for spouses to accommodate each other's needs, especially in matters that may be of importance to one spouse and not to the other, is to mutually agree that they will try to fulfill these kinds of activities and hobbies with other friends. It is recommended to schedule these separate activities for the same time period. This way each spouse would not feel that he/she is left alone by the other spouse.

Appreciation

Appreciation is another very important quality that helps in building a warm, healthy, and lasting marital relationship. Many spouses fail to express their feelings and their gratefulness to Allah *SWT* for the bounties He gave to them. Among these bounties that we tend to forget is having an understanding spouse who is trying his/her best to be close to Allah and to live according to the values of Islam. Expressing gratitude and showing appreciation is highly recommended by Prophet Muhammad *SAAW*. *Abdullah Ibn Amr RAA* reported that the messenger of Allah *SAAW* said,

"لا ينظر الله إلى المرأة لا تشكر زوجها، وهي لا تستغني عنه"

"Allah does not look (with mercy) at a woman who is not grateful to her husband when she cannot live without him"[79]

The prophet *SAAW* always expressed appreciation for what *Khadeejah RAA,* his first wife, did for him, even after her death. He used to say that she supported him when everyone else had deserted him; she believed in him when others did not. He also reminded us that those who don't thank people are not thankful to Allah. He said,

"التحدث بنعمة الله شكر وتركها كفر ومن لا يشكر القليل لا يشكر الكثير

ومن لا يشكر الناس لا يشكر الله والجماعة بركة والفرقة عذاب"

"Speaking of the bounties of Allah shows gratitude; not mentioning them shows rejection; those who are not grateful for the little things will not be grateful for the larger blessings; those who do not thank people, do not thank Allah; being united is a blessing and creating divisions is torture."[80]

Spouses have to appreciate each other's company and use every opportunity to clearly express this appreciation and gratitude. A husband should occasionally mention to his wife

---

[79] An Nesae'i
[80] Al-Bayhaqi

that he misses her and her company whenever he is traveling or he is absent from his home for a few days because of business trips or Islamic commitments. He should let her know that he is grateful to Allah for blessing him with her. On the other hand, a wife should also express her gratitude to Allah *SWT* and clearly indicate to her husband that she appreciates his company and that she is grateful to Allah that he is her husband. Expressing your appreciation and gratefulness to your spouse touches his/her heart and leaves them with warm feelings. This of course has a positive mark on the attitude of your spouse toward you.

Husbands, please try your best to express your appreciation and show gratitude on every possible occasion. Do it when your wife prepares a nice fresh meal that you like. Do it when she shows her understanding when you come late from the office after a long day of work or from attending a long community meeting. Do it when she does routine things like doing the dishes or cleaning up. Do it when she receives and hosts your family when they come for a visit and stay a few days. Do it when she shows her appreciation to your accommodating attitude, if she is busy and couldn't prepare a fresh meal.

Wives, please try your best to express your appreciation and to show gratitude on every possible occasion. Do it when your husband buys a new gift for you. Do it when he reminds you to call any of your family members to check on them and ask about how they are doing. Do it when he insists to call your family first to congratulate them on the occasion of the beginning of *Ramadan* or any of the two *Eids*. Do it when he does some house chores. Do it when he asks you to go out for dinner instead of cooking that day. Do it when he shows his appreciation and gratitude for any of your actions. Do it when he overlooks some of your shortcomings. Do it when he accommodates your needs and puts them ahead of his own. Do it whenever he practices the attitude of appreciation, accommodation, and acceptance. Do it whenever he shows courtesy.

One way of expressing our appreciation to our spouse is recommended by the Prophet *SAAW* is to occasionally exchange gifts. Such a practice creates stronger bonds between spouses and a wonderful feeling of closeness, compassion, and appreciation.

Husbands and wives, this is a great quality and whenever you practice it, it will *insha'a Allah* add a wonderful ingredient to the success, peacefulness, and happiness of your marriage.

Appreciation between spouses is the icing on the delicious cake, the flowers on the dinner table, the decorations in the party room.

Anticipation
This is a skill that both spouses should aspire to learn and practice, especially after living together for a few years. By now each spouse should know quite well what pleases the other spouse, what makes her/him happy, and what makes her/him sad or unhappy. They should know each other's likes and dislikes. They should know each other's habits and the way they react to certain comments and gestures. They should be very well aware of each other's behaviors, practices, and daily routines. When they know these things about each other, they should be able to anticipate each other's reactions in different situations. Practicing this anticipation helps spouses avoid many problems that occasionally arise. Let us take the example of if one of them makes the wrong comment. When the husband anticipates his wife's reaction, he will make sure to be sensitive to her feelings and only say what will make her react happily. By the same token, when the wife anticipates her husband's reaction correctly, because of her knowledge of his personality, she will always try her best to do and say what will make him react pleasantly. It is worthwhile for both spouses to invest time and energy to know and understand the

personality of the other spouse. If one spouse masters this art of correct anticipation based on the knowledge of the other spouse's traits and qualities, s/he could be ready with the right comments or actions on every occasion to make sure that most of the time there is a positive reaction from the other spouse.

Be ready, prepare yourself, and try to know as much as you can about your spouse's character in order to make the right anticipation. This, *insha'a Allah* will keep both of you happy and strengthen your marital bond.

Acceptance
This is another very important ingredient for a successful marriage. Spouses have to accept their partners as is. They have to accept each other's strengths, and they have to accept each other's limitations and shortcomings. There is no perfect human being, as was indicated by the prophet *SAAW*. He said,

"كل ابن آدم خطاء وخير الخطائين التوابون"

"All human beings make mistakes and err. The best of those who err are the ones who repent."[81]

In this life, no one should expect perfection from anybody. This is the nature of human beings. As long as the shortcomings and mistakes are not major and are not related to fundamental Islamic values or to the allowed and the forbidden in Islam, things can be worked out to correct these mistakes and help each other improve in our areas of shortcomings and even overcome them through self-improvement and self-elevation. The cooperation of spouses with each other and their help and support of one another are great assets in correcting these mistakes. While this is being done, acceptance is of utmost importance to keep a good and sincere relationship between spouses and achieve the required spousal trust and closeness.

---

[81] At-Termezi, and Al Hakem

To help each other improve in our areas of shortcomings and reduce our mistakes, it may be helpful to educate ourselves about the conditions of repentance as indicated by scholars. They are as follows:

1. Stop committing the sin or mistake.
2. Express regret for making this mistake.
3. Try our best to avoid repeating this mistake and make commitment to Allah *SWT*, with clear intentions, that we will stop doing this act.
4. Accept responsibility for our action and try to rectify it and repair the damage caused by it.

When spouses practice these steps after making a mistake, it helps them avoid repeating the same mistake in the future and contributes to the well being of the marital relationship. It gives a positive signal to your spouse that you are trying your best to get better in this area, and as such, it improves the acceptance level between spouses.

Other Ingredients and Qualities

Rahmah (meaning compassion, leniency, and kindness)

Rahmah is often translated as "mercy" in English texts; however, we have chosen not to use this word because the word "mercy" in English connotes pity and sympathy, which are not connoted by the Arabic word "*Rahmah*".

This is another very important quality for spousal happiness. In fact, it is one of the two qualities mentioned in the *Qur'an* as the two most important qualities for the foundation of marital relationships. Allah *SWT* says in *Surat Ar Room*,

"وَمِنْ آيَاتِهِ أَنْ خَلَقَ لَكُم مِّنْ أَنفُسِكُمْ أَزْوَاجًا لِّتَسْكُنُوا إِلَيْهَا وَجَعَلَ بَيْنَكُم مَّوَدَّةً وَرَحْمَةً إِنَّ فِي ذَلِكَ لَآيَاتٍ لِّقَوْمٍ يَتَفَكَّرُونَ"

"And among His Signs is this, that He created for you mates from among yourselves, that ye may dwell in tranquility with them, and

118

He has put *Mawadah* and *Rahmah*[82] between your (hearts): verily in that are Signs for those who reflect."[83]

It is not strange for the *Qur'an* to place such great importance on this quality. In fact, the essence of Islam is *Rahmah*. Allah *SWT* summarizes the purpose of the message of the prophet *SAAW* in *Surat Al Anbiaa'* in one word. This word is *Rahmah*.

"وَمَا أَرْسَلْنَاكَ إِلَّا رَحْمَةً لِّلْعَالَمِينَ"

"We sent thee not, but as a *Rahmah* for all creatures."[84]

In another *Surah*, Allah *SWT* indicates to the prophet *SAAW* that dealing with others with *Rahmah* promotes stronger bonds and better relationships. He says,

"فَبِمَا رَحْمَةٍ مِّنَ اللّه لِنتَ لَهُمْ وَلَوْ كُنتَ فَظًّا غَلِيظَ الْقَلْبِ لاَنفَضُّواْ مِنْ حَوْلِكَ فَاعْفُ عَنْهُمْ وَاسْتَغْفِرْ لَهُمْ وَشَاوِرْهُمْ فِي الأَمْرِ فَإِذَا عَزَمْتَ فَتَوَكَّلْ عَلَى اللّه إِنَّ اللّهَ يُحِبُّ الْمُتَوَكِّلِينَ"

"It is part of the *Rahmah* of Allah that thou dost deal gently with them Have you been severe or harsh-hearted, they would have broken away from about thee: so pass over (Their faults), and ask for (Allah's) forgiveness for them; and consult them in affairs (of moment). Then, when thou hast Taken a decision put thy trust in Allah. For Allah loves those who put their trust (in Him).."[85]

Addressing this same quality, the prophet *SAAW* said,

"ليس منا من لم يرحم صغيرنا ولم يوقر كبيرنا"

"He is not considered from us the one who does not have *Rahmah* for our young and the one who does not respect our elders"[86]

---

[82] See the terminology and explanations in this section for the meaning of these words

[83] (Q30, V21)

[84] (Q21, V107)

[85] (Q3, V 159)

[86] Ahmed, Al Hakem and At-Termezi

There are also numerous sayings of the prophet *SAAW* that recommend being gentle, kind, and lenient in all our dealings with others. Among them are the following:

"On the authority of *A'ishah RAA*, (beloved wife of the prophet *SAAW*,) she reported that the messenger of Allah *SAAW* said,

"أن الله رفيق يحب الرفق في الأمر كله"

"Allah is kind and He loves kindness in all affairs."[87]
Also, she reported that the messenger of Allah *SAAW* said,

"يا عائشة إن الله رفيق يحب الرفق ، ويعطي على الرفق مالا يعطي على العنف ، ومالا يعطي على ما سواه"

"Allah is kind and He loves kindness; and confers upon kindness which He does not confer upon severity and does not confer upon anything else besides it (kindness)."[88]

On the authority of *A'ishah RAA,* who narrated that the messenger of Allah *SAAW* said,

"ما كان الرفق في شئ إلا زانه وما نزع من شئ إلا شانه"

"Kindness is not found in anything, but it adds beauty to it, and if it is withdrawn from anything, it defects it."[89]

On the authority of *Gareer Ibn Abdullah RAA* he reported that he heard the messenger of Allah *SAAW* saying,

"من يحرم الرفق يحرم الخير كله"

"Those who are deprived of leniency are deprived of good."[90]
All these texts bear great witness to the importance of being gentle, kind, compassionate, and lenient in our relationships with other human beings. What about our relationships with our spouses? They deserve for us to pay even more attention to these kinds of

---

[87] Agreed upon
[88] Muslim
[89] (Muslim)
[90] (Muslim)

qualities. Each spouse should come forward to please the other spouse. Not only should we practice *Rahmah* in our dealings with our spouses, but we should also practice it in our expectations from them. We should realize their limitations and circumstances. Here are some practical examples illustrating the practice of *Rahmah* with our spouses:

- If one of the spouses has a higher level of energy compared to the other spouse, out of *Rahmah* he/she should not measure his/her spouse based on his/her own high level of energy. People have different potentials and should be considerate to each other's levels of energy. The spouse who has more energy shouldn't request that the other spouse perform more tasks than he/she can. Out of *Rahmah*, Allah *SWT* doesn't burden a soul with more than it can bear. He said,

"لاَ يُكَلِّفُ اللّهُ نَفْسًا إلاَّ وُسْعَهَا"

"Allah does not impose upon any soul a duty but to the extent of its ability."[91] We as humans should learn from this and be merciful to our spouses, as Allah is merciful to each and every one of us.

- When your wife is pregnant, usually she has less energy and she is tired most of the time. Out of *Rahmah*, you shouldn't request that she cook elaborate and fancy dishes that are time-consuming and exhausting. In fact, you should help her and cook for her during these times.

- When your husband is working all day long trying his best to make ends meet, don't overburden him as soon as he comes home with unnecessary issues and problems. Out of *Rahmah*, receive him with a smile and a hug. Give him some good news, and help him to relax and have his dinner in peace with you. Don't nag him, and be considerate to his situation.

---

[91] (Q2, V286)

Love

As promised in the chapter about the process of selection, we are now discussing love.

Love is an emotion, like all other emotions, created by Allah *SWT* for a purpose. Before we examine love as a specific emotion, we need to examine emotions and their characteristics in general.

How emotions work:

Emotions are created by Allah *SWT* to help people achieve their specific goals. However, sometimes adults (we) may not be aware of these goals. For example, the emotion of fear serves a very specific function, that is, to help human beings avoid dangerous or unpleasant situations. In some cases, the reason for fear is obvious and the fear is justifiable; however, there are other cases where the fear doesn't seem logical because the purpose of the fear is not easily recognizable. For example, someone who seems anxious when s/he has to meet new people may seem to be over-reacting and defensive toward others. S/he feels her/his fear is justifiable because s/he knows, from past experience, that a situation with strangers might cause her/him embarrassment. A person in this situation is trying to protect not only her/his physical well-being, but also her/his self-esteem and social status. As we see from this example, a person will subconsciously choose the emotion that suits her/his purpose. This is a subconscious decision, because, inherently, emotions will only work to fulfill their goals if their purpose stays hidden, so it's necessary that the person doesn't admit to herself/himself that s/he selects her/his emotions.

Emotions and Decision-Making:

We also realize that emotions play a big part in decision-making. Every action we take is based on intellectual and emotional motivations. We look for logical reasons to help us choose one side over the other; we think and consider the pros and cons of our future actions. When it's difficult to make a decision, we turn to our emotions, which favor one side over the other. Emotions also give us the extra push to pursue whichever decision we make with motivation. Since it is clear that we're counting on our emotions to be the tie-breakers in our decisions, then it's absolutely crucial that our emotions lead us in the right direction. Some people even depend on their emotions wholly for decision-making, never weighing the pros and cons and always doing what they want to do.

Let us consider the case of a person who has the proper perspective on life, a person who has the true understanding of the purpose of her/his creation as a vicegerent of Allah *SWT*, as indicated in *Surat Al Baqarah* where Allah says,

"وَإِذْ قَالَ رَبُّكَ لِلْمَلاَئِكَة إِنِّي جَاعِلٌ فِي الأَرْضِ خَلِيفَةً"

"And remember when your lord said to the angles: 'Verily, I am going to place mankind generation after generation on earth as my vicegerent'"[92]

If this person takes the prophet *SAAW* as a role model then her/his goals are to achieve happiness in this worldly life and in the eternal life, and, in turn, her/his emotions will be geared toward everything good and wholesome. This will apply also to her/his taste in the other gender. However, if s/he focuses only on instant gratification and short-term gain, taking her/his values and principles from the Hollywood movies, the soap operas, and the songs that surround her/him; her/his emotions will direct her/him toward the same individualistic attitude and selfish lifestyle, and that will again affect the people whom s/he loves.

It is each person's fundamental direction in life that decides her/his emotions, for s/he will subconsciously select the emotions that are appropriate to maintaining and strengthening her/his overall goals.

---

[92] (Q2, V30)

This is very clear in the authentic *Hadeeth* of the prophet *SAAW* which says,

"لا يؤمن أحدكم حتى يكون هواه تبعا لما جئت به"

"None of you is a true believer until his desires and likes are in accordance to what I have brought to you (Islamic teachings)."[93]

Now that we've discussed emotions in a general sense, let's see how these concepts apply to love. Generally, people label any strong emotion of desire, regardless of its merits or faults, as love. This makes love, as an emotion, highly subjective, as it differs from person to person, depending on each person's fundamental aims in life. For example, for a person with a high degree of commitment and moral standing, love represents the highest contribution that one can make to another, a contribution where s/he is willing to give all s/he is and all s/he has. This individual is someone who would love another person based on her/his character and sincerity, an individual who is willing to give and share more than s/he takes. The result of a relationship based on this form of love will be cooperation, mutual respect, and mutual achievement. Love will be a blessing that will help this couple to reach its highest potential.

Meanwhile, for an individual who lacks commitment and interest in the well-being of others, love is an instrument of hostility, a way to use another person for her/his own purposes and wants without the willingness to give back or share. In this case, this individual would love another on the basis of what s/he can offer and provide, be it her/his material wealth, physical beauty, or social prestige and family status. The result of a relationship based on this destructive form of love will be antagonism, disagreement, and misery.

Contrary to the ideas of love that pop culture bombards us with, the ideas of 'love at first sight' and being 'madly in love', we find true, lasting love to be the kind of love where the two people show

---

[93] Muslim

devotion, responsibility, and belongingness and live harmoniously together.

This is not the kind of love promoted by the media, but it is the kind of love that Islamic teachings emphasize and stress. That is why, Allah *SWT* in *Surat Ar Room*, says,

"وَمِنْ آيَاتِهِ أَنْ خَلَقَ لَكُم مِّنْ أَنفُسِكُمْ أَزْوَاجًا لِّتَسْكُنُوا إِلَيْهَا وَجَعَلَ بَيْنَكُم مَّوَدَّةً وَرَحْمَةً إِنَّ فِي ذَلِكَ لَآيَاتٍ لِّقَوْمٍ يَتَفَكَّرُونَ"

"And among His signs is this, that He created for you wives from among yourselves, that you may find repose in them, and He has put between you *Mawadah* and *Rahma*[94]. Verily, in that are signs for people who reflect."[95]

We notice that Allah *SWT* didn't base the marital relationship in love, but He used the word *Mawadah* because it has a much deeper meaning than the word love. It describes the real love that we discussed above which ensures the commitment of both spouses to work for the sake of Allah *SWT* and be righteous people. This is clearly understood when one reflects on the use of the word *Mawadah* or its derivatives in the *Qur'an*. Here is an example:

"إِنَّ الَّذِينَ آمَنُوا وَعَمِلُوا الصَّالِحَاتِ سَيَجْعَلُ لَهُمُ الرَّحْمَنُ وُدًّا"

"Verily, those who believe and work deeds of righteousness, Allah will bestow *Wooda* for them."[96]

The word *Wooda* is from the same root as the word *Mawadah*. Allah *SWT* emphasizes that this kind of great feeling will be bestowed on the believers as a result to their belief and righteous deeds.

---

[94] See the terminology and explanations in this section for the meaning of these words
[95] (Q30, V21)
[96] (Q19, V96)

125

The love intended here is not the love of possessing and controlling, rather it is the love of comforting and considering. Associating the word *Rahmah* with *Mawadah* in the same verse is another witness to the nature of this love.

Finally, one may ask if this means that there is no place for romance in an Islamic marriage? The answer is, of course, that there is a place for romance in an Islamic marriage, but romance is not the main foundation of the marriage. Otherwise, when the fire of romance dies out, the marriage would suffer. The foundation of Islamic marriage is based on more tangible qualities that have the property of continuity and growth within a good marital relationship. At the top of these qualities are *Mawadah* and *Rahmah*.

Forgiveness

Forgiveness is a wonderful quality and essential ingredient for good long-term relationships between people in general and successful marriage unions in particular. It is a great quality and is considered one of the qualities of those who observe their duties toward Allah *SWT* and are mindful of His presence in their lives, *"Al Motaqeen"*. That is why, in *Surat Aal Imran*, Allah says,

"وَسَارِعُواْ إِلَى مَغْفِرَةٍ مِّن رَّبِّكُمْ وَجَنَّةٍ عَرْضُهَا السَّمَاوَاتُ وَالأَرْضُ أُعِدَّتْ لِلْمُتَّقِينَ ۞ الَّذِينَ يُنفِقُونَ فِي السَّرَّاءِ وَالضَّرَّاءِ وَالْكَاظِمِينَ الْغَيْظَ وَالْعَافِينَ عَنِ النَّاسِ وَاللّهُ يُحِبُّ الْمُحْسِنِينَ"

"And be quick in seeking forgiveness from your Lord and a Heaven whose width is as the width of the earth and sky, which is prepared for those who exercise *Taqwa*, those who spend at easy as well as at difficult times, **those who control their anger, and those who pardon people**. Allah certainly loves those who exercise *Ihsan*."[97]

In *Surat Ash Shura*, Allah says,

---

[97] (Q 3, V 133-134)

"وَمَا عِندَ اللَّهِ خَيْرٌ وَأَبْقَى لِلَّذِينَ آمَنُوا وَعَلَى رَبِّهِمْ يَتَوَكَّلُونَ ۞ وَالَّذِينَ يَجْتَنِبُونَ كَبَائِرَ الْإِثْمِ وَالْفَوَاحِشَ وَإِذَا مَا غَضِبُوا هُمْ يَغْفِرُونَ"

"...But that which is with Allah is better and more lasting for those who believe in the Oneness of Allah and put their trust in their Lord. And those who avoid the greater sins and *Al-Fawahish*, **and when they are angry, forgive**."[98]

In addition, in *Surat Al Aa'raf*, Allah instructs the prophet *SAAW* and the believers to exercise this wonderful quality in their interactions with others. Allah says,

"خُذِ الْعَفْوَ وَأْمُرْ بِالْعُرْفِ وَأَعْرِضْ عَنِ الْجَاهِلِينَ"

"Show forgiveness, enjoin what is good and turn away from the foolish (i.e. don't punish them)"[99]

These verses clearly illustrate the importance of forgiving others. These verses indicate that Allah *SWT* considers those who do these acts as the *Mutaqeen*. They also indicate that Allah loves them and promises them a great and lasting reward in the hereafter.

The teachings of Prophet Muhammad *SAAW* further emphasize the importance of forgiving and pardoning generally in human relations and particularly when family members are involved.

It was reported by *Anas Ibn Malik RAA* that the messenger of Allah *SAAW* said,

"لا تقاطعوا ولا تدابروا ولا تباغضوا ولا تحاسدوا وكونوا عباد الله إخوانا، ولا يحل لمسلم أن يهجر أخاه فوق ثلاث"

"Neither nurse mutual hatred, nor envy, nor abandon each other, and be fellow brothers and servants of Allah. It is not lawful for a

---

[98] (Q 42, V 36-37)
[99] (Q 7, V 199)

127

Muslim that he should keep his relation estranged with another Muslim beyond three days."[100]

It was also reported that the prophet *SAAW* said,

"لا يحل لمسلم أن يهجر أخاه فوق ثلاث ،يلتقيان فيعرض هذا ويعرض هذا

،وخيرهما الذي يبدأ بالسلام"

"It is not lawful for a Muslim that he should keep his relation estranged with another Muslim beyond three days. When they meet, each one of them turns his face away, but the best of them is the one who starts to greet the other"[101]

Also it was reported by *Abu Hurairah RAA* that a man said to the messenger of Allah *SAAW,*

"يا رسول الله إن لي قرابة أصلهم ويقطعوني وأحسن إليهم ويسيئون إلي ،

وأحلم عنهم ويجهلون علي فقال : "لئن كنت كما قلت فكأنما تسفهم المل

ولا يزال معك من الله تعالى ظهير عليهم مادمت على ذلك"

"I have relatives with whom I have tried to reunite, but they continue to sever their relationship with me. I try to treat them kindly, but they treat me badly; with them I am gentle, but with me they are rough."

The prophet *SAAW* replied, "If you are as you say, you will not be without support against them from Allah as long as you do so."[102]
It was also narrated by *Ubada Ibn Al-Samet RAA* that the messenger of Allah *SAAW* said,

"ألا أنبئكم بما يشرف الله به البنيان ويرفع الدرجات؟ قالوا: بلى يا رسول الله.

قال: تحلم على من جهل عليك وتعفو عمن ظلمك، وتعطي من حرمك،

وتصل من قطعك"

---

[100] (Agreed upon)
[101] (Agreed upon)
[102] Muslim

128

"Shall I tell you about what would elevate your ranks and increase your honor?"

Those with him replied, "Yes, oh messenger of Allah."
He said, "Exercise forbearance with the one who is ignorant with you, forgive the one who has wronged you, give to the one who didn't give to you, and establish good relations with the one who severs his relations with you."[103]

It was also said,

"التمس لأخيك سبعين عذراً، فإن لم تجد له عذر فقل لعل له عذر لا أعرفه"

"Try to find up to seventy excuses for your brother; and if you can't, say, 'maybe he has an excuse that I'm not aware of.'"[104]
Forgetting and forgiving plays a great role in keeping healthy relationships between family members, especially between spouses. It is natural to have conflicts and differences of opinion on certain issues. These differences should never leave negative imprints on the marital relationship. The best way to ensure this is by exercising forgiveness, forgetting these differences, and not making a big issue out of them. In marital relationships, we need to regularly exercise this, considering the various challenges families are subjected to in North America and the amount of volunteer work Muslims should be doing to help with community development and establish a positive environment for the healthy growth of our children. Following are some practical examples:

- The husband may come home late one day from a community event or from a planning meeting for community activities. The wife may be tired after a long day. She may even have already gone to bed. In this case, it is inconsiderate from the husband to expect her to wake up and serve him his dinner. He should forgive her and warm his dinner plate himself without any feelings of resentment toward her.

---

[103] At-Tabarani
[104] Saying of some of the *Salaf*

129

- On the other hand, it is common for some wives to complain that their husbands are not giving enough time to their family. This is particularly true in the case of active Muslim husbands. Again, instead of harboring feelings of resentment and becoming angry with each other, both should exercise patience in its full meaning, try to be calm at the time of conflict, and at the same time, should search for a comprehensive solution to the problem, particularly, if it is a repetitive one. Practicing forgiveness in situations like this helps in solving the problem in an amicable way and doesn't leave negative imprints on the marital relationship. Blaming, resenting, and expressing rage and anger, doesn't help the family at all in situations like this. On the other hand, exercising patience, forgiveness, and forgetting minor issues will provide the platform needed to resolve the problem and improve the situation.

Trust and Faithfulness

Trust and faithfulness is another very important ingredient for the success of any relationship. In marriage particularly, trust between spouses is crucial in building a very healthy, sound relationship between husband and wife. Trust is a quality to be earned and not demanded. It is foolish for any spouse to think that, just by asking the other spouse to trust him/her, he/she would. It is not enough just to say to your spouse, "Trust me." Spouses really have to work hard to earn each other's trust. For us Muslims, earning this trust would mainly depend on our behavior and not putting ourselves in situations that could be misinterpreted or misunderstood by our spouses and create doubts in their minds.

One great asset we have as Muslims that helps generate an atmosphere of trust and maintain a high level of faithfulness in our family life is the set Islamic etiquettes of gender relations. For this wonderful atmosphere to exist, both spouses must practice these etiquettes. Islam provides us with wonderful guidelines for every aspect of our lives. Gender relations are no different. The verses of the *Qur'an* and the teachings of Prophet Muhammad *SAAW* offer clear guidance on how the two genders should interact with each other. This guidance covers a variety of areas such as the allowed and non-allowed mixing, nature of conversation and tone of voice, dress code for both genders, visitation guidelines, and allowed members of families to visit in the absence of one of the spouses, just to name a few. When all the rules and guidelines are practiced by both spouses when dealing with a person from the opposite gender, it creates and enhances the highest level of trust between them.

In addition, spouses should always be transparent with each other and shouldn't leave any room for doubtful thoughts to develop in each other's minds. It is extremely important that our spouses perceive our actions correctly, especially in certain situations. Actions shouldn't be left unexplained or left to the other spouse to guess at. Otherwise, they may be misunderstood by the other spouse. The prophet *SAAW* gave us the best example in this as indicated in the following *Hadeeth*:

"عن أم المؤمنين صفية بنت حيي رضي الله عنها قالت كان النبي صلى الله عليه

وسلم معتكفا فأتيته أزوره ليلا فحدثته ثم قمت لأنقلب فقام معي ليقلبني فمر

رجلان من الأنصار رضي الله عنهما فلما رأيا النبي صلى الله عليه وسلم أسرعا

فقال صلى الله عليه وسلم: "على رسلكما إنها صفية بنت حيي". فقالا:

سبحان الله يارسول الله. فقال: "إن الشيطان يجري من ابن آدم مجرى الدم وإني

خشيت أن يقذف في قلوبكما شرا – أو قال شيئا"

It was narrated by the mother of the faithful *Safyah RAA* who said, "When the prophet *SAAW* was in *Ietekaf*, I went to visit him at night. After we chatted, he walked me back. Two of the *Ansar* were passing by. When they saw the prophet *SAAW*, they rushed away. He said, 'Do not rush, she is *Safyah Bint Hoyay*'."

They said, "*Subhan Allah*, O prophet of Allah (indicating that they are not suspecting any thing wrong with the prophet *SAAW*.) He said, "The *Shaytan* is as close to the son of *Adam* as if he is running in his blood. I was concerned that he would instill some evil thoughts in your minds."[105]

The above incident is a clear indication that the prophet *SAAW* made sure that those two companions understood that she was his wife. He didn't want their thoughts to wonder and come up with the wrong conclusion. This indicates how important to be transparent and make sure that others perceive your actions correctly, particularly when it is related to interaction with members of the opposite gender.

Open Mindedness and Understanding

Having an open mind, in general, and during discussions with your spouse in particular, is a great asset that helps create strong bonds between spouses. Willingness to exert the effort to understand your spouse's point of view and accommodate different views other than your own are also of great value to the marriage's health and growth. Spouses should never start a discussion of an issue with pre-conceived ideas about the outcome of this discussion. It is of utmost importance to the health of the relationship and the well-being of the marriage that the attitude of both spouses should be one of frankness, open mindedness, and understanding. Spouses should not focus on winning the argument when involved in discussions. They must maintain objectiveness and try to reach the best conclusion. *Imam Shafe'i RAA* was reported to have said, "Whenever I debate an issue with any individual I always pray to Allah that He would make the right ideas about that subject be brought forward by the one I'm debating." One practice that helps ensure objectivity in discussions between spouses is to make sure you don't have your discussions in public. Make sure you discuss your affairs in private, on a one-on-one basis. This way you avoid the extra element of ego-boosting in the discussion, and it is easier to maintain objectivity because nobody else is around to witness who won the argument. Each of the spouses, in this case, should be seeking the truth and the best results out of the discussion. As such,

---

[105] Agreed upon

both will be willing to give up their point of view or winning the argument for the sake of reaching a beneficial resolution out of the discussion. This is exactly what we have been advised by Allah *SWT* in *Surat Saba'*. He says,

"قُلْ إِنَّمَا أَعِظُكُم بِوَاحِدَةٍ أَن تَقُومُوا لِلَّهِ مَثْنَى وَفُرَادَى ثُمَّ تَتَفَكَّرُوا مَا بِصَاحِبِكُم مِّن جِنَّةٍ إِنْ هُوَ إِلَّا نَذِيرٌ لَّكُم بَيْنَ يَدَيْ عَذَابٍ شَدِيدٍ"

"Say: "I do admonish you on one point: that ye do stand up before Allah,- (It may be) **in pairs, or (it may be) singly,- and reflect (within yourselves)**: your Companion is not possessed: he is no less than a Warner to you, in face of a terrible Penalty."[106]

Respect

Islam promotes mutual respect in all areas of life. People are all created equal. The origin of humans is traced back to *Adam* peace be upon him. They are all equal, and there is no difference between one and another in the sight of Allah except on the basis of *Taqwa*. Allah says,

"يَا أَيُّهَا النَّاسُ إِنَّا خَلَقْنَاكُم مِّن ذَكَرٍ وَأُنثَى وَجَعَلْنَاكُمْ شُعُوبًا وَقَبَائِلَ لِتَعَارَفُوا إِنَّ أَكْرَمَكُمْ عِندَ اللَّهِ أَتْقَاكُمْ إِنَّ اللَّهَ عَلِيمٌ خَبِيرٌ"

"O you people, We have created you all out of a male and a female, and have made you into nations and tribes, so that you might come to know one another. Verily the noblest of you in the sight of Allah is the one who is most deeply conscious of Him"[107]

The prophet *SAAW* emphasized the same concept when he said,

"يا أيها الناس ، ألا إن ربكم واحد ، و إن أباكم واحد ، ألا لا فضل لعربي على أعجمي و لا لعجمي على عربي و لا لأحمر على أسود و لا أسود على أحمر إلا بالتقوى..."

---

[106] (Q34, V46)
[107] (Q49, V13)

133

"There is no preference of an Arab over a non-Arab or a non-Arab over an Arab except on the basis of *Taqwa*"[108]

The prophet *SAAW* emphasized the fact of gender equality and mutual respect in every relation between genders when he said,

"إنما النساء شقائق الرجال"

"Certainly women are the twin complements of men"[109]

In more than one verse in the *Qur'an* and saying of Prophet Muhammad *SAAW*, instructions clearly promote mutual respect between spouses. Allah *SWT* says,

"وَلَهُنَّ مِثْلُ الَّذِي عَلَيْهِنَّ بِالْمَعْرُوفِ"

"the rights of the wives with regard to their husband, are equal to the rights of the husbands with regard to their wives"[110]
He also says,

"وَعَاشِرُوهُنَّ بِالْمَعْرُوفِ فَإِن كَرِهْتُمُوهُنَّ فَعَسَى أَن تَكْرَهُواْ شَيْئًا وَيَجْعَلَ اللّهُ فِيهِ خَيْرًا كَثِيرًا"

"Live with them (your wives) on a footing of kindness and equity. If you dislike them it may be that you dislike something in which Allah has placed a great deal of Good."[111]

It is interesting to note that in *Surat Al Baqarah* alone, in the verses discussing the spousal relationship, from verse 226 to verse 241, the word *"Belma'roof* or *Bema'roof"* which means in a respectable, kind, and fair way is mentioned twelve times. This is a clear indication of the importance of using respect in the spousal relationship.

The respect of spouses to each other should manifest itself in various forms and occasions. Both should respect each other's

---

[108] Ahmad
[109] Ahmad
[110] (Q2, V228)
[111] (Q4, V19)

families. They should welcome them and treat them nicely when they come for a visit. None of them should look down at the family of the other or insult any of its members. They should be kind and accommodative to them, especially the mother-in-law and the father-in-law. Another angle of respect related to the in-laws, the husband should respect his wife's right to visit them frequently, should be kind to them, and should exchange gifts with them especially on happy occasions such as *Ramadan* and the *Eids*. The husband should also encourage his wife to treat her blood relatives kindly, be in touch with them, and express concern about their affairs. The wife should also encourage her husband to be good to his family, visit them, present gifts to them, and treat them with kindness. She should never prevent him from doing good things for his family no matter what happens in terms of their feelings toward her.

A wife also should respect her husband's time of rest and comfort and make sure the home environment is not noisy in order to provide him with the needed rest. She should also respect his meal times and make sure that the food is ready, especially if he arrives home daily at a fixed time. A husband should also respect his wife's needs and try to satisfy them. Her need to rest for a while and take a break from the children's care should be respected and accommodated by the husband. He should cooperate with her in this matter and help her with the children. Both spouses should respect the friends of the other spouse as long as s/he is a good Muslim and doesn't interfere in the family affairs or have a negative impact or bad influence on any of them because of her/his bad habits.

A husband should also respect his wife's right of expressing her views on issues and matters related to family affairs. In fact, he should always consult her before making any decisions related to the family and make sure he considers her views before finalizing the decision.

Mutual respect is a very important ingredient that should be observed and practiced in all spousal relationships. It will definitely help spouses have a stronger marital bond and healthy marriage union.

Patience

The word patience and its derivatives are mentioned in the *Qur'an* over 100 times in various locations and on various occasions. Here are some of these verses that encourage believers to exercise patience:

In *Surat Al Baqarah*, Allah says,

"وَلَنَبْلُوَنَّكُم بِشَيْءٍ مِّنَ الْخَوفْ وَالْجُوعِ وَنَقْصٍ مِّنَ الأَمَوَالِ وَالأَنفُسِ وَالثَّمَرَاتِ وَبَشِّرِ الصَّابِرِينَ"

"Be sure that We shall test you with something of fear and hunger, some loss in goods, lives, and the fruits (of your toil), but give glad tiding to those who patiently persevere."[112]

Also in the same *Surah*, Allah says,

"يَا أَيُّهَا الَّذِينَ آمَنُواْ اسْتَعِينُواْ بِالصَّبْرِ وَالصَّلَاةِ إِنَّ اللَّهَ مَعَ الصَّابِرِينَ"

"O you who believe, seek help with patient perseverance and prayer, for Allah is with those who patiently persevere."[113]
In *Surat Aal Imran*, Allah says,

"يَا أَيُّهَا الَّذِينَ آمَنُواْ اصْبِرُواْ وَصَابِرُواْ وَرَابِطُواْ وَاتَّقُواْ اللَّهَ لَعَلَّكُمْ تُفْلِحُونَ"

"O you who believe persevere in patience and constancy; vie in such perseverance; strengthen each other; and fear Allah that you may prosper."[114]

In the same *Surah*, Allah also says,

---

[112] (Q 2, V 155)
[113] (Q 2, V 153)
[114] (Q 3, V 200)

"لَتُبْلَوُنَّ فِي أَمْوَالِكُمْ وَأَنفُسِكُمْ وَلَتَسْمَعُنَّ مِنَ الَّذِينَ أُوتُواْ الْكِتَابَ مِن قَبْلِكُمْ وَمِنَ الَّذِينَ أَشْرَكُواْ أَذًى كَثِيرًا وَإِن تَصْبِرُواْ وَتَتَّقُواْ فَإِنَّ ذَلِكَ مِنْ عَزْمِ الأُمُورِ"

"You shall certainly be tried and tested in your possessions and in yourselves; and you shall hear much that will grieve you, from those who received the book before you and from those who worship partners besides Allah. But if you persevere patiently, and guard against evil, then that indeed is a matter of resolution."[115]

Also in *Surat Az Zumar*, Allah *SWT* says,

"إِنَّمَا يُوَفَّى الصَّابِرُونَ أَجْرَهُم بِغَيْرِ حِسَابٍ"

"Those who patiently persevere will truly receive a reward without measure."[116]

Also In *Surat Al Mu'min*, Allah *SWT* says,

"فَاصْبِرْ إِنَّ وَعْدَ اللَّهِ حَقٌّ وَاسْتَغْفِرْ لِذَنبِكَ وَسَبِّحْ بِحَمْدِ رَبِّكَ بِالْعَشِيِّ وَالْإِبْكَارِ"

"Patiently, then persevere: for the promise of Allah is true: and ask forgiveness for your fault, and celebrate the praises of your Lord in the evening and in the morning."[117]

Also in *Surat Ash Shura*, Allah *SWT* says,

"وَلَمَن صَبَرَ وَغَفَرَ إِنَّ ذَلِكَ لَمِنْ عَزْمِ الْأُمُورِ"

"But indeed if any shows patience and forgives, that would truly be an affair of great resolution."[118]

Also in *Surat Al Ahqaf*, Allah *SWT* says,

"فَاصْبِرْ كَمَا صَبَرَ أُوْلُوا الْعَزْمِ مِنَ الرُّسُلِ وَلَا تَسْتَعْجِل لَّهُمْ كَأَنَّهُمْ يَوْمَ يَرَوْنَ مَا يُوعَدُونَ لَمْ يَلْبَثُوا إِلَّا سَاعَةً مِّن نَّهَارٍ ..."

---

[115] (Q 3, V 186)
[116] (Q 39, V 10)
[117] (Q 40, V 55)
[118] (Q 42, V 43)

"Therefore patiently persevere, as did all messengers of firm resolution; and be in no haste about the unbelievers. On the day that they see the punishment promised them it will be as if they have not tarried more than an hour in a single day...."[119]

Also in *Surat Muhammad*, Allah *SWT* says,

"وَلَنَبْلُوَنَّكُمْ حَتَّى نَعْلَمَ الْمُجَاهِدِينَ مِنكُمْ وَالصَّابِرِينَ وَنَبْلُوَ أَخْبَارَكُمْ"

"And We shall try you until we test those among you who strive their utmost and persevere in patience; and We shall try your reported (mettle)."[120]

Also In *Surat Al Muzzammil*, Allah *SWT* says,

"وَاصْبِرْ عَلَى مَا يَقُولُونَ وَاهْجُرْهُمْ هَجْرًا جَمِيلًا"

"And have patience with what they say, and leave them with noble dignity."[121]

The teachings of Prophet Muhammad *SAAW* emphasize the same concept in different ways. Here are some of the his teachings in this regard:

On the authority of *Abu Malik Al Harith Ibn 'Asim Ash Ash'ari RAA* who related that the messenger of Allah *SAAW* said, "Cleanliness is half of faith. The utterance of 'All praise belongs to Allah' fills the scales of good actions. The utterance of 'Glory be to Allah and all praise belongs to Allah' fills the space between the heavens and the earth. And prayer is light; and charity is the test of faith; **and endurance is a glow**; and the *Qur'an* is a plea supporting or opposing you. Every person begins the morning ready to strike a bargain with his soul taking risk; he either ransoms it or he puts it into perdition."[122]

---

[119] (Q 46, V 35)
[120] (Q 47, V 31)
[121] (Q 73, V 10)
[122] Muslim

It was reported on the authority of *Abu Sa'id Al Khudry RAA* that certain people of the *Ansar* begged of the messenger of Allah *SAAW* and he gave them. Then they again begged of him, and he gave them all what he possessed, and so his means were exhausted. Then the Prophet *SAAW* said, "What I have of good things, I'll not withhold from you. Who so would be abstemious, Allah will keep him abstemious. And who so would be independent, Allah will keep him independent. **And who so would be patient, Allah will give him patience and no one is granted a gift better and more extensive than patience.**"[123]

On the authority of *Abu Yahia Suhaib Ibn Sinan RAA* who relates that the messenger of Allah *SAAW* said, "How excellent is the case of a faithful servant; there is good for him in everything and this is not the case with anyone except him. If prosperity attends him, he expresses gratitude to Allah and that is good for him; and if adversity falls on him, he endures it patiently and that is better for him."[124]

Anas RAA narrated that the messenger of Allah *SAAW* was passing by a woman who was weeping near a grave and said, "Fear Allah and be patient."

She said, "Away from me! My calamity has not befallen on you." Later, the woman was told that he was the prophet *SAAW*, whereupon she came to his door where she found no doorkeeper. She said, "O' prophet of Allah, I was unaware of you."
The messenger of Allah *SAAW* said, "Patience should be exercised at the first stroke of grief."[125]

Anas RAA said he heard the messenger of Allah *SAAW* declaring that Allah *SWT* says, "When I afflict my servant in his two dear

---

[123] Agreed Upon
[124] Muslim
[125] Agreed Upon

things (i.e., his eyes), and he endures patiently, I shall compensate him for them with Paradise."[126]

Abu Hurairah RAA narrated that Prophet Muhammad *SAAW* said, "The strong man is not the one who wrestles, but the strong man is the one who controls himself in a fit of rage."[127]

Khabab Ibn Al Arat RAA narrated, "We lodged a complaint with the messenger of Allah *SAAW* regarding the persecution inflicted on us by the disbelievers of Makkah. He was lying in the shade of the *Ka'bah*, having made a pillow of his sheet. We submitted, 'Why do you not supplicate for our prevalence (over the opponents)?'

He replied, 'From among those before you the man would be seized and held in a pit dug for him in the earth and he would be sawn into two from his head, and his flesh would be torn away from his bones with an iron comb. But in spite of this, he would not wean away from his faith. By Allah, He would bring this matter to its consummation until a rider will travel from *Sana'a* to *Hadramout* fearing nothing except Allah and fear of the wolf concerning his sheep, but you are in hot haste.'"[128]

Patience is very important for all believers in general, and for those with a mission to achieve in particular. Carrying duties and fulfilling missions requires patience and endurance. That is why Allah *SWT* advises even His messengers to equip themselves with patience. Patience is a great virtue for any relationship. Because of the natural differences in personalities, spouses should be patient with each other to ensure a warm family atmosphere and avoid sources of friction and conflicts in their relationship. Spouses will need patience in their interactions at times of hardships as well as times of ease. They will need patience to discuss issues and resolve conflicts without leaving negative imprints on their relationship.

---

[126] Bukhari

[127] Agreed upon

[128] Bukhari

Spouses will need patience when in-laws interfere in the spouses' affairs to ensure that their interference does not cause martial rifts and, at the same time, to deal with them in an honorable and dignified manner without compromising their own rights. They will need patience to deal with their children at various stages of their life. They will need it to handle their teens' problems, particularly in this North American society, with all its pressures. Married life is full of challenges, and there is no doubt that patience is a great virtue to equip ourselves with to ensure living our life safely and fulfilling our duties successfully.

As described by the *Qur'an,* patience is required for us to be able to perform all our acts of pure worship in the proper format at the right time without feeling shy or hesitant to do them in front of others. Patience is required for all believers to stand firm in front of all the hardships they will face when they try to call to the way of Allah *SWT.*

Believers need patience to stand firm when they are faced with any of the tests in this life. After all, we know that life is one trial after another and one test after another. Believers will need patience to resist various temptations in this life, such as their desires and whims.

Tested and Proven Recipes for Various Occassions

The following are some recipes for various situations and occasions using the above ingredients. We recommend that they all be cooked in a pot of *Rahmah* using the heat and warmth of respect, and always served in a plate of *Mawadah.*

Vacation Recipe
In two separate pots of *Rahmah,* both set on the high heat of respect make these two separate mixtures.

Mixture 1:

In the first pot, combine 1 cup each of contentment, satisfaction, and trust & faithfulness with an abundance of sexual gratification. Cover and let simmer.

Mixture 2:
In the second pot, mix 1 cup open mindedness & understanding with 2 cups each of patience and communication together until mixture thickens. Stir in 1 cup each of sharing and compromise.

Combine the mixtures together stirring constantly until they look and taste uniform. Stir in half a cup of courtesy. Add care, adaptation, and acceptance to taste.

Remove pot from heat and sprinkle with contribution, sensitivity, security, and appreciation. Serve on a plate of *Mawadah.*

Baker's Note: Feel free to snack on this often and remember to offer some to your spouse

Visiting In-Laws Recipe
Lightly grease an 8-inch pie plate with adaptation. In a large bowl, beat 1 cup of open-mindedness with 1 cup of understanding, add 2 cups of respect and patience to the mix and blend them all together.

With extra care, stir in 3 tablespoons of commitment, ½ a cup of compromise and a heaping cup of communication. Stir the mixture well, until most of the traces of compromise are concealed.

In a separate bowl, grate ¾ of a cup of acceptance with ½ a cup of appreciation. Sift in 6 teaspoons of accommodation and 1/3 of a cup of forgiveness. Add a dash of courtesy and a generous sprinkle of sensitivity.

Thoroughly blend them all together and bake for 40 minutes in the heat of *Rahmah.* Serve hot on a platter of *Mawadah.*

Baker's note: Should be served two to three times daily in large portions.

During Pregnancy and Delivery Time

Place 1 cup each of commitment, courtesy, communication, and care in a small saucepan and blend together thoroughly. Gently stir in 2 cups of contribution and 11/2 cups of ready to use compromise. Blend all ingredients together well until you get a light, fluffy mixture. In a separate mixing bowl combine 6 heaping tablespoons of sensitivity with 2 large cups of support and ½ cup of sharing. In a medium-sized bowl, melt 1 cup of adaptation and accommodation with a generous amount of appreciation and acceptance.

Combine the 3 mixtures together and beat until consistent and smooth.

Let bake for 90 minutes in the heat of open-mindedness and understanding and respect. When cooled, glaze with forgiveness and top it off with patience and respect.

Baker's Note: Take extra caution when preparing this dish and eat in consistent heaping quantities. Share this dish with all your family members.

During Conflicts

Preheat the oven to 350 Degrees Fahrenheit of the heat of respect. Line a pan of *Rahmah* with adaptation, courtesy, and sensitivity.

In a large mixing bowl, measure 3 cups of patience. In another mixing bowl, combine 2 cups of communication with ¾ of a cup each of forgiveness, open-mindedness & understanding, and compromise (must be measured in, in that order.) Beat the communication mixture together thoroughly until foamy and consistent. Stir the communication mixture into the bowl of patience. Add ½ cup of acceptance. Pour mixture into lined pan and bake in the heat of respect. When fully baked, remove from oven and allow time to cool. When cooled, sprinkle with sharing. Serve in plates of *Mawadah*.

Baker's note: This recipe is very healthy and quite low in fat too. Therefore, use as often as possible.

During Overseas Travel To Visit Family
In a large pot of *Rahmah* and respect, heat 1 cup of anticipation and 6 tblsps open-mindedness and understanding. Add sizable portions of security, care, adaptation, and compromise. Stir from time to time and bring to a boil.

Meanwhile, in a mixing bowl, measure 2 cups of patience. Add ½ a cup of each support, sensitivity, and trust & faithfulness. Mix in a blender until the mixture is uniform.

Add the patience mixture to the communication mixture as soon as the communication mixture comes to a boil. Stir the two mixtures together and bring to a boil.

When the mixture boils add as much sensitivity needed to make the mixture smooth and consistent, stirring constantly. When the mixture is completely smooth, stir in 6 tblsps of accommodation and 7 tblsps of courtesy. Cover and let simmer for five minutes. Add acceptance, sharing, and appreciation to taste.

During Exams and Study Periods
Preheat oven to 350 degrees Fahrenheit of the heat of respect.

In a mixing bowl, mix 1 cup of patience with a ½ a cup each of accommodation, support, and sensitivity. Add ¼ of a cup each of compromise and open-mindedness & understanding.

In a small mixing bowl, measure 2/3 of a cup of forgiveness.
In a large mixing bowl, mix ¾ of each contribution, adaptation and courtesy with 4 tblsps each of acceptance and care.

Add forgiveness to the patience mixture in two parts alternately with the contribution mixture, beginning and ending with the contribution mixture. Mix well.

Spread in a pan of *Rahmah*. Bake in the heat of respect and serve in a plate of *Mawadah*.

Baker's note: This dish should be served at least once a day for as long as the exam period lasts.

During Shopping Trips
In a pot of *Rahmah*, heat ¾ of a cup of patience. Add 3 tblsps of compromise. Cover and let simmer.

In another pot, mix ¾ of a cup each of sharing and accommodation, and 5 tblsps of sensitivity and 4 tblsps of open-mindedness and understanding. Add ¾ of a cup respect. Stir until mixture is uniform. Cover and bring to boil.

Add patience mixture and stir well. Serve on plates of *Mawadah*.

5 - Family Dynamics
and Family Atmosphere

Introduction

One of the prime responsibilities of spouses is to ensure the presence of a positive, comfortable, cozy, and warm family atmosphere where each spouse can be himself/herself and feel supported and loved. This atmosphere is also needed for the well-being and healthy growth of children. Family atmosphere is one of the key factors affecting the formation of children's personalities and molding their character. In their relationship with their parents, children experience society at large. In every family, children will have certain common characteristics; they are the expression of the family atmosphere. That is why family atmosphere is very important. Spouses' moods and interactions are the main contributors to the family atmosphere. It is of utmost importance that both spouses strive very hard with all they can and in every possible way to make sure that the family atmosphere is relaxed, happy, and calm. This is the gate for a stronger bond between spouses themselves and between them and their children. The importance of family atmosphere can't be overemphasized. It is a vital component for not only the health of the husband/wife relationship, but also for the strength of the parent/child bond. As such, spouses have to do their best to achieve this magnificent family atmosphere.

We will discuss the family atmosphere that every serious and sincere couple should work hard to create and seek to maintain during their life together. We will talk about the factors that help create and sustain this atmosphere and the factors that threaten this healthy and warm atmosphere and, in turn, should be completely avoided.

How to Attain This Atmosphere

To achieve this superb family atmosphere, both spouses have to do certain things and have to avoid other things. Here they are in detail:

Things to Do

♦ Eagerly learn and enthusiastically acquire all the above ingredients and use them in the prescribed recipes for various occasions with the proper amount of wisdom and tact. Make up your own working recipes as well (and make sure to use anticipation when making them up!)

♦ Adopt an attitude of light-heartedness and humor, simplicity and tolerance. Try to simplify issues rather than complicate them, and always be solution-oriented.

♦ Always utilize every opportunity to share with the objective of strengthening your marital bond. Performing house chores together, spending leisure time in each other's company, reading in *Seerah* books and reciting *Qur'an* together, and going on trips and vacations together are some of the activities that you should enjoy and be rewarded with a better bond out of their pursuit.

♦ Appreciate the built-in differences in your personalities as two different individuals and as two different genders. Rather than making them a source of friction and conflict, celebrate them and use them complementarily.

♦ Forgive, forget, and find reasons for each other's shortcoming, since no one is perfect.

♦ Be at peace with yourself. Use the process of self-purification (*Tazkiatul Nafs*) described in a later chapter of this book to help you be a better person who can control yourself and always look at the bigger picture.

Things to Avoid

♦ Avoid the nasty three **B**s. The first of them is being **B**lunt in directing, criticizing, or commenting on any issue or matter related to your spouse. For example, if your spouse has bad breath, rather than indicating bluntly that there is a bad smell, you can say the following, "I feel a bad taste and dryness in my mouth. I'm going to have some mint to moisten and freshen my mouth. Would you like me to get you some?" The second is having a **B**laming attitude in your relationship with your spouse. Don't jump to conclusions, always assuming that your spouse is mistaken, and blame her/him regularly for every problem and conflict happening in your relationship. The third is a very ugly attitude. **B**elittling your spouse in public or even in private is an action that you should try your best to avoid. As believers, we are ordered not to ridicule or belittle anybody, let alone our spouses. Allah *SWT* says,

"يَا أَيُّهَا الَّذِينَ آمَنُوا لَا يَسْخَرْ قَوْمٌ مِّن قَوْمٍ عَسَى أَن يَكُونُوا خَيْرًا مِّنْهُمْ وَلَا نِسَاء مِّن نِّسَاء عَسَى أَن يَكُنَّ خَيْرًا مِّنْهُنَّ وَلَا تَلْمِزُوا أَنفُسَكُمْ وَلَا تَنَابَزُوا بِالْأَلْقَابِ بِئْسَ الاسْمُ الْفُسُوقُ بَعْدَ الْإِيمَانِ وَمَن لَّمْ يَتُبْ فَأُوْلَئِكَ هُمُ الظَّالِمُونَ"

"O you who believe, let not a group scoff at another group, it may be that the latter are better than the former. Nor let some women scoff at other women, it may be that the latter are better than the former. Nor defame one another, nor insult one another by nicknames. How bad is it to insult one's brother after having good faith. And whosoever does not repent, then such are indeed wrongdoers"[129]

♦ Avoid the ugly three **P**s. The first of them is to unfairly **P**ick on your spouse's actions and behaviors, whether in public or private. This, no doubt, could lead to unpleasant situations and seriously threaten the family atmosphere and weaken the marital bond. It leaves the spouse who is being targeted with resentment and a sour taste in her/his mouth. Don't pick on your spouse. As a matter of fact we are ordered to try to find reasons for each other. The early Muslims said,

"التمس لأخيك سبعين عذراً، فإن لم تجد له عذر فقل لعل له عذر لا أعرفه"

---

[129] (Q49, V11)

> "Try to find up to seventy reasons for your brother; and if you can't, say, 'Maybe he has an excuse that I'm not aware of'"[130]

To illustrate our point further, here are few practical examples on spouses picking on each other:

- Ameenah and her husband Mustafa are visiting another couple in their home. Their friends serve them dinner and dessert & coffee. The couple is enjoying a nice time with their friends and chatting. When the dessert is served, the hosting wife comments that she hopes that they like the cake, as it is her specialty. After taking a fork of his cake, Mustafa smiles and says that he likes it very much. Ameenah agrees, saying that it tastes fabulous. Mustafa then adds, "Remember the last time you baked a cake, Ameenah? I spent the whole day looking forward to this chocolate cake and then it was burnt and dry. I had the worst stomach ache after that cake." Mustafa shakes his head, and then adds to Ameenah, "You should spend some more time with Sister Farzanah. Learn this recipe from her."

Here Mustafa picks on Ameenah in public, which is something to avoid completely in all circumstances. Ameenah feels wounded and humiliated by this and will carry this resentment for a long time to come.

- Jamal comes home after a terrible day at work. When Safia, his wife, asks him what is wrong, he opens up and tells her about the conflicts that have been going on and how everything exploded today between a co-worker and him. After listening to his complaints, Safia tells Jamal that there was a lot he could have done to prevent this problem. "You shouldn't have said anything to him in the first place," she says. "Don't you remember? I've told you so many times not to get into these

---

[130] Saying of some of the *Salaf*

discussions at work. Every time, all that happens is that you end up fighting with someone. You keep making enemies and you can stop it. It's not like this was all his fault."

Here Jamal needed Safia's support after an emotionally draining day. Instead, Safia picked on him in his time of need by blaming him for the problem and telling him he should have known better. If Safia's advice was truly needed, she should have delivered it at a different time and in a completely different manner.

After this conversation, Jamal feels judged, ridiculed, and hurt. He will not be opening up to Safia about his feelings or problems again any time soon.

- Anisa and her husband Kareem are having dinner together at home. As Anisa reaches for a second serving of potatoes, Kareem raises his eyebrows and makes a joke. "Anisa!" he exclaims. "I don't have the money to buy you an entire new wardrobe, and all your clothes are getting too small as it is!"

Here Kareem picks on Anisa's eating habits. While this may be a legitimate problem that Kareem wants to address, the way he does it is completely unacceptable. First of all, eating habits and weight are very sensitive subjects between spouses and especially so for women. The joke Kareem makes is hurtful and destructive. If he would like to address this problem, it should be done away from the dinner table and the discussion needs to be a sensitive, fair, and respectful one.

The second of these ugly **P**s is being **P**articular, rather than being easy-going in your dealings and interactions.

"رحم الله عبداً سمحاً إذا باع وإذا اشترى وإذا اقتضى"

"Allah will have mercy on an easy-going servant of His when he sells and when he buys and when he asks for his rights"[131]

To illustrate our point further, here are two practical examples on spouses being very particular while dealing with each other:

- Rafeeq is very particular about the way he likes his meals. After a long day at work, he is tired and looking forward to dinner. His wife Sarah calls him to the table after he has washed up. As he sits down, he notices that the table is set rather awkwardly. "Why would you put the spoons on the left side of the plates when we eat with our right hands?" he asks. Sarah shrugs and serves Rafeeq his dinner. She turns to serve the food to the children before finally sitting down and serving her own dinner. As he eats his food Rafeeq shakes his head. "Sarah, please, I've told you so many times that I don't like the vegetables to be so saucy. There's too much sauce on them. And next time, cut the salad in small pieces, these tomato chunks are huge."

- Asma is happy that her husband is helping around the house. Today, as they tidy the house, Mohamed is doing the dusting and the dishes. He starts with the dusting. Asma finishes cleaning the bathroom and walks into the living room to see that Mohamed has started dusting the lower shelves on the bookshelf and is working his way up. "No, no, Mohamed," she shakes her head. "Do it the other way around. Work from top to bottom or else all the dust just settles below anyway." Mohamed switches to do the top shelves first, but stops when he gets to the middle, having already done the bottom shelves before Asma had seen him. "Aren't you going to complete it? You dusted them before but, you know, the dust from the top shelves came on them again." Mohamed sighs and dusts the bottom

---

[131] Al Bukhari

shelves again. Then he heads into the kitchen to do the dishes. Humming to himself, he washes and rinses. Just as he finishes the dishes, Asma walks into the kitchen. Looking at the countertop around the sink, she lets out a big sigh and grabs a washcloth. She wipes the counter dry and squeezes the water out of the cloth and walks back out of the kitchen. "I was about to do that," Mohamed mutters. "If you'd just waited a few seconds." Mohamed is left standing in the kitchen, wondering why he should do any housework at all when all it does is make her so angry and bossy.

In both cases, the spouse that is particular makes the other spouse feel completely unappreciated.

The third of these is being a **Perfectionist**, when you always expect more from your spouse and don't take your spouse's abilities into consideration. Remember that the prophet *SAAW* said,

"اذا أمرتكم بشيئ فاتوا منه ما استطعتم"

"Whatever I have ordered you, try to do as much as you can, and whatever I forbid you, try to avoid fully"[132]

Prophet Muhammad *SAAW* also gave us a clear example of those who try to be perfectionists, as reported in *Albazzar,* when he said, "The hasty one neither covers the desired distance, nor spares the back of his means of transportation." The "hasty one" was explained by the scholars as the one who lost the companionship of his fellow travelers because he caused the beast he was riding to be fatigued. A perfectionist is similar to the hasty one; he or she asks others to do more than they can bear, and in the process, causes them to be fatigued. This is not healthy behaviour in any relationship, and especially between spouses.

---

[132] Agreed upon and Narrated also in the book of *Tag*

Again, to illustrate our point, here is an example on spouses being perfectionists while dealing with each other:

"Anwar has always wanted the best for Mona, his wife. Every Friday he wants Mona to come to *Jum'a* prayers with him so that she can earn rewards, stay connected, and increase her knowledge. When he is going to *Qiam* prayers, he also pushes her to attend. At the same time, Anwar expects that Mona keep the kids always looking clean and fresh, with their hair combed and their clothes tidy. He expects to come home everyday to a tidy house with the dinner ready to be served. Anwar also likes to visit family members and friends or have them over to visit twice a week. When Mona objects or says that she's not up to it, he insists, reminding her of how important *silat rahim* (staying in touch with family) is in Islam.

All of the things that Anwar wants for his wife and himself are good and useful. However it is not possible for Mona to do all of these things together, considering her time and energy.

Her husband should think over the things that he would like her to do and prioritize what is the most important to him and what can be sacrificed for the sake of the more important things. Then he should discuss these things with Mona and together they should decide what their priorities are. After they have prioritized, then Anwar should encourage her to do the important things, but he should not push her or make her feel guilty when she cannot do them. When she doesn't do the things that Anwar expected and encouraged her to do, he should be understanding and supportive. This attitude will make her want to do it if she can to make him happy, because she will feel valued and loved, not pressured."

When spouses pick on each other, are particular, or are perfectionists in their expectations of each other, this break down the respect and trust in the relationship and puts up barriers to the comfort and safety that spouses should feel in their relationship.

♦ Never forget that you are spouses, husband and wife. No matter who you are and what profession you do or how high your position in your job is, when you come back from your job, don't carry your work attitude with you home. At home, you are husband and wife. Spouses' shares in life in terms of being very important or having prominent positions in their workplace should not affect how they treat each other: rich or poor, famous or not. Some examples of potentially problematic jobs are as follows: a husband/wife who has a senior position in his/her job, or a high ranking police or army official who is used to giving out orders harshly and shouting, or a spouse in a very prestigious business position. In all of these cases, as soon as you are home, remember, you are husband and wife and forget your position in the workplace. This also applies when one spouses is unemployed or between jobs.

♦ Never deal with your spouse based on the family status of either of you. Subtle comments from spouses that indicate that s/he is of higher social status because her/his family is more famous or rich should be completely avoided. Both should never forget that all people are equal. We all came from Adam. The only measure of worth in Allah's sight is piety. He says,

"يَا أَيُّهَا النَّاسُ إِنَّا خَلَقْنَاكُم مِّن ذَكَرٍ وَأُنثَى وَجَعَلْنَاكُمْ شُعُوبًا وَقَبَائِلَ لِتَعَارَفُوا إِنَّ أَكْرَمَكُمْ عِندَ اللَّهِ أَتْقَاكُمْ إِنَّ اللَّهَ عَلِيمٌ خَبِيرٌ"

"O mankind! We created you from a single (pair) of a male and a female, and made you into nations and tribes, that ye may know each other (not that ye may despise (each other). Verily the most honored of you in the sight of Allah is (he who is) the most righteous of you. And Allah has full knowledge and is well acquainted (with all things)."[133]
The prophet *SAAW* said,

"الناس سواسية كأسنان المشط"

---

[133] (Q49, V13)

"People are equal like the teeth of the comb"[134]

The marriage of *Zaid Ibn Harithah RAA* and *Zainab Bint Jahsh RAA* is a clear indication of this concept. *Zainab* was the cousin of Prophet Mohammad *SAAW*. She was from a family with very high social status. As for *Zaid*, he used to be a slave until he was freed by the prophet *SAAW*. In spite of this fact and all the social pressures of the society then, the prophet *SAAW* married them.

◆ Try your best not to embarrass your spouse, no matter what the cause is. Embarrassing one another will only ruin the marital relationship and weaken the spousal bond. It leaves bad memories and a sour taste in spouses' mouths. It diminishes the respect among spouses and leads to miserable relationships and an unhappy family atmosphere. The prophet *SAAW* never embarrassed anybody in public or private, no matter how bad the mistake of this person was. He always tried to advise individuals in private in the best possible manner. If he had to correct a situation in public, he never embarrassed the person who made the mistake by mentioning his name, but he would say,

"ما بال أقوام يفعلون كذا وكذا"

"Why are some people doing such and such?"[135]

◆ Avoid ignoring your spouse. Avoid ignoring needs, feelings, and conflicts. If there is a conflict, attend to the issue at hand and try to resolve the conflict using the proper Islamic ways described in chapter seven. Ignoring conflicts doesn't make them go away; they may accumulate and cause even bigger problems. Ignoring feelings signals to your spouse that you don't care about him/her. That is unacceptable, since caring is crucial in establishing a strong marital relationship and a

[134] *Tohaf Ale'qool*, page 368
[135] Abu Dawood

155

comfortable family atmosphere. Ignoring needs of our family members is an un-Islamic attitude. The prophet *SAAW* said,

"All of you are guardians and are responsible for your wards. The ruler is a guardian of his subjects and the man is a guardian for his family; the lady is a guardian and is responsible for her husband's house and his offspring; and so all of you are guardians and are responsible for your wards"[136]

♦ Avoid nagging and irritating your spouse especially if your spouse is tired and exhausted after a long day of work or is busy during a time of executing and finishing house chores. If you have something you want to discuss with your spouse, try to find a suitable time for the discussion and the right setting to make sure that you get the proper output from the discussion and reach the expected productive conclusion rather than just annoying and frustrating your spouse. Nagging only spoils the loving and cozy marital relationship and pollutes the family atmosphere. Do your best to avoid nagging.

♦ Avoid being a loner. Marriage is about being in a relationship, and family atmosphere is about productive and lovely socialization. Being a loner contributes harmfully and negatively to family atmosphere. Sharing, chatting, and discussing with your spouse, creates an atmosphere of trust, an atmosphere of companionship and friendly relationships. Being a loner doesn't promote the proper environment and the needed warmness you want to inject into your marital relationship in order to have healthy family dynamics, and a pleasant and agreeable family atmosphere.

♦ Reflect deeply on the meaning of verse 187 of *Surat Al-Baqarah*, where the Qur'an sums up the husband-wife relationship very simply but very eloquently and beautifully when it says:

---

[136] Al Bukhari

"They (your wives) are your garment and you are their garment." (2:187)

This simple but beautiful simile covers succinctly several aspects of spousal relationship. First of all, a dress or garment is not a part of the human being wearing it; it is something external. Be that as it may, it is the closest thing to a human being. A dress describes its wearer; it gives him or her a personality. Like a dress, a husband and wife are closest to each other and should reflect each other's personality.

A dress covers, conceals, and protects. It covers our nakedness and it conceals our blemishes. It protects us from the external surroundings. Like a dress, a husband and wife provide this covering, concealment, and protection to each other.

A dress provides comfort and meets the needs of the person he is wearing. In winter it is heavy enough and provides the wearer warmth, and in summer, it is light enough to reduce the effect of heat on the body. Like a dress, husband and wife should be a source of comfort and satisfaction of each other's needs.

A dress adapts to the body of the person wearing it. It provides the right fit, so the wearer would look at his or her best. Like a dress, a husband and wife with each other should try to adapt to various situations to make their life successful, happy, and harmonious.

A dress is a source of pleasure and beauty. It not only gives the wearer a unique personality, it also enhances and beautifies that personality. Like a dress, a husband and wife become each other's adornments. They expose each other's personality in the best possible light.

Finally, a dress does not destroy what it covers; rather, it adorns, protects and complements. In a similar manner, the husband and wife do not suffocate each other by their closeness and

157

togetherness; rather they strengthen and support each other, complement and enrich each other, help to bring out the best in each other in all spheres of life and interactions.

6 - Essential Spousal Obligations

Introduction

In this chapter *insha'a Allah*, we will discuss essential spousal obligations. We take the approach of looking at the family as a team. That is why we opted to discuss spousal obligations rather than talking about the duties of the husband toward the wife and the duties of the wife toward the husband or the rights of the husband and the rights of the wife. After all Allah tells us in *Surat Al Baqarah,* in the context of discussing women's rights in the marital union,

$$\text{"وَلَهُنَّ مِثْلُ الَّذِي عَلَيْهِنَّ بِالْمَعْرُوفِ"}$$

" And women have the same right as the duty they have to fulfill according to what is equitable."[137] The verse goes on to indicate that men have an extra degree over them. This is the degree of *Qawamah*, which is the responsibility to maintain, protect, and provide for the family financially. As such, they have the right to make the final decision after consulting with their wives.

Based on this, we feel that it is more appropriate to talk about spousal obligations of both spouses as a team rather than considering them as two separate individuals. We are hoping that this approach, if adopted by Muslim spouses, will *insha'a Allah* make their relationship more harmonious, enhance their marital bond, and strengthen their marriage union.

Based on the above understanding, most of the spousal obligations are mutual or shared, which means that, with the exception of a few special duties, whatever the wife has to do, the husband has to reciprocate with something similar, and whatever the husband has to do, the wife also has to reciprocate with something similar.

---

[137] (Q2, V228)

It is our intention to emphasize and highlight more of these obligations that will, without doubt, if observed by both spouses, bring spousal peace and harmony into their sacred marital union. It is not our intention to record a detailed list of these duties, since they have already been covered in many of the available *Fiqh* books in Islamic literature, and since some of them are already covered in various sections of this book such as the Ingredients' section and the case studies. We recommend either <u>*Fiqh Al Sunnah*</u> of *Sh. Sayed Sabeq* or the <u>Muslim Family Series</u> of Dr *Muhammad Al-Jibaly* for a more exhaustive list of these duties and rights. Both references are listed in our reference section at the end of this book.

Let us now explore the most important shared and mutual spousal obligations in more detail.

Essential Shared Obligations

The following are a few of the most important and crucial shared obligations. We feel that if both spouses fulfill these shared obligations in the best possible way to the best of their abilities, keeping in mind that it is their duty to do so, their marital union will *insha'a Allah* be successful and their spousal relationship will be very rewarding and fulfilling

Help Each Other Be Better Muslims

This obligation was discussed in great detail in the second chapter of this book. Every institution in Islam should contribute to the ultimate purpose of the existence of human beings, which is to fully submit to Allah and be his vicegerent in this worldly life. The institution of marriage is no different. As such, spouses should do their best to help each other be better Muslims, cooperate in goodness, enjoin what is good and forbid what is wrong. Numerous practical examples were given in chapter two. Here, we add the following situations that are very important in the North American environment:

◆ The importance of acquiring knowledge in Islam cannot be overemphasized. The first verse of *Qur'an* revealed talks about the most important tool of acquiring knowledge: **reading**. The first five verses of *Qur'an* revealed emphasize three tools of acquiring knowledge: **reading, teaching, and the use of the pen**. Every book of *Hadeeth* includes a chapter about knowledge and the importance of acquiring knowledge; this chapter usually comes after the chapter about belief. These chapters include hundreds of the sayings of prophet Muhammad *SAAW* that encourage seeking knowledge. In North America, since Muslims are a minority, sources of acquiring knowledge are somewhat limited. As such, it is very important for spouses to help each other in this area. We especially recommend that each of them attend a regular study circle in the mosque or an Islamic center. It is also of utmost importance that the husband makes sure that he allows his wife to attend such study circles and makes it easy for her by helping out with the children during the time of the *Halaqah*. It is also of great importance that both make sure to attend national and regional conventions where they have a higher chance of learning from learned scholars and listening to discussions of vital issues and problems related to the affairs of Muslims in North America. The benefit of these gatherings extends beyond just listening to good lectures. Usually there are book fairs and collections of useful materials to help both spouses in their quest for knowledge. These conventions also provide a wonderful environment for the children. It is a worthwhile investment of your time, with tested and proven successful results in the lives of many Muslim families in North America. The money spent in traveling to these conferences and conventions should never be an obstacle for families seeking to enhance their level of Islamic knowledge. This is one of the best investments a family can make.

◆ Participation in Islamic nature camps or group nightly prayers is another thing that families should do their best to achieve. Wives should not be deprived from attending. Organizers of these activities should ensure that it is done in a facility that can accommodate both brothers and sisters. Husbands should help in the organization to ensure the suitability of the arrangement for the wives attendance. They should encourage their spouses to attend as much as possible.

♦ *Taraweeh* prayers and *Qiam Al Lail* during the month of *Ramadan* are other important spiritual gatherings that both husband and wife should try to participate in to enhance their spiritual levels.

Treat Each Other With Respect, Kindness, and Compassion

Being treated with respect and kindness is every spouse's right. Since the husband is given the responsibility of *Qawamah*, and he is usually in the position of power, Allah *SWT* reminds him to deal with his wife in a fair and equitable way:

"وَعَاشِرُوهُنَّ بِالْمَعْرُوفِ فَإِن كَرِهْتُمُوهُنَّ فَعَسَى أَن تَكْرَهُواْ شَيْئًا وَيَجْعَلَ اللّهُ فِيهِ خَيْرًا كَثِيرًا"

" Live with them (your wives) on a footing of kindness and equity. If you dislike them, it may be that you dislike something in which Allah has placed a great deal of Good."[138]

Prophet Muhammad *SAAW* gave similar instructions, indicating that respect is due for both men and women because they are *Shaqae'q*, i.e. they are twins. He said,

"إِنَّمَا النِّسَاءُ شَقَائِقُ الرِّجَالِ"

" Women are the twin complements of men."[139]

He also recommended that men should not dislike their wives. He said,

" لا يَفْرُكُ مُؤْمِنٌ مُؤْمِنَةً، إِنْ كَرِهَ مِنْهَا خُلُقاً رَضِيَ مِنْهَا آخَرَ"

---

[138] (Q4, V19)
[139] Ahmad

162

"A believing man must not dislike a believing woman. If he dislikes one of her traits, he should remember that there are other traits that he likes."[140]

He *SAAW* also emphasized that the best Muslims are those who are best to their wives. He said,

"أكمل المؤمنين إيماناً أحسنهم خلقاً، وخياركم خياركم لنسائهم خلقا"

"The believers who show the most perfect faith are those who have the best character and the best of you are those who are best to their wives."[141]

We should also remember that the prophet *SAAW* said,

"خيركم خيركم لأهله وأنا خيركم لأهلي"

"The best of you is he who is best to his family, and I'm the best among you to my family."[142]

Although most of these instructions are directed at men, as we said at the beginning of this chapter, the basic rule according to the verse of *Surat Al Baqarah*, "[a]nd women have the same right as the duty they have to fulfill according to what is equitable,"[143] is that these are shared obligations and a wife should be kind to her husband just as her husband is ordered to be kind to her.

The wife also has to respect her husband just as he has to respect her. The respect of spouses to each other should manifest itself in various forms and occasions. Both should respect each other's families. They should welcome the families when they come for visits and always treat them nicely. None of them should look down at the family of the other or insult any of its members. They should be kind and accommodative to the families, especially the mothers-in-law and the fathers-in-law. Another angle of respect related to the in-laws is that a husband should respect his wife's

---

[140] Muslim
[141] At-Termezi
[142] At-Termezi
[143] (Q2, V228)

right to visit her family frequently, and he should be kind to them and exchange gifts with them, especially on happy occasions such as *Ramadan* and *Eids*. The husband should also encourage his wife to treat her blood relatives kindly, be in touch with them often, and express her concern about their affairs. The wife should also encourage her husband to be good to his family, visit them, present gifts to them, and treat them with kindness. She should never prevent him from doing good things for his family no matter what happens in terms of his family's feelings toward her.

A wife should respect her husband's time of rest and comfort and make sure the home environment is not noisy in order to provide him with the opportunity to rest. She should also respect his meal time and try as much as possible to have the food ready upon his return, especially if he arrives home daily at a fixed time. This advice about meal times should not be taken in isolation from the other qualities we have discussed in chapter four. If there are other priorities that have been agreed upon by both spouses, this should be taken into consideration. A husband should also respect his wife's needs and try to satisfy them. Her need to rest for a while and take a break from caring for the children should be respected and accommodated by the husband. He should cooperate with her in this matter and help her with the children. Each spouse should respect the other spouse's friends as long as s/he is a good person and doesn't interfere in the family affairs or have a negative impact or bad influence on any of them because of his/her own bad habits.

A husband also should respect his wife's right to express her views on issues and matters related to family affairs. In fact, he should always consult with her before making any decisions related to the family and make sure he takes her views into consideration before finalizing these decisions.

Fulfill Each Other's Physical Intimate Needs and Desires
This aspect of the obligations was dealt with in great detail in chapter four, "**Tested and Proven Recipe for a Successful Marriage.**" It is one of the magical seven Ss: Sexual gratification.

We refer you to this section for further details. There is a common belief among some Muslims that the prophet *SAAW* instructed women to fulfill the physical intimate desire of her husband no matter what the situation is and didn't instruct the man with similar instruction. Because of this we would like to add here one saying of the prophet *SAAW* to husbands indicating the importance of fulfilling the wife's physical intimate desire and need and an incident from the *Seerah* witnessing to this fact.

The prophet *SAAW* said,

"إذا جامع أحدكم أهله فليصدقها فإن قضى حاجته قبل أن تقضي حاجتها فلا يعجلها حتى تقضي حاجتها"

"When one of you has sexual intimacy with his wife, let him be true to her; so that, if he feels fulfilled/satisfied before she does, then he should not rush her, and he should wait until she feels fulfilled"[144]

This is a very clear indication that this obligation is a shared one. A husband has to satisfy his wife's physical need and desire, and the wife has to satisfy her husband's need and desire in this area. Here is a wonderful story from *Seerah* during the time of *Omar Ibn Al Khattab RAA* to witness to this meaning:

It was narrated after *Muhammad Ibn Ma'n Al-Ghafary* that he said, "A woman came to *Omar Ibn Al Khattab RAA* and said, 'O commander of the faithful, my husband fasts during the day and stands up in prayer during the night and I hate to complain against him while he is involved in Allah's obedience.' *Omar RAA* said, "What a wonderful husband yours is." The lady repeated her statement again, and *Omar RAA* repeated the same answer. *Ka'b Al Asady* said to him, "O commander of the faithful, this lady is complaining against her husband because he is not fulfilling his duty as a husband."

---

[144] Abu Ya'ley

Omar RAA said, "Since you understood what she meant, you should judge between them." *Ka'b RAA* called upon her husband, and, when he came, *Ka'b* told him that his wife was complaining about him. The man asked "Is her complaint related to me not providing her with food or drink?" *Ka'b* said, "No."

The lady then said,

ألهى خليلي عن فراشي مسجده	يأيها القاضي الحكيم رشده
فاقض القضا كعب ولا تردده	زهده في مضجعي تعبــــده
فلست في أمر النساء أحمــده	نهاره وليله ما يرقـــــــده

The meaning of these verses in nutshell is that because her husband is busy with his worship day and night, he doesn't satisfy her intimate physical needs.

The man said,

أني امرؤ أذهلني ما نــــــزل	زهدني في النساء وفي الحـــــجل
وفي كتاب الله تخويف جلل	في سورة النحل وفي السبع الطول

Again, the meaning in a nutshell is that he is scared from the *Qur'anic* revelations in various chapters, and, because of this, he is not interested any more in engaging in such acts, and he wants to worship continuously.

Ka'b RAA said,

إن لها حق عليك يا رجل

نصيبها في أربع لمن عقل

فاعطها ذلك ودع عنك العلل

This means that his wife has legitimate right on him and he has no excuse not to satisfy her needs. Then *Ka'b RAA* said, "Allah *SWT* permitted you to marry up to four wives; thus you have three nights to worship Allah and give her the fourth night to satisfy her needs."

166

Omar RAA was amazed at the intelligence of *Ka'b RAA* both in understanding the complaint of the lady and in the way he judged between her and her husband. He said, 'Because of this I'm appointing you as the Judge for *Basrah!*'"

Provide Good Companionship
This is another important shared obligation of both spouses. They should provide each other with good companionship. Sharing good times together like going for a long nature walk, discussing light-hearted matters with a sense of humor, and chatting regularly are very effective ways of providing wonderful companionship to each other. Some spouses mistakenly think that they only should discuss when they have to make a decision regarding serious matters or come up with a solution to a family problem. This is not right. Talking and chatting for the sake of being closer to each other and strengthening the spousal bond is encouraged in Islam. As a matter of fact, there is a very lengthy *Hadeeth* reported in *Al Bukhari, Muslim,* and *Al Nesae'y* called *Hadeeth Um Zare'*. In this *Hadeeth, A'ishah RAA* told of eleven ladies who sat together talking about their husbands and how they treated them. The last of those ladies was named *Um Zare'*. The prophet *SAAW* didn't object to *A'ishah* talking about this, because he wants to teach us that, sometimes, we have to provide companionship to our wives and listen to what they are saying attentively, even if it may not be very important to us. Not only did the prophet *SAAW* listen to this long *Hadeeth* from *A'ishah*, but he also comforted her at the end by telling her, "I am to you as *Abu Zare'* is to *Um Zare'*, but I'll not divorce you." The prophet *SAAW* said this because, in the story, *Abu Zare'* treated *Um Zare'* nicely, but, in the end, he divorced her and married another lady.

Providing good companionship to our spouses is also clearly illustrated in the entertainment provided by the prophet *SAAW* to *A'ishah RAA*. He allowed her to watch the Abyssinians enact a performance, (similar to that of a martial arts performance), in his mosque. He also raced with her more than once as was reported by

Ahmad and *Abu Dawood*. It was also reported by Ahmad that the prophet *SAAW* said,

"كل شئ يلهو به ابن آدم فهو باطل، إلا ثلاثاً: رميه عن قوسه وتأديبه فرسه

وملاعبته أهله، فإنهن من الحق"

"All gaming actions for people are falsehood except three things: Shooting with your arch, training your horse, and entertaining/ /playing with your spouse. These are from the truth."[145]

In addition, it was reported by *Jabir Ibn Abdullah* and *Jabir Ibn Umayr* that the prophet *SAAW* said,

"كل شيء ليس فيه ذكر الله فهو لغو وسهو ولعب، إلا أربع خصال: ملاعبة

الرجل امرأته وتأديب الرجل فرسه، ومشيه بين الفرضين وتعليم الرجل

السباحة"

"Everything that does not involve remembrance of Allah is futile, senseless, and wasted, except for four acts: a man entertaining his wife, a man training his horse, a man walking between two posts (when practicing archery), and a man teaching another man swimming"[146]

To emphasize the importance of companionship and entertainment, when *Jabir RAA* told the prophet *SAAW* that he married a lady that was married before, the prophet *SAAW* told him,

"فهلا بكراً تلاعبها وتلاعبك"

"You should have married a virgin to entertain each other"[147]

Proper Understanding of the *Qawamah* Concept

This is a very important shared obligation of both spouses. We feel that there is a great number of Muslim spouses who don't understand the concept of *Qawamah* in Islam. Most spouses go to

[145] Ahmad and *Sunnan*
[146] An Nessae'i
[147] Ahmad

one extreme or the other in misunderstanding this concept. One extreme is represented in men who think that the meaning of *Qawamah* is to boss their wives around and to order them to do whatever they want and the wives have no choice but to obey and accept the husbands' views on everything. The second extreme is represented by ladies who are following the feminist movement and don't want to recognize that their husbands have certain status and responsibility given to them by Allah *SWT* to provide family protection and maintenance. They refuse to recognize that there are natural differences between males and females and want to go against the rights and responsibilities given by Allah to men via this status of *Qawamah*. Both of these positions are extremes and are not accepted by Islam. It is of utmost importance that both spouses understand properly what *Qawamah* means, its privileges, its responsibilities, and its consequences. It simply means maintenance and protection, as indicated by Dr. *Badawi* in his valuable booklet, *Status of Women in Islam.*

He writes, "The rules of married life in Islam are clear and in harmony with upright human nature. In consideration of the physiological and psychological make up of men and women, both have equal rights and claims on one another, except for one responsibility, that of leadership. This is a matter which is natural in any collective life and which is consistent with the nature of man. The *Qur'an* thus states,

"وَلَهُنَّ مِثْلُ الَّذِي عَلَيْهِنَّ بِالْمَعْرُوفِ وَلِلرِّجَالِ عَلَيْهِنَّ دَرَجَةٌ"

'And they (women) have rights similar to those (of men) over them, and men are a degree above them.'[148]

Such degree is *Qawamah* (maintenance and protection). This refers to that natural difference between the sexes, which entitles the weaker sex to protection. It implies no superiority or advantage before the law. Yet, a man's role of leadership in relation to his family does not mean that a husband is a dictator over his wife.

---

[148] (Q2, V228)

Islam emphasizes the importance of taking counsel and mutual agreement in family decisions. The *Qur'an* gives us an example:

$$\text{"فَإِنْ أَرَادَا فِصَالًا عَن تَرَاضٍ مِّنْهُمَا وَتَشَاوُرٍ فَلاَ جُنَاحَ عَلَيْهِمَا"}$$

'...If they (husband and wife) desire to wean the child by mutual consent and after consultation, there is no blame on them...'[149]"

Muslim scholars usually interpret this degree of *Qawamah* in conjunction with another *Qur'anic* passage:

$$\text{"الرِّجَالُ قَوَّامُونَ عَلَى النِّسَاءِ بِمَا فَضَّلَ اللّهُ بَعْضَهُمْ عَلَى بَعْضٍ وَبِمَا أَنفَقُواْ مِنْ}$$
$$\text{أَمْوَالِهِمْ"}$$

"Men shall take full care of women with the bounties which Allah has bestowed more abundantly on the former than on the latter and with what they may spend out of their possessions"[150]

It is to be emphasized that this is just a division of labor and role differentiation. It does not, in any way, mean any categorical discrimination or superiority of one sex to the other.[151]

Although this degree of *Qawamah* gives the man the authority to make the final decisions in matters related to family, it also entrusts him with the responsibility to consult with his wife and to provide protection and maintenance to the family in the best way possible.

Proper Understanding of the Status of Women in Islam
In our view and after being involved in many counseling cases with Muslim families in North America, we feel that this is a very crucial shared responsibility. It is of utmost importance that both spouses should have the proper understanding of the status of women in Islam. Neglect of this matter by either of the spouses is, undoubtedly, a source of continuous conflicts and family rifts in many cases. Our experiences indicate that as soon as both spouses

---

[149] (Q2, V233)
[150] (Q4, V34)
[151] See *Islam in Focus* by Hammudah 'Abd al 'Ati

understand properly the status of women in Islam, they avoid a great source of family feud.

The Islamic library is rich with ample literature related to this subject. We advise all spouses to consult such literature. In addition to this, here is a summary of a research paper written on the subject by our daughter *Hoda* for her high school class, Families in Canadian Society:

"In Islam, the woman's personal status is revered. For over fourteen centuries Islam has taken into consideration all of her needs as a person. Her spiritual rights, intellectual rights, legal rights, financial rights, and emotional rights are clearly stated in Islamic Law.

Islam recognizes women's spirituality in many ways. In the Qur'an itself there are many verses indicating the importance of the woman's spirituality:

> Surely for men who submit to God and for women who submit to god, for believing men and believing women, for devout men and devout women, for truthful men and truthful women, for steadfast men and steadfast women, for humble men and humble women, for charitable men and charitable women, for men who fast and women who fast, for men who guard their chastity and women who guard, for men who remember God much and for women who remember – for them God has prepared forgiveness and a mighty reward (Qur'an 33:35) (Heeran and Lemu 14,15)

From this verse, it is clear that women are considered to be spiritual beings. The same moral and religious duties that are expected from men are also expected from women (Badawi 9). Many verses in the Qur'an encourage women to develop the spiritual side of their person. '{If any do deeds of righteousness, be they male or female, and have faith, they will enter paradise and

not the least injustice will be done to them} (Qur'an 4:124)'
(Badawi 10). By promising an entry into paradise to the righteous
women, two things are established: women have souls and women
should enrich their souls. In Islam, it is the person's soul and
spiritual status that determine whether or not s/he will enter
paradise. Through this verse it is evident that, not only does Islam
recognize the woman as a spiritual being, but it also greatly
encourages her to pursue her spirituality by offering paradise as a
reward to those of high spiritual status. Sumaya Umm Ammar is an
excellent example of a woman holding an extremely high spiritual
status, as she was the first ever Muslim to sacrifice her life rather
than give up her faith. Khadijah, the wife of the Prophet, was
the first person to become Muslim. The first person to accept the
faith and the first martyr - both of these spiritual honors are held
by women in Islam (Sheriff 6). A woman's spiritual status is an
honored and respected part of a woman's character, but it is
certainly not viewed as the only part of her character.

Along with her spiritual being, a Muslim woman is also
encouraged to develop herself as an intellectual being. The Prophet
Muhammad said, 'The search for knowledge is a duty for every
Muslim, (male or female)' (Heeran and Lemu 15). Islam does not
just say that a woman's intellect is important, it sets up society in
a way that women naturally come to value their intellect. The
hijab, the dress code which Muslim women adhere to, covers the
woman's entire body in a modest manner with the exception of her
hands and face. One of the purposes of the *hijab* is to give women
the right to be judged on their intellect and personality rather than
their physical beauty. Since their intellect and personality is
the basis on which they are being treated, Muslim women find
it important to better themselves intellectually. There is much
evidence of this in the history of Islam. 'Aisha, the wife of the
Prophet, was one of the most eminent scholars. She gave advice to
people in all spheres of life, and men traveled great distances
to seek knowledge from her. Her intellectual ability is famous
in Islamic history' (Nazlee 59). Many women in Islam are
remembered for their great intellectual standings. It is the duty of

all Muslims, be they male or female to 'Seek knowledge from the cradle to the grave,' as Prophet Muhammad has told them to (Heeran and Lemu 15). Thus, it is obvious, through the advice of the Prophet, the divine rule of dress, and the example of women in Islamic history, that a Muslim woman's intellectual status is highly valued.

Islam also realizes that, in order to be emotionally healthy, every woman needs to have a positive self-image. This is another reason for the divine rule of *hijab*. Because the *hijab* hides a woman's physical beauty, appearance does not become the focus of her worth. This is a great blessing for Muslim women because when women depend on physical beauty for self-worth, they are always disappointed. Firstly, not all women can achieve whatever society's definition of physical beauty is and so some women will feel bad about themselves because no matter how hard they try, they cannot become beautiful. Secondly, some women will be so determined to become beautiful that they will develop emotional complexes that may lead to health problems such as bulimia and anorexia. Thirdly, even the women who do fulfill society's expectation of being physically beautiful will be let down, because beauty fades with age and with it fades their self-esteem. In Islam, the goal is to become beautiful on the inside rather than the outside. Inner beauty is achieved through bettering one's self, a process which is completely within the woman's control. This way all women have a fair chance of achieving their goal in spite of any outside factors, and, in turn, they achieve a lasting sense of self-worth.

Not only does Islam care for the woman's emotional, intellectual, and spiritual well-being, it also guarantees women full legal and financial rights. Under Islamic law, a woman is regarded as her own 'individual personality . . . not a mere adjunct of her husband or father' (Sheriff 13). If she commits a crime, she will be penalized; 'the Qur'an tells us that her penalty is no more or less than a man's' (Sheriff 13). In the same instance, if she is wronged then she is entitled to compensation. Muslim women have had the

right to vote and act as representatives in parliament for over
fourteen hundred years (Sheriff 13).

In terms of financial rights, Islam grants the woman complete
financial security throughout her life as well as the right to own
and control her own money and property, the right to pay equity,
and the right to inherit. She is guaranteed complete financial
security by the divine rule in Islam that sets males financially
responsible for their female relatives such as wives, daughters,
mothers, sisters, etc. All Muslim women also have the full right to
own property, which they may buy, sell, or lease at their will. Any
money that a woman earns is hers and she is under no obligation to
spend any amount of it on her household or family (Badawi 16).
Muslim women are also free from financial discrimination in the
workplace. 'Islam . . does not countenance discrimination in pay
merely on the basis of gender; a woman should be paid whatever
the going rate is in her particular field' (Nazlee 62). The Qur'an
makes it clear that women have the right to inherit. '{From what is
left by parents and those nearest related, there is a share for men
and a share for women, whether the property be small or large – a
determinate share} (Qur'an 4:7)' (Badawi 17). Females inherit less
than males do, but they retain their entire share for investment and
financial security; they are not legally required to spend any of that
money, not even to support their own livelihood, whereas males
are financially responsible for all their female relatives.

Through these rules it is apparent that Islam liberates the woman as
a person from all aspects; it encourages her spiritual and
intellectual growth; it looks after her emotional health and provides
her with a solid sense of self-esteem; it regards her as her own
respectful entity in the eyes of the law, grants her full legal rights,
and guarantees her financial security and power over her own
personal property. Keeping in mind the rights given to the woman
as a person, it is no surprise that Islam views the woman's role
within the family as an extremely important one. Through many of
Prophet Muhammad's sayings and actions and many verses in the
Qur'an, it is evident that the woman is highly esteemed in the

family in her different roles, whether she is a daughter, a wife, or a mother.

Islam is responsible for a revolutionary change in attitude of parents toward their daughters. In pre-Islamic times, female infanticide was widely practiced throughout the Arabian Peninsula. The Qur'an forbade and ended this practice. '{When the female infant buried alive is questioned for what crime she was killed . . .} (Qur'an 81: 8-9)' (Badawi 21). This chapter in the Qur'an is listing the different things that will happen on judgement day. By including the question of why the female infant was buried alive, the Qur'an brings the crime of burying one's daughter alive to the highest of courts: the court before God. This shows that the crime of female infanticide is extremely serious.

The Qur'an did not stop at forbidding female infanticide; it went further to condemn the unwelcoming attitude that some parents had when they found out that their newborn was a girl:

> When news is brought to one of them of the birth of a female child, his face darkens and he is filled with inward grief! With shame he hides himself from his people because of the bad news he has had! Shall he retain her on sufferance and contempt or bury her in the dust? Ah! What an evil choice they decide on! (Qur'an 16:58-59)

This verse, along with sayings of Prophet Muhammad, showed parents that it was part of their religious duty to support their daughters and to treat them fairly and kindly. The prophet said, 'Whosoever has a daughter and does not bury her alive, does not insult her, and does not favour his son over her, Allah will enter him into Paradise' (Badawi 21-22). By making kindness to daughters part of a parent's religious duty, Islam changed the culture of the Arabs; girls are now greatly valued by their fathers.

> This is shown in what the prophet . . says about his daughter Fatima, "Fatima is part of me; what makes her angry makes me angry.", "Fatima is part of me; what makes

175

me sad, makes her sad, and what pleases me, pleases her" and "surely my daughter is part of me; I fear what frightens her, and I am harmed by what harms her." (Al Qaradawy 52)

Prophet Muhammad is the living example of Islam and, in turn, a role model for all Muslims. The attitude that he displays toward his daughter is that which all Muslims try to emulate. Through the various teachings, parents' attitudes toward their daughters changed and they came to realize that a daughter, like a son, was a blessing from God (Al Qaradawy 49).

Just as the Muslim woman is treated with love and respect in her family of orientation, she continues to receive this same gentle treatment with her family of procreation, first as a wife and then, if she so chooses, as a mother. Islam looks out for the wife's safety and happiness. "Marriage is intended not as an arena for the battle of the sexes, nor as a means of imprisoning women and treating them harshly, but as an institution which will offer security and stability to both partners . ." (Khattab 38).

Looking out for the wife's happiness, the Qur'an outlawed the pre-Islamic Arabian practice that the stepson of the deceased father inherited the widow like she was part of the property:

> O you who believe! You are forbidden to inherit women against their will. Nor should you treat them with harshness, that you may take away part of the marital gift you have given them, except when they have been guilty of open lewdness; on the contrary, live with them on a footing of kindness and equality . . (Qur'an 4:19) (Badawi 25)

Islam granted women the right to accept or refuse marriage. The woman's consent is a prerequisite to the validity of the marriage; if a woman is forced into a marriage without her permission, then the marriage can be annulled if she so wishes. In fact, at the time of the prophet, a lady came to him to complain that her father had forced her into her marriage without her consent. Prophet

Muhammad told her that if she wanted to, she could invalidate the marriage (Badawi 23). It is obvious that the woman has the full right to choose her husband, but what about after she is married? What is her status as a wife?

Islam repeatedly emphasizes good treatment to wives. The Qur'an says, 'And among His signs is this, that He created for you mates from among yourselves that you may dwell in tranquility with them, and He has put love and compassion between your hearts' (30:21). The relationship between husband and wife should be built on mutual care, consideration, respect, and affection. The Qur'an even advises husbands to be kind to their wives when they are not on good terms with them. '{Live with them in kindness; even if you dislike them, perhaps you dislike something in which God has placed much good} (4:19)' (Heeran and Lemu 20). The prophet said, 'The best among you are those who are kindest to their wives.' By saying this, again, Prophet Muhammad has made it clear that part of a man's religious measure is how well he treats his wife. It is narrated that the amount of references of the prophet doing things to please his wives is roughly equal to the amount of references there are of his wives doing things to please him (Heeran and Lemu 17). From the above Qur'anic verses and sayings of the prophet, one can conclude that, according to Islamic teachings, the wife's opinion, safety, and happiness is of great importance.

Women in the Muslim family are cherished as daughters and wives, but no role is as glorious as that of a Muslim mother. 'Motherhood is regarded as the most noble and honorable calling in society' (Nazlee 51) with good reason. The mother is the early character-trainer of children; she has a lasting effect on the attitudes and behaviors of the next generation (Heeran and Lemu 19). God has made honoring the mother a virtue; in the Qur'an, the right of the mother is stated and restated in many different chapters so as to show the importance of honoring one's mother. '{And we have enjoined on man to be dutiful and good to his parents. His mother bore him in weakness and hardship upon weakness and hardship, and his weaning is in two years – give

177

thanks to Me and to your parents . .}(31:14)' (Al Qaradawy 43). Another example in the Qur'an that illustrates the importance of respecting the mother is '{Reverence God through Whom you demand your mutual rights and reverence the wombs that bore you . .} (4:1)' (Sheriff 9).

Not only was it emphasized in the Qur'an that one should give the utmost respect to one's mother, but it was also reinforced in the prophet's teachings. The prophet once said that Paradise lies at the feet of the mother. This means that Paradise awaits those who cherish and respect their mothers. The mother's right over her children is such that they owe her more than they can ever repay her.

One time a man approached Prophet Muhammad and asked him, "Who is most deserving of my care?" The prophet replied, "Your mother". "Then who?" asked the man "Your mother," answered the prophet. "After her?" the man asked again. "Your mother," the prophet replied for the third time. "Then?" asked the man. "Then your father," the prophet replied (Heeran and Lemu 20). It is then very clear that a Muslim mother can expect security and excellent care from her children in her time of need.

As a mother, a wife, a daughter, as a legal entity, as an emotional, intellectual, and spiritual being, as an independent person or as a family member, however a woman chooses to see herself, under Islamic law she is liberated in all aspects of her person. From the Qur'an, Islamic history, and the sayings and actions of Prophet Muhammad, it is indisputable that a Muslim woman is a valued member of the family and society as a whole.

WORKS CITED

Al Qaradawy, Yusuf. The Status of Women in Islam. Trans. Mohammed Gemea'ah.
    Cairo: Islamic Home Publishing & Distribution, 1997.

Badawi, Jamal. Gender Equity in Islam: Basic Principles. Plainfield, Indiana: American
    Trust Publications, 1995.

Khattab, Huda. The Muslim Woman's Hand Book. London: Ta-Ha Publishers, 1993.

Lemu, B. Aisha and Fatima Heeran. Woman in Islam. Leicester, United Kingdom: The
    Islamic Foundation, 1978.

Nazlee, Sajda. Feminism and Muslim Women. ed. Huda Khattab. London: Ta-Ha
    Publishers, 1996.

Sheriff, Sarah. Women's Rights in Islam. 1989. London: Ta-Ha Publishers, 1996."

Some Essential Wife's Obligations

In the following few paragraphs, we will emphasize some of the wife's essential obligations in the marital union. Again, these obligations are mainly for the well being of the family. Women are entrusted with them because of their nature. Allah *SWT* created them to fulfill these obligations in the best possible way. This by no mean indicates that women are inferior to men. In Islam, both sexes are equal but not identical. As such, there are certain differences in their obligations. These differences are complementary to ensure the proper family life, minimize family conflicts, provide a healthy atmosphere to keep the foundation of the society strong, and, finally, lead to a stronger, healthier, and more productive Muslim community. Here are some of these obligations:

Main Caregiver of the Children

Although in Islam, the responsibility of the children's upbringing is a shared responsibility between both spouses, there is no doubt that women are the main caregivers in the family because of their nature. They are the ones who take care of the children. They carry them during pregnancy, they deliver them, and they nurse them when they are babies. It is not natural to ask the men to provide any of these basic needs, especially when the child is very young. The *Qur'an* illustrates this in the following verse:

"وَالْوَالِدَاتُ يُرْضِعْنَ أَوْلاَدَهُنَّ حَوْلَيْنِ كَامِلَيْنِ لِمَنْ أَرَادَ أَن يُتِمَّ الرَّضَاعَةَ وَعَلَى الْمَوْلُودِ لَهُ رِزْقُهُنَّ وَكِسْوَتُهُنَّ بِالْمَعْرُوف لاَ تُكَلَّفُ نَفْسٌ إِلاَّ وُسْعَهَا لاَ تُضَآرَّ وَالِدَةٌ بِوَلَدِهَا وَلاَ مَوْلُودٌ لَّهُ بِوَلَدِه"

"Mothers shall suckle their children for two whole years; (that is) for those who wish to complete the suckling. The duty of feeding and clothing nursing mothers in a seemly manner is upon the father of the child. No one should be charged beyond his capacity. A mother should not be made to suffer because of her child, nor should he to whom the child is born (be made to suffer) because of his child."[152]

Of course, the father's help and support is needed, especially during the pregnancy period, the delivery, and in the early days after birth when the baby wakes up frequently during the night for feedings. The father should give his wife a break from the overwhelming daily chores and household tasks. When the children grow older, the father's involvement in his children's lives becomes more essential.

---

[152] (Q2, V233)

It is unrealistic from a woman to expect that her husband would spend the same amount of time with his children as she does, particularly if the woman is a housewife and the man is holding a full time job outside the house. The husband's main involvement is in discussing with his wife and agreeing together on the ways and methods they will use to bring up their children. Tasks should then be divided between both of them, but the final responsibility of follow-up is in the mother's hands. She is the main caregiver of the children, and she should make it easier for her husband to help her in this task as much as he can, without adopting a blaming attitude toward him.

Obedience

Islam requires the wife to obey her husband as long as he doesn't ask or request anything un-Islamic from her. The wife is rewarded for such obedience greatly. There are numerous teachings of prophet Muhammad *SAAW* instructing women to obey their husbands. Here are some examples:

It was reported by *Abdel Rahman Ibn Aouf RAA* that the prophet *SAAW* said,

" إذا صلت المرأة خمسها و صامت شهرها و حفظت فرجها و أطاعت زوجها

قيل لها : ادخلي من أي أبواب الجنة شئت"

"When a woman prays her five (prayers), fasts her month (*Ramadan*), preserves her chastity, and obeys her husband, she will be told (in the Day of Judgment), "Enter *Jannah* from any of its gates"[153]

It was also narrated by *Abde Rahman Ibn Aouf RAA* and others that the prophet *SAAW* said,

"إذا صلت المرأة خمسها و صامت شهرها و حفظت فرجها و أطاعت زوجها

دخلت الجنة"

---

[153] Ahmad, and Ibn Hibban

"When a woman prays her five (prayers), fasts her month (*Ramadan*), preserves her chastity, and obeys her husband, she will enter *Jannah*"[154]

In addition, it was reported by *Um Salamah RAA* that she said that she heard the prophet *SAAW* say,

"أيما امرأة ماتت وزوجها عنها راض دخلت الجنة"

"When a woman dies while her husband is pleased with her, she will enter Jannah"[155]

This obedience is required by women in every aspect of their marital life, as long as the husband's request does not contradict any Islamic injunctions, as indicated before. Obedience to fulfill the physical intimate needs of the husband is particularly emphasized as we discussed in detail in a previous chapter. It is also important to point out that disobeying the husband for no legitimate reason is considered a sin, and could cause the prayer to be unacceptable by Allah. It was reported by *Ibn Omar RAA* who said that the prophet *SAAW* said that there are two people whose prayers will not be accepted and one of them is a woman who disobeys her husband, until she returns to his obedience[156]

It is also important to point out that the husband should be reasonable in his requests and should take into consideration his wife's condition. It is not recommended to over burden you spouse with unrealistic orders. Having said this, the wife should try her best to obey her husband whenever possible. Here are some examples:
- ◆ When your husband requests that you go together to visit his family, always try to obey him. In fact, you should even try to initiate the visit yourself. This kind of action will, no doubt, create warm feelings and a stronger bond between you and your husband.

---

[154] Ahmad, Al-Bazzar and others
[155] Ibn Magah, At-Termezi, and Al Hakim
[156] Al Tabarany and Al Hakim

♦ When your husband asks you not to associate with certain individuals because of fear of their bad influence, you should respect his desire and obey him as long as he explains the reasons and he is not just reacting to a certain unpleasant incident between him and those individuals. Even if you are not 100 percent convinced of his logic, it is better to obey him; then you can review the matter with him later rather than causing a family conflict and hurting your relationship.

♦ It is important not to refuse your husband's request for physical intimate relation for no legitimate reason. Try to always satisfy his needs. You don't have to be fully (100%) in the mood for this act. In some situations, you may be tired, rather than bluntly saying, "No, I'm exhausted." It is better to engage with your husband to satisfy his need with your body, even if your mind is not fully there.

Obeying your husband is an act of obedience to Allah *SWT*, if you do it with the right intention. It leaves a positive impact on him that you are trying your best to accommodate his needs, and he will, *insha'a Allah*, reciprocate by being more considerate, more accommodative, and more accepting of your reasons for declining in the future which will enhance the family bond and keep it healthy.

It is important here to point out that some husbands abuse such a privilege and in the name of obedience, mistreat their wives with requests that are, at the very least, not reasonable. They boss them around and keep ordering them to do things and if the wife says "I'm tired," or "I can't do this now", the husband complains that she is not obeying him. Some of them may even say: "You have to obey me; otherwise you won't go to paradise". As an example of this, a husband may be watching his favorite TV program after dinner, while the wife may be busy cleaning the kitchen and preparing the milk formula for their baby, who is crying. Rather than preparing a cup of tea for himself, he orders his wife to prepare one for him right away, saying, "Make me a cup of tea." If she says, "I'm busy preparing the formula for the baby," he may consider this an act of disobedience from her. This is clearly unfair. This is not what is meant by obedience. Your wife is not a slave. The husband has to be considerate and sensitive to the wife's conditions. Another example is when a husband, after dinner, asks his wife to go with him to visit a member of his family or a close relative. The wife may be exhausted from a long day of work and attending to children. She may respond by saying, "Can we do this on another evening?" Rather than being considerate and understanding her reasons for this, some husbands may consider this as an act of disobedience on their wives' part.

Acceptance and Respect of the Husband's *Qawamah*

The concept of *Qawamah* was discussed in detail earlier. It is of great importance and vital significance to the healthy family atmosphere that the wife acknowledges and respects her husband's *Qawamah*. This respect manifests itself in acceptance of the final decisions he makes with respect to the family affairs. As long as the husband is fulfilling the responsibilities of *Qawamah*, in terms of family maintenance, family protection, and consultation before making decisions that affect the family, the wife should respect and accept his final decision even if it is different from what she had desired and hoped for. Not accepting or respecting the husband's *Qawamah,* will only lead to a power struggle within the family and contaminate the family atmosphere. Be true to your husband when he consults with you in any matter. Do your homework and provide him with the best advice you can. Remember two heads thinking and discussing are much better than one. However, don't harbor feeling of resentment if the decision made is not the one you wanted.

Some Essential Husband's Obligations

As we did in the case of the wife, in the following few paragraphs, we will emphasize some of the husband's essential obligations in the marital union. Again, these obligations are mainly for the well being of the family. Men are entrusted with them because of their nature. Allah SWT created them to fulfill these obligations in the best possible way. Again, we emphasize that this by no mean indicates that men are superior to women. In Islam, both sexes are equal but not identical. As such, there are certain differences in their obligations. These differences are complementary to ensure the proper family life, minimize family conflicts, provide a healthy atmosphere to keep the foundation of the society strong, and, finally, lead to a stronger, healthier, and more productive Muslim community. Here are some of these obligations:

Main Financial Supporter of Family
Allah *SWT* entrusted men with the responsibility of providing, maintaining, and protecting the family. Because of their nature, they are asked to go out, work hard, and earn a living for themselves and their families. This protection and financial support is clearly indicated in *Surat An Nesaa'*:

"الرِّجَالُ قَوَّامُونَ عَلَى النِّسَاء بِمَا فَضَّلَ اللّهُ بَعْضَهُمْ عَلَى بَعْضٍ وَبِمَا أَنفَقُواْ مِنْ أَمْوَالِهِمْ"

"Men shall take full care of women with the bounties which Allah has bestowed more abundantly on the former than on the latter and with what they may spend out of their possessions"[157]
Jabir RAA reported that the prophet *SAAW* said,

"اتقوا الله في النساء، فإنكم أخذتموهن بأمانة الله، واستحللتم فروجهن بكلمة الله ولهن عليكم رزقهن وكسوتهن بالمعروف"

" Have *Taqwa* of Allah in regard to your women. Indeed, you took them in marriage through a trust with Allah and had access to their private parts by Allah's permission. They have a right on you that you provide them with food and clothing in a fitting manner"[158]

---

[157] (Q4, V34)
[158] Muslim and Abu Dawood

185

Most scholars agree that the above teachings of the *Qur'an* and *Sunnah* indicate that accommodation, food, and clothing provided by the husband to his family should be comparable to other families who have the same standard of living. The middle way is always the better way. This means that excessiveness in spending and a lavish way of living should be avoided. In the same time, being miserly and stingy is not acceptable behavior by the husband and should be avoided. There are numerous teachings of the prophet *SAAW* encouraging believers to spend and provide for their families. Not only that, but they also indicate that this act is considered an act of charity and that men are rewarded for it. It was narrated by *Abu Hurairah RAA* that the prophet *SAAW* said,

"دينار أنفقته في سبيل الله ودينار أنفقته في رقبة ودينار تصدقت به على مسكين

ودينار أنفقته على أهلك أعظمها أجرا الذي أنفقته على أهلك"

" A *Dinar* that you spend for the sake of Allah, a *Dinar* that you used to free a slave, a *Dinar* you spend on a needy person, and a *Dinar* that you spend on your family; the one that will be rewarded most is the one you spend on your family"[159]

The prophet *SAAW* also indicated that it is a great sin for somebody not to take care of those individuals for which he is responsible. He said,

"كفى بالمرء إثما أن يضيع من يقوت"

" It is enough sin for somebody not to take care of those whom he is in charge of their maintenance"[160]

Serving and Helping
This is another important obligation on husbands. It is illustrated clearly in the life of the prophet *SAAW*. He used to help with the house chores such as mending his garments and fixing his shoes. It was reported by *Al-Aswad Ibn Yazeed RAA* that he asked *A'ishah RAA*,

---

[159] Muslim
[160] Abu Dawood, AN Nesae'y, and Al Hakim

"أي شيء كان يصنع النبي صلى الله عليه وسلم إذا دخل بيته قالت:
كان يكون في مهنة أهله"

" What did the prophet *SAAW* used to do when he entered his house?" She said, "The prophet used to be in servitude of his family"[161]

The only time that would prevent him from being in the service of his family would be the time of prayer, as was indicated by *A'ishah RAA* in the rest of the same *Hadeeth* she said,

"كان يكون في مهنة أهله فإذا حضرت الصلاة قام فصلى"

"he used to be serving his family, but when prayer time comes, he would go for prayer"[162]

There is a great lesson for all husbands in the manners of the prophet *SAAW*. After all, we should take him as our role model as indicated in the *Qur'an*:

لَقَدْ كَانَ لَكُمْ فِي رَسُولِ اللَّهِ أُسْوَةٌ حَسَنَةٌ لِّمَن كَانَ يَرْجُو اللَّهَ وَالْيَوْمَ الْآخِرَ وَذَكَرَ اللَّهَ كَثِيرًا

"Certainly you have in the messenger of Allah the best example of character for those whose hope is in the Hereafter and engage in the remembrance of Allah much"[163]

It is important for husbands to provide this kind of help to their wives, especially in North America where most families are nuclear families and do not enjoy the presence of extended family. Husbands should plan and program their time intelligently to find the opportunity to fulfill such needs and provide this important support for their wives.

---

[161] Al Bukhari
[162] Al Bukhari
[163] (Q33, V21)

187

It is worthwhile here to note that one of the unacceptable behaviors of husbands living in North America, particularly those from Middle Eastern origins, is the amount of time they spend socializing with their friends compared to the amount of time helping their families. Some of them meet on a regular basis with their friends and also play soccer or other sports more than once a week with their friends; at the same time, they ignore their families' need for support and help. They value these socializing activities and place a higher priority on them than on their families' needs. There is nothing wrong with meeting friends and playing sports occasionally; what is wrong is the higher frequency of these meetings and the position of these activities on the list of priorities. Everything in moderation is good and acceptable as long as other duties are not neglected.

Proper Use of *Qawamah* and
Proper Fulfillment of *Qawamah*'s Responsibility
Just as we asked the wife to respect her husband's *Qawamah,* it is also important for the husband to exercise it in the proper way. He should fulfill its responsibilities and obligations before using its authorities. It is of vital importance that husbands have the right attitude toward this aspect of marriage life. *Qawamah* is a trust and a responsibility from Allah that He, in His wisdom, entrusted men with in the marital union. It is not an honorary status given to men, but it is an obligation and accountability to be fulfilled. Here is a list of **Do**s and **Don't**s that we feel husbands should observe with respect to the application of *Qawamah*:

Do
- Provide family protection
- Provide family maintenance
- Provide family support
- Consult with wife in all family matters before making any decision

Don't
- Boss your wife around and order her left, right and center

◆ Make commitments that require her presence without getting her permission
◆ Make decisions without consulting her
◆ Give the impression that her views don't matter much

Here is a practical example of proper use of *Qawamah*:

"*Abbas* is a hard working husband. He is holding a reasonable position with a high tech firm in a small town. He has lived with his wife *Sayedah* and his two young children in this small town for the last ten years. *Sayedah* has developed a good relationship with several families in the area and became good friends with them. They get together regularly for various activities and they visit each other's houses often. She is very happy with these friendships and considers most of them as her family since she doesn't have family members living close by.

Abbas has been working with this firm for the last ten years and is still in the same position. He has been trying hard to move up the ladder, but his attempts haven't born any fruits in spite of all his efforts. He feels that there is no future for him staying in this firm. He has been talking about this to *Sayedah* for the last couple of years, who has been asking him to be patient and try harder. Recently, and after a long discussion with *Sayedah*, he decided to look for a job elsewhere. He started sending his resume to various firms with the hope of finding a better position, even if it was in another city. After a few interviews with various hiring managers at different companies, he finally received an attractive offer from one firm in a completely different State. In addition to a considerable increase in his salary, the potential of moving to higher position in the company is very real. The offer also included a trip for his family to the company's location to check out the new city, look for a new house, and find out if they will be happy moving to this new location. *Abbas* and *Sayedah* took the trip and together had a tour in the city, found out that there is more   than one Islamic center, and visited some of them. They also checked out the schooling for their children and they found more than one good school in the vicinity of *Abbas's* new work place.

Abbas is very happy with this new opportunity and thinks it is very good to accept the offer. However, whenever he discusses the matter with *Sayedah* to finalize his response, she says, "I don't want to move to a new place where I have no friends. It will be so bad to miss all my good friends. It will take so long to have the same kind of friends in this new place." *Abbas* tries to convince *Sayedah* that the new city has a bigger Muslim community, and the new position also has many advantages that will reflect positively on the whole family. However, she is not fully convinced because of the friends' issue.

The matter can't stay unresolved forever. A decision has to be made by *Abbas* as the head of the family who is entrusted by Allah *SWT* to provide, protect, take care of, and be responsible for his family affairs. At this point, it is clear that *Abbas* fulfilled the requirements of *Qawamah* in terms of doing the proper research and consulting with his family members before finalizing the decision. If *Abbas* decides to move the family to the new location and accept the new job offer, even with *Sayedah* not fully convinced, he is using the *Qawamah* properly and *Sayedah* should accept his decision and help him and the family to start their new stage of their life."

Here is another practical example of improper use of *Qawamah*:

"*Khaleel* is happily married to *Saleema*. They have two children who are school aged. He just started a new job with a new company a few months ago. As such, he is only allowed to take two vacation weeks a year. Last year and the year before, the whole family spent their holidays visiting *Khaleel's* parents who live in a close by State. *Saleema's* parents live in Europe, and *alhamdulellah*, for her peace of mind (she thought), there is a direct flight between the city they live in and her parents' city in Europe. Since *Khaleel* just joined this new firm a few months ago, he can't take his vacation time except after the start of the school year. *Saleema* was hoping to visit her parents during the summer vacation this year, since the last time they visited was over three years ago. *Saleema* suggested to *Khaleel* that she, with the children, could visit her parents during the summer vacation. He response was, "no we should wait until next summer and we can all go together." *Saleema* begged him to allow her and the children to go this summer because her parents are old and her father particularly is sick, as well as the fact that she hasn't seen them for over three years. *Khaleel* said, "No, I don't feel comfortable with you traveling alone. I know it is safe and it is only one flight without stopovers or connections, but I still don't feel comfortable with this arrangement." *Saleema* tried every possible way she could think of to convince *Khaleel*, but he adamantly refused to discuss the issue further, saying "I've made my decision. You are not traveling this summer. End of discussion."

The above case certainly indicates an improper use of *Qawamah* on *Khaleel*'s part.

Exercising *Qawamah* properly will *insha'a Allah* strengthen the family bond and enhance the quality of marital relationship.

Finally, we feel that it is important for both spouses to have a fair idea on physiological differences between men and women. We trust that most would have already learned this during their school years from biology books and that we don't have to spend time discussing this issue here. For those who didn't, we recommend consulting with Dr. *Muhammad al-Jibaly* family series, particularly book two.

7 (*Tazkeiatu Annafs*)
Purifying and Cleansing Soul

Introduction

For us to be able to carry out the responsibility of being spouses and to always try to find and use the best ways in dealing with our spouses, it is a must that we go through a process of purification of ourselves and try to regularly cleanse our souls. This will, *insha'a Allah*, strengthen us and help us perform various tasks related to our family life with ease and without many conflicts with our spouses. It is a known fact in Islam that purification of oneself is the best support mechanism for a strong and capable personality. That is the reason we are covering this topic in this chapter. Our goal is to provide the reader with some practical tips to help her/him exercise this process of self-searching and soul cleansing. The ultimate objective is to be able to put our fingers on and identify the sources of our negative spousal behavior and make a commitment to correct ourselves and minimize our shortcomings in this area.

Before we start this, let us define the term *Tazkeiatu Annafs* and find out what the *Qur'an* and *Sunnah* say about purification and soul cleansing.

Definition of *Tazkeiatu Annafs*

Let us start our discussion with a simple definition of that term *Tazkeiatu Annafs*. Here are our findings from the literature:

Ibn Taimiyyah states that the root word of *Tazkeiah* is *Zakaah*, *which* means an increase in goodness. However, he notes, goodness does not increase unless evil is abandoned and avoided, in the same way that a crop does not grow unless the silt is removed from it. Similarly, a soul and deeds can't be purified until what negates that purification is removed.[164]

It is useful here to also quote the definition of purification of the soul as stated by *J Zarbozo* in his valuable book, *Purification of the Soul*. He says, "Purification of the soul equals the process in which the healthy elements found in the soul are fostered, built upon and added to while any invading contaminants are removed or controlled such that the person worships Allah properly and fulfills his purpose in life, which can culminate in the ultimate expression of the true *Ihsan*."

The Qur'an and Tazkeiah

Purification of the soul is mentioned in the *Qur'an* in several locations. It is emphasized as one of the important tasks the messengers' have to perform. The prayer of messenger *Ibraheem SAAW* is a clear indication to this fact. He said,

"رَبَّنَا وَابْعَثْ فِيهِمْ رَسُولاً مِّنْهُمْ يَتْلُو عَلَيْهِمْ آيَاتِكَ وَيُعَلِّمُهُمُ الْكِتَابَ وَالْحِكْمَةَ وَيُزَكِّيهِمْ إِنَّكَ أَنتَ الْعَزِيزُ الْحَكِيمُ"

"Our Lord! send amongst them a Messenger of their own, who shall rehearse Thy Signs to them and instruct them in scripture and wisdom, **and sanctify them**: For Thou art the Exalted in Might, the Wise."[165]

Allah *SWT* emphasizes the same message again in the same chapter. He says,

"كَمَا أَرْسَلْنَا فِيكُمْ رَسُولاً مِّنكُمْ يَتْلُو عَلَيْكُمْ آيَاتِنَا وَيُزَكِّيكُمْ وَيُعَلِّمُكُمُ الْكِتَابَ وَالْحِكْمَةَ وَيُعَلِّمُكُم مَّا لَمْ تَكُونُواْ تَعْلَمُونَ"

"A similar (favour have ye already received) in that We have sent among you a Messenger of your own, rehearsing to you Our

---

[164] Majmooah Al-Fatawa
[165] (Q2, V129)

193

Signs, **and sanctifying you**, and instructing you in Scripture and Wisdom, and in new knowledge."[166]

Allah *SWT* emphasizes this fact again in another Chapter of the *Qur'an:*

"هُوَ الَّذِي بَعَثَ فِي الْأُمِّيِّينَ رَسُولًا مِّنْهُمْ يَتْلُو عَلَيْهِمْ آيَاتِهِ وَيُزَكِّيهِمْ وَيُعَلِّمُهُمُ الْكِتَابَ وَالْحِكْمَةَ وَإِن كَانُوا مِن قَبْلُ لَفِي ضَلَالٍ مُّبِينٍ ۝ وَآخَرِينَ مِنْهُمْ لَمَّا يَلْحَقُوا بِهِمْ وَهُوَ الْعَزِيزُ الْحَكِيمُ"

"It is He Who has sent amongst the Unlettered a messenger from among themselves, to rehearse to them His Signs, **to sanctify them**, and to instruct them in Scripture and Wisdom,- although they had been, before, in manifest error. **As well as (to confer all these benefits upon) others of them, who have not already joined them**: And He is exalted in Might, Wise"[167]

In this verse, it is clear that the process of purification of the soul is not only limited to the prophet *SAAW* and those around him, but it is a continuous task, applicable to all Muslim generations that come after the prophet *SAAW*. It is then, the responsibility of all Muslim individuals to seek help in performing this process. They should subject themselves to the methods by which they can purify and cleanse their souls. This is usually done through learning and following the teachings of the sincere and dedicated scholars of the time.

In another *Surah* Allah *SWT* says,

"وَنَفْسٍ وَمَا سَوَّاهَا فَأَلْهَمَهَا فُجُورَهَا وَتَقْوَاهَا قَدْ أَفْلَحَ مَن زَكَّاهَا وَقَدْ خَابَ مَن دَسَّاهَا"

"By the soul and proportion and order given to it, and its inspiration as to its wrong and its right; **Truly he succeeds that purifies it**, and fails that he corrupts it."[168]

This verse clearly indicates that people are able to purify and cleanse themselves and to elevate their souls to the highest levels of purity, and, at the same time, they are also able to corrupt themselves. This depends on what they do and how they conduct themselves. If they take steps toward the right direction and strive to improve themselves, Allah *SWT* stretches His hand to give them the needed support and to guide them to the Straight Path. If they decide not to follow the guidance of Allah *SWT*, they are usually left to themselves without Allah's support and they usually end up corrupting themselves.

The *Sunnah* and *Tazkeiah*

Prophet Muhammad's *SAAW* teachings and his life as a model for us are wonderful illustrations of the orders of the *Qur'an* in every area of our life and particularly in the area of self-purification. He *SAAW* understood his mission and knew that without being closer to Allah *SWT*, without purifying himself and helping his companions purify themselves, it will be very difficult to carry the enormous responsibility and noble task of propagating the word of Allah *SWT* to all humankind. Allah entrusted the prophet *SAAW* and his companions with this massive obligation, and He has to make sure that they are well prepared to fulfill it to the best of their ability. Self-purification and soul cleansing was the proper tool and the proven exercise to give them the strength required to carry out this enormous task. This is clearly reflected in the verses of the *Qur'an* that instruct the prophet *SAAW* to stand up for night prayers as a way to prepare himself for the huge duty of propagating the call for Allah *SWT*:

---

[168] (Q91, V 7-10)

"يَا أَيُّهَا الْمُزَّمِّل قُمِ اللَّيْلَ إِلَّا قَلِيلًا نِصْفَهُ أَوِ انقُصْ مِنْهُ قَلِيلًا أَوْ زِدْ عَلَيْهِ وَرَتِّلِ
الْقُرْآنَ تَرْتِيلًا إِنَّا سَنُلْقِي عَلَيْكَ قَوْلًا ثَقِيلًا إِنَّ نَاشِئَةَ اللَّيْلِ هِيَ أَشَدُّ وَطْئًا
وَأَقْوَمُ قِيلًا إِنَّ لَكَ فِي النَّهَارِ سَبْحًا طَوِيلًا وَاذْكُرِ اسْمَ رَبِّكَ وَتَبَتَّلْ إِلَيْهِ تَبْتِيلًا"

"O thou folded in garments. Stand (to prayer) by night, but not
all night, Half of it,- or a little less. Or add to it, and recite the
Qur'an as it ought to be recited. Soon shall We send down to
thee a weighty Message. Surely the rising by night is the firmest
way to tread and the best corrective of speech. True, there is for
thee by day prolonged occupation with ordinary duties: But keep
in remembrance the name of thy Lord and devote thyself to Him
whole-heartedly."[169]

The prophet *SAAW* did exactly this, and he instructed and trained
his companions to do the same, as confirmed by Allah later in the
same chapter of the *Qur'an*:

"إِنَّ رَبَّكَ يَعْلَمُ أَنَّكَ تَقُومُ أَدْنَى مِن ثُلُثِي اللَّيْلِ وَنِصْفَهُ وَثُلُثَهُ وَطَائِفَةٌ مِّنَ الَّذِينَ
مَعَكَ"

"Surely your Lord knows that you pass in prayer nearly two-
thirds of the night, and (sometimes) half of it, and (sometimes) a
third of it, and (also) a party of those with you...."[170]

Not only did the prophet *SAAW* do this, but also he instructed his
companions to engage themselves much in the remembrance of
Allah *SWT* and to regularly recite the words of Allah as
instructed by the *Qur'an*. The prophet *SAAW* also taught his
companions to repeat certain sentences of *Thikr* on various
occasions and during certain times of the day such as in the early
morning and before sunset. In fact, there is a *Dua'a* that a
believer should say for almost every occasion to the extent that
all her/his life would be continuous remembrance of Allah *SWT*.
This is a source of great strength because of how close it makes

---

[169] (Q73, V1-8)
[170] (Q73, V20)

us to Allah all the time. Here are some of these wonderful prayers as a sample of what the *Sunnah* has taught us in the way of soul cleansing and how to be close to Allah with this permanent relationship:

It was narrated by *Abu Hurairah RAA* that he said that the messenger of Allah *SAAW* said,

"من قال حين يمسي ثلاث مرات: أعوذ بكلمات الله التامات من شر ما خلق

لم تضره حُمة تلك الليلة"

"Who ever says three times at the evening, 'I seek refuge in the perfect words of Allah from the evil of that which He has created,' nothing would hurt him that night"[171]

It was also reported by *Othman Ibn A'fan RAA* that the messenger of Allah *SAAW* said,

"ما من عبد يقول في صباح كل يوم ومساء كل ليلة: بسم الله الذي

لا يضر مع اسمه شيء في الأرض ولا في السماء وهو السميع العليم

ثلاث مرات فلن يضره شئ"

"Any servant of Allah who says in the morning and in the evening, 'In the name of Allah, with whose name nothing on the earth or in heaven can cause any harm and He is the All-Hearer, the All-Knower three times,' nothing would hurt him"[172]

When we ride our cars, or any means of transportation, we are instructed to say,

"سُبْحانَ الَّذي سَخَّرَ لَنا هَذَا وَمَا كُنَّا لَهُ مُقْرِنين وَإِنَّا إِلَى رَبِّنَا لَمُنقَلِبُونَ"

"Glory be to Him Who made this subservient to us and we were not able to do it. And surely to our Lord we must return."[173]

---

[171] Ibn Heban
[172] Abu Dawood and At-Termezi
[173] (Q43, V13,14)

When we wake up in the morning, we are instructed to say,

"أصبحنا وأصبح الملك لله، والحمد لله لا شريك له، لا إله إلا هو وإليه النشور"

"Morning has risen upon us and sovereignty is all Allah's. Praise is due to Allah alone, He has no partner. There is no god but him, unto whom is the return."[174]

We are also instructed to say the following before sunset,

"أمسينا وأمسى الملك لله، والحمد لله لا شريك له، لا إله إلا هو وإليه المصير"

"Evening has befallen on us and sovereignty is all Allah's. Praise is due to Allah alone, He has no partner. There is no god but him, unto whom is the return."[175]

When we look at a mirror, we should say,

"اللهم كما حسنت خلقي فحسن خلقي وحرم وجهي على النار، الحمد لله الذي سوى خلقي فعدله، وكرم صورة وجهي فأحسنها وجعلني من المسلمين"

"O Allah, as you beautified the way I look. Please perfect my manners and protect my face from Hell fire. Praise be to Allah who created me upright, honored my face and beautified it, and made me Muslim."[176]

The life of prophet Muhammad *SAAW* provides us with the best practical example for self-purification and soul cleansing. It is of utmost importance for us to always refer to his example in every occasion to find out how he behaved or responded to certain events and situations and learn from his example. One should not think that he can come up with new ways of self-purification that

---

[174] Al-Bazzar
[175] Al-Bazzar
[176] Ibn Heban and At Tabarany

are better and more suitable than the ways described to us by the prophet *SAAW*. This is a very serious defect in the belief of those with such mentality. It is an indication that they think that the prophet *SAAW* didn't do his job properly. Let us all follow his guidance and take him as our role model because it is the best way to achieve felicity *insha'a Allah* in this life and in the life after.

Process of *Tazkeiah*

Since the main purpose of the purification process is to get closer to Allah in order to be a stronger believer who can fulfill his purpose of existence and attend to every task in the best possible way, the following saying of prophet Muhammad *SAAW* should act as our guide for this process. *Abu Hurairah* narrated that the prophet *SAAW* said,

إن الله عز وجل قال : "من عادى لي وليا فقد آذنته بالحرب وما تقرب إلي عبدي بشيء أحب إلي مما افترضت عليه، وما يزال عبدي يتقرب إلي بالنوافل حتى أحبه، فإذا أحببته كنت سمعه الذي يسمع به وبصره الذي يبصر به، ويده التي يبطش بها، ورجله التي يمشي بها، وإن سألني لأعطينه ولئن استعاذني لأعيذنه"

"Allah *SWT* says, 'The one who becomes an enemy of my close friend, I'll wage war on him. The best act My servant would draw close to me is what I made obligatory on him. My servant will continue to get closer to me by doing extra acts of obedience *Nawafel* until I love him. When I love him, I become his sense of hearing that he uses to hear, I become his sense of sight that he uses to see, I become his hand that he uses to fight, and I become his leg that he uses to walk. If he asks Me, I'll grant his request, and if he seeks refuge in Me, I'll grant him this refuge"[177]

---

[177] Al Bukhari

This great *Hadeeth* will be our guide in the process of *Tazkeiatu Annafs*. It is very clear from the text that being close to Allah *SWT* is the greatest source of strength. Also, for anyone to be close to Allah s/he has to fulfill certain acts of pure worship. The more s/he does, practices, performs, and exercises these acts, the closer s/he will be to Allah *SWT* with the ultimate goal to achieve Allah's love. Following are those acts in the order of importance as indicated by the *Hadeeth*:

♦ Obligatory worships such as the regular five daily prayers, the obligatory fasting of the month of *Ramadan*, the obligatory charity "*Zakat*", and the obligatory trip to perform *Hajj* for those who can afford it physically, financially, and emotionally. It is important here to emphasize that we should try to perfect our acts of worship to get closer to Allah. The prayer should be performed properly, with complete presence of heart and feelings, without being sidetracked by worldly distraction as much as possible. The *Khoshooe'* during prayer is a very important element to achieve perfection. Reflecting on every word you say and every verse you recite during the prayer is very important to achieve closeness to Allah *SWT*. The same level of concentration should be exercised in performing other acts of pure worship such as fasting, obligatory charity, and *Hajj*. Avoiding all acts that could violate our fast, for example, or render it vain, is highly recommended. We should try our best to understand the purposes of these acts of pure worship and make sure to perform them in a more complete way to achieve these purposes.

♦ Extra un-obligatory acts of worship. These are called *Nawafel*. It includes every prayer you make over and above the obligatory prayers and the regular *Sunnan* of the prophet *SAAW*, including the night prayers that is highly recommended in so many texts of the *Qur'an* and teachings of the prophet *SAAW*. Most of his companions observed the night prayers and practiced them regularly. It also includes the extra fasting one would perform in days other than the days of *Ramadan* and the days that make up for missed days in *Ramadan*. It includes extra spending for the sake of Allah over and above the obligatory *Zakat*. It is also important here to remind the reader that these extra acts of worship should be performed properly as was indicated in the obligatory acts of worship. We should always try to achieve perfection in all our deeds to get the real benefit out of such acts.

♦ Since the goal is to accomplish Allah's love, any acts that bring Allah's love are highly recommended. This will lead us to increase our closeness to Him, to attain His love, and to deserve His guidance, His support, and His protection. Let us check in the *Qur'an* and the teachings of prophet Muhammad *SAAW* to find out what the various categories of people who deserve the love of Allah *SWT* are:

In numerous locations in the *Qur'an*, Allah says,

"إِنَّ اللَّهَ يُحِبُّ الْمُحْسِنِينَ"

" Allah loves the doers of good (*Al Muhseneen*)."[178]

In addition, Allah *SWT* says,

"إِنَّ اللَّهَ يُحِبُّ الْمُتَّقِينَ"

" Allah loves those who are conscious of Him (*Al Mutaqeen*)."[179]

He also says,

"إِنَّ اللَّهَ يُحِبُّ الْمُقْسِطِينَ"

" Allah loves those who act equitably (*Al Muqseteen*)."[180]

He *SWT* also says,

"إِنَّ اللَّهَ يُحِبُّ التَّوَّابِينَ وَيُحِبُّ الْمُتَطَهِّرِينَ"

" Allah loves those who turn unto Him in repentance (*At Tawabeen*)."[181]

---

[178] (Q2, V195, Q3, V134 and148, Q5, V13 and V93)
[179] (Q3, 76, Q9, V4, and 7)
[180] (Q5, V42, Q49, V9, Q60, V8)

"Allah loves those who keep themselves pure (*Al Mutatuhereen*)."[182]

"وَاللّٰهُ يُحِبُّ الصَّابِرِينَ"

"Allah loves those who are patient (*As Saabireen*)."[183]

"إِنَّ اللّٰهَ يُحِبُّ الْمُتَوَكِّلِينَ"

"Allah loves those who place their trust in Him (*Al Muttawakeleen*)."[184]

"وَاللّٰهُ يُحِبُّ الْمُطَّهِّرِينَ"

"Allah loves those who keep themselves pure (*Al Muttuhereen*)."[185]

The above are some of the categories of believers whom Allah *SWT* loves according to the *Qur'an*. For one to realize the love of Allah, s/he should try her/his best to practice the above qualities and be from *Al Muhseneen, Al Mutaqeen, Al Muqseteen, At Tawabeen, Al Mutatuhereen, As Saabireen,* and *Al Muttawakeleen.* This will, no doubt *insha'a Allah*, bring the love of Allah *SWT* and make her/him a close friend of His (*Waley*) who deserves His support, guidance, and *Tawfeeq*.

Here are some more of the sayings of the prophet *SAAW* regarding those who will be blessed with Allah's love:

It was reported by *A'ishah RAA* that the prophet *SAAW* said,

"إِنَّ اللهَ يُحِبُّ الْمُلِحِّينَ فِي الدُّعَاءِ"

"Allah loves the servants who insist in their *dua'a*"[186]

---

[181] (Q2, V222)
[182] (Q2, V222)
[183] (Q3, V146)
[184] (Q3, V159)
[185] (Q9, V108)
[186] Al-awzae'y

It was also reported by *Sa'd Ibn Abi Waqqas RAA* that the prophet *SAAW* said,

"إن الله يحب العبد التقي الغني الخفي"

"Allah loves the servant who has *Taqwa*, who is content and satisfied, and who does good deeds inconspicuously"[187]

Since our goal is to earn the love of Allah, it may also be of great benefit to find out the various categories of people that Allah dislikes. This would help us avoid being from them, which will automatically translate into more love from Allah *SWT*.
Allah *SWT* says,

"وَاللّهُ لاَ يُحبُّ كُلَّ كَفَّارٍ أَثِيمٍ"

"Allah does not love any ungrateful sinner."[188]

He *SWT* also says,

"فَإِنَّ اللّهَ لاَ يُحبُّ الْكَافرِينَ"

"Allah does not love those who reject Faith."[189]

He *SWT* also says,

"وَاللّهُ لاَ يُحبُّ الظَّالمِينَ"

"..and Allah does not love the unjust."[190]

He *SWT* also says,

"إنَّ اللّهَ لاَ يُحبُّ مَن كَانَ مُخْتَالاً فَخُورًا"

"Surely Allah does not love him who is proud, boastful."[191]

He *SWT* also says,

"إنَّ اللّهَ لاَ يُحبُّ مَن كَانَ خَوَّانًا أَثِيمًا"

---

[187] Muslim
[188] (Q2, V276)
[189] (Q3, V32)
[190] (Q3, V75, Q42, V40)
[191] (Q4, V36)

"Surely Allah does not love him who is treacherous, sinful"[192]

He *SWT* also says,

"وَاللّهُ لاَ يُحِبُّ الْمُفْسِدِينَ"

"Allah does not love the mischief-makers."[193]

He *SWT* also says,

"إِنَّ اللّهَ لاَ يُحِبُّ الْمُعْتَدِينَ"

"Surely Allah does not love those who exceed the limits."[194]

He *SWT* also says,

"إِنَّهُ لاَ يُحِبُّ الْمُسْرِفِينَ"

"Surely He does not love the wasteful."[195]

He *SWT* also says in various locations of the *Qur'an* that He doesn't love the treacherous, the arrogant, or the proud. He also doesn't love the unfaithful and the ungrateful, nor does He love the exultant, nor those who brag and boast.

Spouses generally should avoid all of the above qualities and traits in their interactions with other people and particularly in their interactions with each other. This way they can achieve the love of Allah and deserve His help, His guidance, and His support. With the help, guidance, and support of Allah both spouses would *insha'a Allah* strive to always do the right thing and avoid any sources of conflict in their relationship. *Insha'a Allah* their marital life will be successful, they will be able to apply the recommendations in this book, and they will live happily and fulfill the purpose of their existence in the best possible way.

---

[192] (Q4, V107)
[193] (Q5, V64, Q28, V77)
[194] (Q5, V87, Q7, V55)
[195] (Q6, V141)

Be at Peace with Yourself

In addition to engaging in the above acts of obligatory worship, performing extra *Nawafel*, remembering Allah much via utilizing the proper *Dua'as* that we were taught by the prophet *SAAW* for different occasions, and observing various traits which brings the love of Allah *SWT* into our lives, we should also try to be at peace with ourselves and achieve a higher level of *Taqwa* via the following process:

Making Commitment *"Mo'ahadah"*
Understanding our prayer components is a very important aspect of improving our commitment to being good Muslims who try their best to fulfill their duties to the best of their abilities. We should remember that every time we do our prayers we recite the first chapter of the *Qur'an*. One of the verses we recite is,

"إِيَّاكَ نَعْبُدُ وإِيَّاكَ نَسْتَعِينُ"

"Thee (alone) we worship; Thee (alone) we ask for help."[196]

This is a commitment that we make at least seventeen times every day with Allah. It is of a paramount importance that we honor our commitments and fulfill our contracts. Allah says,

"يَا أَيُّهَا الَّذِينَ آمَنُواْ أَوْفُواْ بِالْعُقُودِ"

"O ye who believe! fulfill (all) obligations"[197]
He also says,

"وَأَوْفُواْ بِعَهْدِ اللّه إِذَا عَاهَدتُّمْ وَلاَ تَنقُضُواْ الأَيْمَانَ بَعْدَ تَوْكِيدِهَا وَقَدْ جَعَلْتُمُ اللّهَ عَلَيْكُمْ كَفِيلاً إِنَّ اللّهَ يَعْلَمُ مَا تَفْعَلُونَ"

"And be true to your bond with Allah whenever you bind yourselves with a pledge, and don't break your oaths after having freely confirmed them and having called upon Allah to be

---

[196] (Q1, V5)
[197] (Q5, V1)

witness to your good faith: behold Allah knows all that you do"[198]

Having the proper understanding of this pledge that we repeat several times daily, will without doubt help us observe our actions during the day to make sure they adhere to the articles of the contract between us and the Almighty. This will enhance our level of *Taqwa* and make us closer to Allah, and consequently it will *insha'a Allah* put us in a better position to fulfill our obligations and be the best we can be.

Watching Over Oneself *"Moraqabah"*

This is another important element and vital component of the *Taqwa* enhancers. Observing our actions, being on guard of what we do, and feeling that Allah is with us all the time are very important and help us to always behave in the right way. Allah reminds us to be aware of His presence and His awareness of what we do all the time to help us be alert and observe what we do regularly. He says,

$$\text{"الَّذِي يَرَاكَ حِينَ تَقُومُ وَتَقَلُّبَكَ فِي السَّاجِدِينَ"}$$

"Who sees you when you stand alone, and who sees your behavior among those who prostrate themselves to Him"[199]
He also says,

$$\text{"يَعْلَمُ خَائِنَةَ الْأَعْيُنِ وَمَا تُخْفِي الصُّدُورُ"}$$

"He is aware of the most stealthy glance, and of all that the hearts would conceal"[200]
He also says,

$$\text{"وَلَقَدْ خَلَقْنَا الْإِنسَانَ وَنَعْلَمُ مَا تُوَسْوِسُ بِهِ نَفْسُهُ وَنَحْنُ أَقْرَبُ إِلَيْهِ مِنْ حَبْلِ الْوَرِيدِ"}$$

---

[198] (Q16, V91)
[199] (Q26, V218-219)
[200] (Q40, V19)

"Verily, it is We who have created man, and We know what his innermost self whispers within him: for We are closer to him than his neck-vein."[201]

He also says,

"وَأَسِرُّوا قَوْلَكُمْ أَوِ اجْهَرُوا بِهِ إِنَّهُ عَلِيمٌ بِذَاتِ الصُّدُورِ"

"And whether you keep your sayings secret or state them openly, He has full knowledge indeed of all that is in your hearts"[202]

Being aware of this fact will help the individual always think about what s/he is doing and make sure that s/he is performing it well and with the right intention. This will undoubtedly lead to closeness to Allah *SWT* and help enhance the level of *Taqwa*.

Reviewing, Assessing, and Evaluating One's Actions "*Mohasabah*"

The concept of *Mohasabah* is a very important one in Islam. It takes its roots from the following verse:

"يَا أَيُّهَا الَّذِينَ آمَنُوا اتَّقُوا اللَّهَ وَلْتَنظُرْ نَفْسٌ مَّا قَدَّمَتْ لِغَدٍ وَاتَّقُوا اللَّهَ إِنَّ اللَّهَ خَبِيرٌ بِمَا تَعْمَلُونَ"

"O you who attained to faith. Remain conscious to Allah (Have *Taqwa*), and let every human being look to what he sends ahead for the morrow. And, once again remain conscious to Allah (Have *Taqwa*) for Allah is fully aware of all that you do"[203]

The prophet *SAAW* also emphasized that we should always assess and evaluate our actions and deeds. In fact, he labeled the person who doesn't do this as *Ghafel or A'jez, which* means careless, complacent, and unable. It was narrated by *Shaddad Ibn Awes RAA* that the prophet *SAAW* said,

---

[201] (Q50, V16)
[202] (Q67, V13)
[203] (Q59, V18)

207

"الكيس من دان نفسه وعمل لما بعد الموت والعاجز من أتبع نفسه هواها ثم
تمنى على الله"

" A wise person is one who blames himself for his shortcomings
and works hard for what comes after death, while a careless and
complacent person (*Ghafel*) or unable person (*A'jez*) is one who
follows his whims and desires and keeps hoping in the mercy of
Allah"

Omar Ibn Al-Khattab RAA used to say,

"حاسبوا أنفسكم قبل أن تحاسبوا ، وزنوا أعمالكم قبل أن توزنوا ، فإن
أهون عليكم في الحساب غدًا أن تحاسبوا أنفسكم اليوم ، وتزينوا للعرض
الأكبر "يومئذٍ تعرضون لا تخفى منكم خافية"

"Review, evaluate, and assess yourself before you will be
assessed. Weigh your deeds before they are weighed against you,
and prepare yourself for the day where you will be fully
exposed."[204]

Al Hassan Al Basry used to say,

"المؤمن قوام على نفسه، يحاسب نفسه لله، وإنما خف الحساب يوم القيامة
على قوم حاسبوا أنفسهم في الدنيا، وإنما شق الحساب يوم القيامة على قوم
أخذوا هذا الأمر من غير محاسبة"

"A believer observes himself and maintains his good deeds. He
always reviews, assesses, and evaluates his status. Those who do
this in life will have an easy time on the Day of Judgment. And
those who don't, will have a difficult time on the Day of
Judgment."

The following is reported in the tablets of *Ibraheem*:

---

[204] Ahmad

"ينبغي للعاقل ما لم يكن مغلوباً على عقله أن يكون له أربع ساعات ساعة
يناجي فيها ربه ، وساعة يحاسب فيها نفسه ، وساعة يتفكر في صنع الله ،
وساعة يخلو فيها لحاجته من المطعم والمشرب"

"A wise person should divide his time to four portions; one portion to supplicate to his Lord, a second portion to review, evaluate, and assess himself, the third portion to reflect upon the creation of Allah, and the fourth portion to work and earn his living"[205]

We should remember that one day we will be fully exposed as Allah says in *Surat Al Haqah*:

"يَوْمَئِذٍ تُعْرَضُونَ لَا تَخْفَى مِنكُمْ خَافِيَةٌ"

"On that day you shall be exposed to view-- no secret of yours shall remain hidden."[206]

Because of this, it is a wise practice for believers to assess and review their actions regularly. Relationships can be enhanced if actions are monitored and rectified as soon as faults are discovered and rectification is needed. Scholars recommend that a process of *Mohasabah* be implemented to help improve and enhance the level of our *Taqwa* and closeness to Allah. This process should be done frequently to achieve the best possible results. It involves both spouses assessing their actions individually first and then together. They should have a list of questions to ask themselves at the end of the day, maybe, or the end of the week. This list of questions should cover their daily activities to find out how good their days are and whether there is room for improvement. The following are examples of questions that their list should cover:

♦ Did I perform my daily prayers on time?
♦ Did I donate money and charity for the sake of Allah?
♦ Did I think about what I want to say before speaking?

---

[205] Ibn Heban and Al-Hakem
[206] (Q69, V18)

- Did I hurt the feelings of my spouse in any way?
- Did I express my love and appreciation to my spouse?
- Did I thank my spouse for his/her efforts to help me?
- Did I thank my spouse for being patient with me during the stressful time at the end of my project in the office?
- Did I speak nicely about my spouse's family?
- Did I treat my spouse kindly?
- Did I satisfy my spouse's needs?
- Did I.......?
- Did I.......?

These are samples of the questions that every spouse should ask him/herself to evaluate his/her performance during that specific day or week. If the answers are good, we should be thankful to Allah *SWT*. If we find out that there are shortcomings in our performance, we should make a strong commitment to improve, correct our mistakes, and perform better in the future.

Punishing Oneself for Mistakes Committed *"Mo'aqabah"*

When one makes mistake after mistake and they go without punishment, it reinforces his/her negative behavior. Allah *SWT* uses both rewards and punishments as tools of *Tarbiyah* to correct the behavior of the believers. He told us that there are benefits in executing punishment against wrong doers. He says,

"وَلَكُمْ فِي الْقِصَاصِ حَيَاةٌ يَا أُولِيْ الأَلْبَابِ لَعَلَّكُمْ تَتَّقُونَ"

"And there is life for you in (the law of) retaliation, O men of understanding, that you may guard yourselves."[207]

This is an invitation for us to discipline ourselves particularly when we make mistakes. The companions of the prophet *SAAW* used to do exactly this when they made mistakes to force themselves to remember such mistakes in the future and not repeat them. *Omar Ibn Al-Khattab RAA* once entered one of his gardens for a walk. He enjoyed the walk to the extent that he

---

[207] (Q2, V179)

missed the congregation prayer of *Asr*. He punished himself by donating this garden for charity and the needy. Others did similar acts to purify themselves and avoid repeating negative behaviors. This is a lesson for us. After we do the process of *Mohasabah*, if we find certain shortcomings, it may be a good idea to discipline ourselves by depriving ourselves from certain privileges for a period of time to help in the process of improving ourselves and enhancing our *Taqwa* level.

Striving for the Best "*Mojahadah*"

Changing one's behavior and performance requires effort and struggle. That is why *Mojahadah* is an essential component of *Taqwa* enhancement and elevation. Allah says,

"وَالَّذِينَ جَاهَدُوا فِينَا لَنَهْدِيَنَّهُمْ سُبُلَنَا وَإِنَّ اللَّهَ لَمَعَ الْمُحْسِنِينَ"

"As for those who strive in Us, We surely guide them to Our paths, and lo! Allah is with the good."[208]

Through exercising *Mojahadah*, Allah *SWT* helps us and guides us to the straight path. He gives us the needed support to deal with others in the best manner and helps us react to various situations in the proper way.

The prophet *SAAW* gave us the best example as he strove hard to improve himself and get closer to Allah via extra good deeds. He used to stand up for prayer at night for long hours. When *A'ishah RAA* told him that Allah has forgiven his sins, he then said, "Shouldn't I be a grateful servant of Allah?"

Also, *Rabea'h Ibn Ka'b* said,

كنت أبيت مع رسول الله فأتيته بوضوئه وحاجته فقال لي: "سل". فقلت: أسألك مرافقتك في الجنة قال: "أو غير ذلك" قلت: هو ذاك قال: "فأعني على نفسك بكثرة السجود"

---

[208] (Q29, V69)

"I used to stay overnight with the prophet *SAAW*. I used to bring the water for his *Wudo'*. I asked him to be his companion in paradise. He said, 'Help me fulfill your request by prostrating much to Allah.'"[209]

Efforts to improve yourself and correct your shortcomings through exercising *Mojahadah* will not go unnoticed by your spouse. It will be appreciated and, hopefully, reciprocated. This will *insha'a Allah* contribute to the will being of the relationship and strengthen the martial union.

The above five steps of *Mo'ahadah, Moraqabah, Mohasabah, Mo'aqabah,* and *Mojahadah* are a great source of *Taqwa* enhancement and closeness to Allah *SWT*. With *Mo'ahadah*, we stay straight according to Allah's injunctions. With *Moraqabah*, we feel the presence of Allah all the time. With *Mohasabah*, we free ourselves from our shortcomings, observe our duties toward others, and fulfill them. With *Mo'aqabah*, we wane ourselves from committing mistakes and force ourselves to be upright. With *Mojahadah*, we rejuvenate ourselves, continue to be active, and earn Allah's guidance and support.

Self-search

This is another useful exercise to help spouses in the process of purification. Each spouse should ask her/himself certain questions to try to find out and identify the sources of the negative spousal behavior s/he has. These behavioral patterns could be the result of certain life experiences at various stages of the life of the individual. They could be the result of experiences during his/her childhood years, teen years, or even adult years. As such, the questions should cover all stages of the individual's life to make sure all sources of negative spousal behaviors are identified in order to be able to take the steps needed to correct them.

---

[209] Muslim

To help you with this exercise, here are two sample checklists; the first is for husbands, and the second is for wives. Spouses should be able to come up with other questions to help themselves search for different elements and hidden reasons that cause them to behave in a certain way toward their spouses. They should be able to evaluate the effect of this behavior on their marital relationship. They should also try to sort out their behavioral patterns into positive and negative. Finally, they should reinforce positive ones and learn new positive behavioral patterns to replace the negative ones.

Sample Checklist for Husbands

♦ During my childhood and teen years . . .
   o My father always expressed love, respect, and affection to my mother in front of us.
   o My father never expressed love, respect, or affection to my mother.
   o My mother always prepared fresh meals every day for the family.
   o My mother always had the dinner ready on the table before my father's arrival.
   o My father always made decisions related to the family without discussing them with my mother.
   o My father always consulted my mother, and even us sometimes, before making any decisions related to family.
   o My father always stayed home after dinner finishing his own work or reading his favorite paper. He never took my mother or us out for visits and entertainment.
   o My father always found time to take us out to the park or go for a walk with my mother.
   o My father always went out alone almost every day after dinner to socialize with his friends.

♦ As an adult . . .

    o I don't feel the need to do any extra acts of worship other than the obligatory ones.

    o I don't feel the need to review my behaviors/ actions. I always think that whatever I do is right and there is no need for me to change. My wife should change.

    o I feel that I have enough knowledge, and there is no need for me to acquire any more knowledge. Life can go on without the need to learn and understand new stuff.

    o I feel that cleaning the house and preparing food is the wife's most important duty. I have no obligation to help her.

Sample Checklist for Wives

♦ During my childhood and teen years . . .

    o My mother never had dinner ready when my father came home, although my father always arrived home at the same time every day.

    o My mother always argued with my father in front of us and showed her disrespect to his views and wishes.

    o My mother never argued with my father in front of us. She always dealt with him in a respectful manner and instructed us to do the same.

    o My parents discussed family decisions openly and sometimes included us in the discussions.

    o My mother often got frustrated and shouted at my father.

    o My mother never let us play in the living room because she didn't want us to make a mess. This was always a source of conflict between her and my father.

    o My mother always complained that she couldn't pursue her career. Her resentment about having to stay home was very obvious, though she and my father made this decision together.

- ♦ As an adult . . .
  - o I don't feel the need to do any extra acts of worship other than the obligatory ones.
  - o I don't feel the need to review my behaviors/actions. I always think that whatever I do is right and there is no need for me to change. My husband should change.
  - o I feel I have enough knowledge, and there is no need for me to acquire any more knowledge. Life can go on without the need to learn and understand new stuff.
  - o I feel that cleaning the house and preparing food is the wife's most important duty.
  - o I feel frustrated that part of my job is to clean the house and prepare the food.
  - o When there is a conflict between myself and my husband, I feel that I always have to consult with my mother.

Remember that the purpose of the self-search is to discover the sources of your negative behavior toward your spouse and try to replace it with positive behavior.

Proper Islamic Conflict Resolution

Proper conflict resolution is very important to follow when there is a difference of opinion or any conflict between husband and wife. Each spouse has to abide by the teachings of the prophet *SAAW* and allow their spouse to present her/his case and her/his point of view while the other spouse is attentively listening. Then they can try to reach an agreement that is acceptable to every body. When they reach the agreement, both will more likely honor their part of the agreement because they feel that they both participated in the decision-making process. On the other hand, if one spouse tries to impose his/her own point of view without giving the other spouse a fair chance to present his/her case, the spouse who is not given a chance to express his/her opinion may not be eager to implement the final decision. In addition, using proper conflict resolution ensures a wonderful warm family atmosphere and keeps the marital relationship strong and healthy.

Islam provides a wonderful framework and valuable guidelines for conflict resolution. This is important for both spouses to learn, since even in the most successful marriages, conflicts do happen between partners. A'ishah RAA reported that one day Allah's messenger SAAW said to her,

"إني لأعلم إذا كنت عني راضية، وإذا كنت علي غضبى"؛ فقلت: ومن أين تعرف ذلك؟ قال: " أما إذا كنت علي راضية فإنك تقولين: لا ورب محمد، وإذا كنت غضبى قلت: لا ورب إبراهيم ". قالت: قلت: أجل والله يا رسول الله ما أهجر إلا اسمك.

"Indeed, I know when you are pleased with me, and when you are angry: When you are pleased with me you say (while making an oath), 'No, by the Lord of Muhammad.' And when you are angry with me you say, 'No, by the Lord of Ibraheem.'"

She replied, "Yes indeed, by Allah, O Allah's messenger! I don't abandon (when angry) except your name."[210]

Using proper conflict resolution methods and techniques, which are based on Qur'anic teachings as well as the teachings of Prophet Muhammad SAAW, will ensure a higher rate of success with our spouses. It will also help us keep a strong bond between us as partners, keep an open channel of communication between us as spouses, and create a warm,

---

[210] Muslim, Al Bukhari and Ahmad

healthy family atmosphere. A good family atmosphere is also important and conducive to the better upbringing of children. This is another crucial reason for spouses to familiarize themselves with the Islamic methodology of dealing with conflicts. We try to address this issue in the next few pages.

Islamic Guidelines for Conflict Resolution

A successful Islamic conflict management and resolution technique utilizes a combination of an open mind and heart, accommodation, suspension of judgment, forgiveness, gentleness, calmness, and above all anger control. It also tries to get to the core of the problem and find the proper, permanent solution rather than provide a superficial treatment that deals only with the symptoms of the problem. Let us now discuss some conflict resolution guidelines in detail and see how we can benefit from them as spouses.

Take Initiative

Whenever a conflict takes place between two Muslims, the one who takes the initiative to resolve the problem and starts by greeting the other party is considered the better person, according to the teachings of Prophet Muhammad, *SAAW*. *Abu Ayub, RAA*, relates that the messenger of Allah *SAAW* said,

"لا يحل لمسلم أن يهجر أخاه فوق ثلاث، يلتقيان فيعرض هذا ويعرض هذا،

وخيرهما الذي يبدأ بالسلام"

"It is not proper for a Muslim to keep away from his Muslim brother for more than three days so much so that when they meet they move away from each other. The better of them is the one who is first to salute the other."[211]

It was also reported by *Abu Hurairah RAA* that the messenger of Allah *SAAW* said,

---

[211] Bukhari and Muslim

"لا يحل لمسلم أن يهجر أخاه فوق ثلاث، فإن مرت به ثلاث فليلقه فليسلم
عليه، فإن رد عليه السلام فقد اشتركا في الأجر، وإن لم يرد عليه فقد باء
بالإثم، وخرج المسلم من الهجر"

"It is not lawful for a Muslim to be angry with his brother
for more than three days. When they meet after three days, he
should greet him. If he responds to the greeting, both will be
rewarded. If he doesn't respond, he will be a sinner and the
first one is free from this sin."[212]

Forgive and Forget
In *Surat Aal Imran*, Allah says,

"وَسَارِعُواْ إِلَى مَغْفِرَةٍ مِّن رَّبِّكُمْ وَجَنَّةٍ عَرْضُهَا السَّمَاوَاتُ وَالأَرْضُ أُعِدَّتْ
لِلْمُتَّقِينَ ۞ الَّذِينَ يُنفِقُونَ فِي السَّرَّاءِ وَالضَّرَّاءِ وَالْكَاظِمِينَ الْغَيْظَ وَالْعَافِينَ عَنِ
النَّاسِ وَاللَّهُ يُحِبُّ الْمُحْسِنِينَ"

"And be quick in seeking forgiveness from your Lord and a
Heaven whose width is as the width of the earth and sky,
which is prepared for those who exercise *Taqwa*, those who
spend at easy as well as at difficult times, **those who control
their anger, and those who pardon people**. Allah certainly
loves those who exercise *Ihsan*."[213]

In *Surat Ash Shura*, Allah says,

"وَمَا عِندَ اللَّهِ خَيْرٌ وَأَبْقَى لِلَّذِينَ آمَنُوا وَعَلَى رَبِّهِمْ يَتَوَكَّلُونَ ۞ وَالَّذِينَ يَجْتَنِبُونَ
كَبَائِرَ الْإِثْمِ وَالْفَوَاحِشَ وَإِذَا مَا غَضِبُوا هُمْ يَغْفِرُونَ"

"...But that which is with Allah is better and more lasting for
those who believe in the Oneness of Allah and put their trust

---

[212] Abu Dawoud
[213] (Q 3, V 133-134)

in their Lord. And those who avoid the greater sins and *Al-Fawahish*, **and when they are angry, forgive.**"[214]

In *Surat Al Aa'raf*, Allah says,

"خُذِ الْعَفْوَ وَأْمُرْ بِالْعُرْفِ وَأَعْرِضْ عَنِ الْجَاهِلِينَ"

"Show forgiveness, enjoin what is good, and turn away from the foolish (i.e. don't punish them)"[215]

These verses clearly illustrate the importance of forgiving others. It considers those who do such acts as the *Mutaqeen*. It also indicates that Allah loves them and promises them a great and lasting reward in the hereafter.

The teachings of Prophet Muhammad *SAAW* further emphasize the importance of forgiving and pardoning in human relations in general and particularly when it involves family members. It was reported by *Anas Ibn Malik RAA* that the messenger of Allah *SAAW* said,

"لا تقاطعوا ولا تدابروا ولا تباغضوا ولا تحاسدوا وكونوا عباد الله إخوانا،

ولا يحل لمسلم أن يهجر أخاه فوق ثلاث"

"Neither nurse mutual hatred, nor envy, nor abandon each other, and be fellow brothers and servants of Allah. It is not lawful for a Muslim that he should keep his relation estranged with another Muslim beyond three days." [216]

Also it was reported by *Abu Hurairah RAA* that a man said to the messenger of Allah *SAAW*,

---

[214] (Q 42, V 36-37)
[215] (Q 7, V 199)
[216] Agreed upon

يا رسول الله إن لي قرابة أصلهم ويقطعوني وأحسن إليهم ويسيئون إلي،

وأحلم عنهم ويجهلون علي فقال : "لئن كنت كما قلت فكأنما تسفهم الملّ

ولا يزال معك من الله تعالى ظهير عليهم مادمت على ذلك"

"I have relatives with whom I have tried to reunite, but they continue to sever their relationship with me. I try to treat them kindly, but they treat me badly, with them I am gentle, but with me they are rough."

The prophet *SAAW* replied, "If you are as you say, you will not be without support against them from Allah, as long as you do so."[217]

It was also narrated by *Ubada Ibn Al-Samet RAA* that the messenger of Allah *SAAW* said,

"ألا أنبئكم بما يشرف الله به البنيان ويرفع الدرجات؟ قالوا: بلى يا رسول

الله. قال: تحلم على من جهل عليك وتعفو عمن ظلمك، وتعطي من

حرمك، وتصل من قطعك"

"Shall I tell you about what would elevate your ranks and increase your honor?"

Those with him replied, "Yes, oh messenger of Allah." He said, "Exercise forbearance with the one who is ignorant with you, forgive the one who has wronged you, give to the one who didn't give you, and establish good relations with the one who severs his relations with you." [218]

Forgetting and forgiving play a great role in enhancing healthy relationships between family members.

---

[217] Muslim
[218] At-Tabarani

Control Your Anger

Among the great advice of the prophet *SAAW* is the advice not to be angry.

On the authority of *Abu Hurairah RAA* who narrated that a man asked the Messenger of Allah *SAAW* to give him a piece of advice, he said,

أوصني. قال: "لا تغضب" فردد مرارا قال: "لا تغضب"

"Don't be angry." The man repeated his question several times and the prophet *SAAW* replied, "Don't be angry."[219]

In another agreed upon *Hadeeth*, the prophet *SAAW* defined the strong person as the one who controls himself in a fit of rage and not the one who wrestles others.

عن أبي هريرة رضي الله عنه أن رسول الله صلى الله عليه وسلم قال: "ليس الشديد بالصرعة إنما الشديد الذي يملك نفسه عند الغضب"

On the authority of *Mu'ath Ibn Anas RAA* who narrated that the prophet *SAAW* said,

"من كظم غيظا وهو قادر على أن ينفذه دعاه الله سبحانه وتعالى على رؤوس الخلائق يوم القيامة حتى يخيره من الحور العين ما شاء"

"The one who swallows up anger will be called out by Allah, the Exalted, to the forefront of the creatures on the Day of Resurrection and will be put to option about any pure-eyed virgin, he would like."[220]

Not only did the prophet *SAAW* warn us against getting angry, but he also taught us the best anger management techniques:
- Seek refuge with Allah from Satan: On the authority of *Suliman Ibn Surd RAA* two people began to quarrel with each other in front of the prophet, *SAAW*. One of

---

[219] Bukhari
[220] Abu Dawoud and At-Termithy

221

them was so angry that his face had turned red and the veins on his neck were swollen. The messenger of Allah *SAAW* said,

"إني لأعرف كلمة لو قالها لذهب عنه الذي يجد. أعوذ بالله من الشيطان

الرجيم. فقال الرجل: وهل ترى بي من جنون؟"

"I know of a phrase that, if he were to utter it, his fit of rage would be relaxed, and that phrase is 'I seek refuge with Allah from Satan, the accursed.'" So the companions said to him, "the messenger of Allah said, 'seek refuge with Allah from Satan, the outcast.'"[221]

- Change your position: It was narrated that the messenger of Allah *SAAW* said,

"إذا غضب أحدكم وهو قائم فليجلس، فإذا ذهب عنه الغضب وإلا

فليضطجع"

"if one of you gets angry while he's standing, let him sit down, and if he is still angry, let him lie down."[222]

- Perform *wudu'*: It was narrated that the prophet *SAAW* said,

" إن الغضب من الشيطان وإن الشيطان خلق من النار وإنما تطفأ النار بالماء،

فإذا غضب أحدكم فليتوضأ"

"Anger is from Satan and Satan is created from fire, and fire is extinguished by water; so if one of you becomes angry let him perform *wudu'*."[223]

- Be silent: It was narrated that the prophet *SAAW* said,

---

[221] Agreed upon
[222] Ahmad
[223] Abu Dawoud

"إذا غَضِبَ أحدكم فليسكت"

"If one of you gets angry, let him be silent."[224]

Spouses should make use of all of these wonderful techniques in managing their anger when they're in a conflict with each other. They should not be quick to react when they are upset with one another, but should use one of the above strategies instead. It may be difficult at first, and it does take training, but these techniques are very helpful and make it a lot easier to avoid unnecessary problems. Spouses should even try to help each other in learning and training themselves to exercise these methods of anger management.

No Name-Calling
Allah *SWT* tells us in *Surat Al Hujorat*,

"وَلَا تَنَابَزُوا بِالْأَلْقَابِ"

"Do not call each others names or humiliate one another."[225]
This applies to everyone, but it applies even more to us in the way we deal with our spouses. Humiliation destroys our spouses' self-esteems, leaves a sour taste in their mouth, and increases resentment between spouses. We don't want our spouses to end up having weak personalities or to be resentful toward us or toward the marital relationship. We all want strong and confident family members to be able to face the challenges of this society and live as committed Muslims who have positive influences on others as our ancestors did. They were able to show other societies they migrated to the beauty of Islam. In fact, Islam spread in South East Asia via the good manners and strong personalities of early Muslims who migrated to this part of the world and made it their home. We have plenty to learn from them and should take them as role models *insha'a Allah*. Also, the prophet *SAAW*

---

[224] Ahmad
[225] (Q 49, V 11)

was described as a person who never used foul language or cursed others.

A'ishah RAA reported that the messenger of Allah *SAAW* said,

"أبغض الرجال إلى الله الألد الخصم"

"The most hated man to Allah is the stubbornly, quarrelsome"[226]

The use of active listening techniques described in chapter four under the communication ingredient is also helpful in conflict resolution and tends to keep problems from escalating.

Following the above guidelines and accommodating others' views helps greatly in ensuring that spouses are objective and deal with the root of the problem and not only the symptoms. This will ensure a win-win situation and both husband and wife will feel that they are part of the process. As such, they both will tend to honor their parts of the agreement.

Practical Steps for Conflict Resolution

In addition to observing the above Islamic etiquettes of conflict resolution, here are some steps that we recommend both husband and wife follow when they are trying to resolve a conflict.

1. Keep your cool. Try to stay calm with the help of the anger management techniques previously mentioned.
2. Reflect, and put your finger on the root cause of the problem. Ask yourself repeatedly why this is happening until you find the real cause of the problem. Make sure you identify the cause and not one of the symptoms of the problem. Again, this could be done by repeatedly asking yourself

---

[226] Al Bukhari and Muslim

"Why?" Every time you come up with an answer to your question, ask yourself "Why?" again until you can't find an answer for the question. In this case the last answer you came up with is the real cause of the problem

3. Get yourself to accept the fact that there is a problem and you may be part of the cause of this problem. Don't automatically assume that you are innocent, and the other party is the guilty one.
4. Set up a proper time for both of you to discuss the problem. Make sure that the time selected meets the following criteria:
   a) Good for both of you, and get your spouse's agreement
   b) Long enough to discuss the problem in detail
   c) No other distractions are expected around that time
   d) Both of you are rested, ready to discuss, and dedicated to finding a workable solution to the conflict
5. Focus on the current problem and be solution oriented. Don't be historical, which means that you remind your partner of problems from the past.
6. Use the best methods in your discussions. Allah *SWT* says,

$$\text{"ادْفَعْ بِالَّتِي هِيَ أَحْسَنُ"}$$

"And rebel with which is best"[227] which means the following:
   a) No name calling
   b) No blaming
   c) No finger pointing
   d) Not even a subtle signal at any of the above

[227] (Q41, V34)

7. Remember that your real enemy is *Shaytan*, not your spouse. He is trying his best to create divisions between spouses. His ultimate success, which he brags of to his leader *Iblees,* the accursed, is to start conflicts and cause problems between husband and wife.

"وَقُل لِّعِبَادِي يَقُولُواْ الَّتِي هِيَ أَحْسَنُ إِنَّ الشَّيْطَانَ يَنزَغُ بَيْنَهُمْ"

"Say to My servants that they should (only) say those things that are best: for Satan doth sow dissensions among them: For Satan is to man an avowed enemy."[228]

8. Put your ego aside and be objective when discussing your problem. Try to use the collaborative dialogue that was discussed earlier under communication. Remember that the family institution is a sacred bond that each spouse should do her/his best to keep intact and healthy.

9. Remember that those who forgive, forget, and pardon others are considered from the poised ones for whom Allah prepared a great reward: a paradise that's width is as large as the heavens and the earth

No matter what happens, never go to bed with angry feelings toward your spouse. If you can't discuss the problem the same evening because of a shortage of time, at least set a suitable time to discuss it together later. This will help you to go to bed at night without ill feelings toward your spouse. Don't forget that this quality could lead you to paradise *insha'a Allah.*

---

[228] (Q17, V51)

8 - Common Marital Problems (Case Studies)

1- My wife talks too much

Laila is a committed wife who likes her husband *Abbas* very much. The couple has two little children aged one and three. They have one car that *Abbas* uses to go to work, *Laila* doesn't drive and she feels stuck at home with the children. *Laila* waits daily for *Abbas* to come back from his office in hopes of talking and chatting with him.

As soon as her husband arrives home, she starts talking and talking and talking without giving any consideration to the fact that her husband is probably tired and exhausted from a long day in the office. This behavior is very irritating to *Abbas*. He likes to rest for an hour or so as soon as he comes home but *Laila* doesn't give him the chance to do so. She always starts complaining about being alone for the whole day and says that he is not giving her enough attention or listening to her. *Laila* also complains that *Abbas* often goes out in the evening for other commitments. *Laila* tells him, "You don't love me any more, I'm here at home all day long and you don't even want to listen to me."

This problem is causing a lot of friction between *Abbas* and *Laila*. *Abbas* has repeatedly asked *Laila* to give him a chance to unwind from the pressures of work for an hour or so. *Laila,* on the other hand, feels and insists that it is her right after a long day of being alone with the children to get some attention and affection from *Abbas* right away.

Questions
1) Do you think this situation represents a problem?
2) What is the source of this problem?
3) What would your advice to *Abbas* be?
4) What would your advice to *Laila* be?
5) Do you have other suggestions to help avoid such a situation?

2- I would love to help my husband be a grateful son to his mom, but!

Raheemah and *Ahmad* have been married for five years and have one son, *Haytham* who is two years old. *Raheemah* and *Ahmad* are compatible in many areas and enjoy each other's company. Both of them are determined to live their lives according to Islam in order to earn Allah's pleasure.

Ahmad's mother has lived with them since they got married. Both of them agree that it is important to be very accommodative to *Ahmad*'s mother and make her feel at home.

Ahmad's mom is a very helpful person and likes to be in charge. *Raheemah* feels that *Ahmad*'s mom is always telling her what she should or shouldn't do regarding almost everything: housekeeping, cleaning, cooking, hosting guests, and so on. This makes *Raheemah* feel as though she can't do anything right. *Ahmad*'s mom also knows what *Ahmad* likes and always rushes to do these things for him which makes *Raheemah* feel insufficient.

If *Raheemah* feels like going to her room to lie down and read a book, or talking to her sister over the phone, she is always concerned that *Ahmad*'s mom will get offended.

Raheemah and *Ahmad* have been in agreement all along that they will raise their children using Islamic parenting techniques, even if they have to do things differently from their cultural practices. Whenever *Haytham* cries and *Raheemah* ignores his temper, *Ahmad*'s mom rushes to him and gives him what he desires in order to stop him from crying. Though *Raheemah* doesn't agree with this parenting method, she keeps quiet.

Raheemah has tried to talk to her husband about all of these situations over the course of the five years they have been married, but *Ahmad*'s response has always been, "Be patient, I don't want my mom to get offended."

Recently when *Ahmad*'s mom made a comment to *Raheemah* about how she should have cut the fruits before serving them, *Raheemah* answered politely saying, "It doesn't really matter. Fruits can be served in several ways." Later that evening, *Ahmad*'s mom commented to *Ahmad* that *Raheemah* doesn't like her living with them and that she is not accepting her help. *Ahmad* got upset with his wife *Raheemah* and asked her, "Why can't you treat my mother properly? Don't you know how important this is to me? Don't you know that paradise is under the mother's feet? I can't get to paradise if she is not pleased with me."

Questions
1) Is this a common problem when one of the in-laws lives with their married child?
2) Is this a serious problem and why?
3) What is the source of this problem?
4) How do you think the mother, *Ahmad*, and *Raheemah* feel in the midst of this situation?
5) What do you think the environment is like in *Ahmad* and *Raheemah*'s home? How is that going to affect little *Haytham*?
6) What could be done to improve the situation, if anything?
7) What would your advice to *Ahmad* and *Raheemah* be?

3- The Sister-in-law Dilemma

Waheeba and *Ali* have been married for the last four years. Their married life has been satisfactory without major problems. Ali has a sister whose name is *Safa'*. Occasionally *Waheeba* and *Safa'* get into arguments because of different points of view. Those arguments usually create an unpleasant situation within the house. At times, it even leads to an argument between *Waheeba* and *Ali*.

Waheeba feels that most of the time, *Ali* takes his sister *Safa'*s side. She feels that this is not fair, however, she has never discussed this thoroughly with *Ali*. One day, after a disagreement between *Waheeba* and *Safa'*, *Ali* interfered and ended the argument by instructing *Waheeba* to stop the discussion and apologize to *Safa'*. *Waheeba* felt very frustrated by *Ali*'s behavior. She shouted in a very disappointed voice: "You always take your sister's side. You are not being fair." She then rushed to her room crying and closed her door.

Questions
1) Do you think there is a problem in *Ali* and
Waheeba's relationship?
2) What do you think the reason for the problem is?
3) What would your advice to *Waheeba* be?
4) What would your advice to *Ali* be?
5) Do you know a situation similar to this one?
6) Do you think anything could have been done
to prevent such a problem from taking place?

4- If you don't eat it warm, you don't understand a thing!!

Hilal and *Hassenah* have been married for three years and they have a one-year-old daughter named *Safia*. Both *Hilal* and *Hassenah* are doing their post graduate studies at university. They often argue and fight together for no apparent reason.

One evening, *Hilal* and *Hassenah* invited some family friends over. Just before the arrival of the guests, *Hassenah* rushed to bake some desserts to serve to their guests. Shortly after the guests arrived, *Hilal* said to *Hassenah*, "Bring us the dessert now, it tastes so good when it's still warm." *Hassenah* answered,

"You want me to serve it warm. No way, this dessert should always be served cold." *Hilal* retorted, "What are you talking about, we always ate it hot at our home. Come on bring it now." *Hassenah* snapped back, "Anybody who eats it hot doesn't understand a thing!!!" *Hilal* hollered, "You're the one who doesn't understand a thing!" At this point the guests got quite embarrassed and uncomfortable and left after a short while, feeling bad about what had happened.

Questions
1) In your opinion, do you think the way *Hilal* and *Hassenah* treat each other represents a problem or not?
2) Do you think little fights between spouses stimulates the marriage or harms the marriage?
3) What do you think the reason for all these fights is?
4) How do you think both *Hilal* and *Hassenah* feel about fighting all the time and in front of their guests?
5) How do you think the guests feel about *Hilal* and *Hassenah* fighting while they are visiting?
6) What is your advice to *Hilal* and what is your advice to *Hassenah*?

5- I feel like we are growing apart

Zahida and *Tarek* have been married for four years and they have a son, *Ali*, who is one year old. *Zahida* is very concerned about her family, she feels that her relationship with *Tarek* is not at the level where it should be. *Zahida* feels that her and her husband are growing apart.

Before *Zahida* and *Tarek* got married, they spent a lot of time planning their life. They discussed their priorities and agreed that they will share their lives together. They both promised themselves that they wouldn't let "it" happen to them. They never wanted to turn into "the two strangers living under the same roof with a bunch of kids".

231

Since they got married, both *Zahida* and *Tarek* have been very busy and under a lot of pressure. *Tarek* has been working long hours to prove himself at work, while *Zahida* has been studying hard to get her college degree. They did not have much spare time, but with the little spare time they had, *Tarek* always wanted to spend it quietly with his wife at home or go on the internet, while *Zahida* desired to spend it going out on a walk or taking a hike at the park. Whichever way they ended up spending the time, one of them was always unsatisfied and displeased.

One year ago, Allah *SWT* blessed the couple with baby *Ali*. *Zahida* and *Tarek* were very happy to be blessed with *Ali* and are doing their best to take good care of him, which requires lots of time, particularly from *Zahida*

Tarek complains that even after *Ali* goes to bed, *Zahida* talks about him and nothing else and that this is beginning to annoy him very much. *Tarek* feels that as a couple they don't know how to talk about anything but *Ali*. *Tarek* tried a few times, without success, to try to get *Zahida* to talk about other subjects saying "*Zahida*, do you notice that all you ever talk about is *Ali*"? On the other hand, *Zahida* complains that *Tarek* doesn't put enough effort into sharing in the activities she enjoys. She says that other than eating and sleeping, they do nothing together.

Questions:
1) Is this a common problem
2) Is this a serious problem
3) What do you think the cause of the problem is?
4) *Tarek* and *Zahida* made a promise to themselves before they got married. What can they do to fulfill this promise?
5) Do you know of a similar situation?

6- He only thinks of his parents

Alia' and *Hamdy* have been married for the last 6 years with no major problems. *Hamdy's* parents are old and live in a different country. *Hamdy* is very kind to his parents. He calls them regularly over the phone at least once a week and sends expensive gifts to them frequently, at least once a month. He also tries to visit them every year during his vacation.

Because of the time he spends thinking, talking, visiting, and sending gifts to his parents, *Alia'* feels that *Hamdy* is neglecting some of his basic duties toward his family. This issue is becoming a continuous source of friction between *Alia'* and *Hamdy*.

Whenever *Alia'* asks *Hamdy* to put more time into the children's affairs and to pay more attention to his family's needs, he tells her, "I have to be good to my parents first and foremost, and in what ever time is left over I'll help the family."

Alia' complained to her parents about *Hamdy's* practice. Her parents replied by asking, "What is wrong with being good to your parents? You should help him rather than complain about it."

Alia' feels that what *Hamdy* is doing is going overboard and that he should allocate enough time for his immediate family. *Alia'* doesn't know what to do.

Questions
1) Do you think this is a common problem?
2) What do you think the reason for the problem is?
3) What would your advice to *Hamdy* be?
4) What would your advice to *Alia'* be?
5) Is there anything that could have been done to avoid such a problem?

7- My husband is rarely home

Hasan is a successful professional who works hard to provide for his family and help give a good image to Non-Muslims about Muslims in North America. He is married to *Na'eema* who is a home-maker.

Due to *Hasan*'s long working hours, *Na'eema* spends all day long lonely at home. She is bored with her life and doesn't know what to do. When *Hasan* comes back home, he is very exhausted and can't spend much time with *Na'eema* or help out with the house chores.

Because of this, *Na'eema* feels frustrated and her relationship with *Hasan* is strained. On the other hand *Hasan* feels he is under pressure from his office work and that he doesn't receive any support from *Na'eema* when he comes home.

Questions
1) Do you think this is a common problem?
2) What do you think the reason for the problem is?
3) How would you solve this problem?
4) What would your advice to *Na'eema* be?
5) What would your advice to *Hasan* be?

8- I can't enjoy a thing around him

Faten is a practicing Muslim lady who is married to *Sameer*, also a practicing Muslim. The couple has 3 children. *Faten* recently sought marriage counseling for herself and her husband. *Sameer* has a good job and works hard to ensure financial stability for his family. He is an achiever who likes to take his family for trips and buy them expensive clothing.

Faten complains that she is not enjoying her life because *Sameer* is always picking on her and blaming her for not doing a good enough job. He is very demanding; he wants the house to be tidy, clean, and spotless at all times. He wants the children to be A-plus students, well-behaved, and neat and orderly. He demands that *Faten* always prepares tasty, hot meals every day for the family. He also expects her to be cheerful and provide him with good company and requests that she stay up late at night to chat with him until he is ready to go to sleep. *Sameer* has very high expectations from his wife and never overlooks any shortcomings. She often feels insulted by his comments about her.

Sameer complains that *Faten* does not try hard enough, and that she keeps quiet for long hours and seems withdrawn and distant from him. She has little enthusiasm to visit family or friends or to stay up late to talk with him.

Questions
1) Do you believe that this is a serious problem?
2) What do you think the reason for the problem is?
3) How do you think *Faten* is feeling?
4) How important do you think good communication is in order to achieve a successful marriage?
5) What would your advice to *Sameer* be?
6) What would your advice to *Faten* be?

9- Where did my wife go?

Safia and *Hussain* got married four months ago. One morning, *Safia* went out to meet her friend *Haifaa'* so the two could go shopping together. *Safia* arranged with her husband *Hussain* that she would drive him to his work that day so she could keep the car with her. When *Haifaa'* arrived at the shopping mall, she brought another friend with her and introduced *Fatimah* to *Safia*. After they finished shopping, *Safia* offered to drive the two ladies back home. She dropped off *Haifaa'* first, and when she arrived at *Fatimah*'s home, *Fatimah* invited *Safia* to come in for a cup of tea. *Safia* tried to apologize, but *Fatimah* insisted. Finally, *Safia* accepted the invitation for fear of offending *Fatimah*. She stayed for a short visit.

When she returned home, she found a message from her husband *Hussain* on the voice mail. *Hussain* sounded very worried. He was trying to locate *Safia* for a while but didn't know where she was. *Safia* called her husband to let him know that she had arrived back home safely.

In the evening, when *Hussain* came home, they talked over the days events. *Hussain* told *Safia* not to go inside any home without letting him know first. This upset *Safia* because she felt this is too much control from *Hussain*.

Questions
1) Why do you think that *Hussain* got worried?
2) Why do you think *Safia* was upset? Would you feel upset if you were in her situation?
3) Do you think *Hussain's* worry is justified?
4) What is your advice to both *Safia* and *Hussain*

9- Anatomy of The Problems (Case Studies)

1- My wife talks too much

1- Do you think this situation represents a problem?
Yes, this situation represents a minor problem that could get bigger if it is not dealt with properly.

2- What is the source of this problem?
We think the problem is caused by lack of effective communication between *Laila* and *Abbas*.

3- What would your advice to *Abbas* be?
Abbas needs to work on creating a common understanding between himself and *Laila* regarding what happens after he comes home from work. *Abbas* has only been making comments in passing that express his need for some time to unwind and rest after work. It is very clear from *Laila*'s actions that she doesn't recognize this need. In this case, it's time for *Abbas* to move to a higher, clearer, level of communication. Maybe *Abbas* should set a time for a meeting with *Laila* where they can both discuss their different needs and come to a compromise that they can both agree on. The compromise could be something similar to the following: for a few days of the week, *Abbas* will have his rest after work, and then he will spend time with the family, either at home, or they can all go out together. For the remaining weekdays, *Abbas* will rest after work and then continue with his own activities. Another suggestion could be that *Abbas* drives *Laila* to a relative or a friend's house in the evenings when he is occupied by his own activities.

4- What would your advice to *Laila* be?
Laila needs to realize that when *Abbas* leaves home to go to work, he is not out enjoying himself and relaxing. Most probably, his work is tiring and takes a great deal of effort from him. *Laila* should be keen about providing a good environment

for *Abbas* to get the rest he needs. By doing this, *Laila* is contributing to the success of her marriage.

5- Do you have other suggestions to help avoid such a situation?
It is clear from the case that *Laila* feels that her life is empty. She lacks communication with adults. Here are some suggestions that could enrich *Laila*'s life and make her feel that she is doing something worthwhile:

♦ *Laila* should use part of her time to educate herself and increase her Islamic, parenting, and general knowledge. The plan should include *Qur'anic* memorization, *Ahadeeth* and *Tafseer*, learning positive parenting skills, etc. *Abbas* can help her in developing an educational plan with clear daily goals in order to give her day some structure. This will help *Laila* feel that she is achieving something valuable throughout her days.

♦ By applying the knowledge she learned about positive parenting skills with her children, *Laila* will be occupied in a very noble task and will spend more time helping her children grow up healthy and confident. Such an activity would fill her life and make her feel worthy.

♦ *Laila* should build a circle of friends with whom she can get in touch with over the phone, the internet, and occasionally visit. This will help decrease her need to chat and talk with *Abbas* when he is tired.

♦ *Abbas* could also help the situation by expressing his appreciation for the time and effort *Laila* contributes with the children and house chores.

♦ *Laila* and *Abbas* should work together to help *Laila* get her driver's license, which will make it possible for her to use the car sometimes on the weekends and after work. As well, whenever possible, *Laila* can drive *Abbas* to the office and use the car during the day.

Many stay-at-home young mothers don't usually see or feel the results of their efforts. Whatever they do today, they have to do again tomorrow and it never seems to end. The need to feel that they are achieving something and the need for some structure throughout their day are both pressing needs. This is why having a schedule for memorization and learning helps the mom. This schedule will also help make her more open to understanding the dad's situation.

Another important family issue that is relevant here, is that both husband and wife should feel comfortable enough to rest and unwind in their home. It is expected that they help each other feel this way. When *Laila* respects *Abbas's* need for rest, he will feel that she cares about him personally, not just about what he can provide for her. By the same token, when *Abbas* respects *Laila's* needs, she will feel that he cares for her personally, and not just about what she can provide for him. This will create a better understanding and a good long-term relationship between the two spouses.

2) I would love to help my husband be a grateful son to his mom, but!

1- Is this a common problem when one of the in-laws lives with their married child?
It looks like this is a common problem, particularly when the mother-in-law is living with her married son.

2- Is this a serious problem and why?
Yes, this is a serious problem because it strongly interferes with the relationship between the two spouses and destroys the feelings of compassion and kindness between them.

3- What is the source of this problem?
The problem is caused by *Ahmad's* mother's dominating nature and by a lack of leadership on *Ahmad's* side.

4- How do you think the mother, *Ahmad*, and *Raheemah* feel in the midst of this situation?

♦ *Ahmad*'s mom is in a power struggle with *Raheemah* in hopes of keeping the position of the one who is running the house. She is probably restless and unsatisfied.

♦ *Raheemah* is likely feeling upset, frustrated, disrespected, and helpless. She also probably feels disappointed and let down by her husband.

♦ *Ahmad* is likely feeling caught in the middle, confused, and that he can't please either his mom or his wife.

5- What do you think the environment is like in *Ahmad* and *Raheemah*'s home? How is that going to affect little *Haytham*?
The home environment is most likely tense, which will affect little *Haytham* negatively.

6- What can be done to improve the situation if anything?
In order to improve the situation, cooperation from the three parties involved is required. Also, applying Islamic rules and etiquettes is a must.

7- What would your advice to *Ahmad* and *Raheemah* be?
With the proper Islamic understanding, the right intentions, and sincerity, a problem like this one can be solved so that everyone can have peace of mind, enjoy life, and be rewarded from Allah *SWT*. It is in the best interest of *Ahmad*, *Raheemah*, and the mother to keep in mind that they are all accountable for every action that they do and will either be rewarded or punished for it. By looking at the situation from this perspective, much of the confusion will be cleared and many issues clarified. Problems like power struggles and inflexibility will disappear. No one will avoid offending a family member at the expense of standing by what is right. Every one will be willing to cooperate and reach out to the other family members in order to keep the evil one out of their relationship. All family members need to keep in mind that the evil one (*Shaytan*) will do his best to manipulate them and cause problems among them. We need to be alert to this fact and not take each other as enemies but, instead, unite against

Shaytan's manipulation. Here is a brief summary of related Islamic principles:

♦ The main purpose of forming a family is to establish and implement Allah's rules and etiquettes.

♦ Compassion, kindness, and love have to be the basis for the relationship between the husband and the wife. Both of them are required to take the steps that will maintain it.

♦ Every family member has basic general rights and duties that apply to all Muslims including the right to be treated with dignity and fairness. While applying the recommendations from *Qur'an* and *Ahadeeth* related to using the best manners with parents and being grateful to them, the basic rights of the spouse should still apply, and there should be no contradictions between the two.

♦ Justice and fairness is a basic Islamic principle for all relationships and dealings, including family relations. Allah *SWT* has instructed Muslims to be just in all situations. Also, the Prophet *SAAW* instructed us not to commit injustice because it is darkness on the day of judgment. He also taught us that one of the names of the day of judgment is the day of settling accounts on which each person will take their rights back from the person who wronged them or dealt with them unfairly.

♦ The relationship between husband and wife is highly targeted by the *shaytan*. The Prophet *SAAW* described this when he said that the closest evil ones to *Iblees* are the ones who cause divisions between husbands and wives.

♦ The husband, being the family leader and having the responsibility of *Qawamah,* has to take the steps required to ensure that justice is applied and observed within his family. Allah has given rights to the mother and the wife even in inheritance; balancing all of these rights is very important. In the absence of the husband's leadership, serious and damaging consequences take place where . . .

    o Family members start losing the sense that they should live and function as one unit.

- o Individualism becomes the way to do things and every family member feels that they only need to think about themselves, look for their best interest, and act accordingly.
- o A sense of carelessness and being cold toward other family members prevails over the family.
- o Little differences become big problems that take over the family environment.
- o The family becomes dysfunctional and everybody suffers.

Let us now see what specific things *Ahmad, Raheemah,* and the mother can do in order to keep their family functioning on the basis of compassion, love, and kindness.
Ahmad is advised to do the following:

♦ Fulfill his *Qawamah* role and work with both his mother and *Raheemah* to ensure that justice and fairness is observed in the family.

♦ Educate himself in order to have a clear, accurate, and true understanding of his duties toward his parents and toward his wife and learn how to balance all the rights of the different family members.

♦ *Ahmad* needs to listen to both his mother and his wife in order to have a fair judgment on the situation. He should not get upset at one of them as soon as he hears a complaint about her from the other one, before he listens to the other side of the story.

♦ *Ahmad* needs to realize that he is not doing his mother any favors by letting her behave the way she pleases when it comes to *Raheemah*'s rights. Hurting *Raheemah* and destroying the family are both bad deeds that won't help his Mother on the day of judgment. *Ahmad* needs to advise his mother regarding this matter as the Prophet *SAAW* said, "Support your brother whether he is being wronged or he is wronging somebody else."

The prophet was then told "we know how to support him when he is being wronged, but how do we support him when he is wronging others?"

The prophet replied, "By preventing him from wronging others."

♦ In this case, as the mother is the one who is unjustly complaining about the wife, *Ahmad* needs to assure the mother that *Raheemah* is very happy with the mother's stay and that she appreciates her help very much. *Ahmad* should also tell the mother that *Raheemah* likes her and that she's trying her best to make her happy, but she also needs some room to do things her way, and he should ask the mother to help with that. *Ahmad* also needs to comfort *Raheemah* with regards to his mother's interference in her life and express to her how much he really appreciates her patience and cooperation in dealing with his mom.

♦ *Ahmad* needs to be patient and make a lot of *dua'a* to Allah *SWT*.

Raheemah is advised to do the following:

♦ Make a lot of *dua'a* to Allah *SWT* to give her patience and ease the situation. She should remember that Allah rewards her every time she tries to control herself and do the right thing.

♦ Ask her husband for advice and suggestions on how to deal with the situation. She should be careful, however, not to show anger or resentment toward her husband or his mom, but keep her cool while dealing with this situation.

♦ *Raheemah* should try to deal with her mother-in-law in the best way, following the *Qur'anic* advice from *Surat Fussilat*[229]. She should be proactive and go the extra mile in order to make the mother feel that she really likes and appreciates her. *Raheemah* could, for example, make a point of asking the mother in a cheerful way "How are you this morning?" She could prepare a cup of tea, or a cup of

---

[229] (Q41, V34)

juice for her, take her shopping and ask for her advice, or buy her little gifts every now and then. *Raheemah* could even call *Ahmad*'s mother Mom, after getting her own mother's consent. All these kinds of actions from *Raheemah* will assure the mother that *Raheemah* welcomes her as part of the family and will remove any insecurities that the mother might have. The key here is to do all these things with patience and a smile and not to expect *Ahmad*'s mother to change right away; after all, *Raheemah* is rewarded by Allah for every kind action she does.

The mother is advised to do the following:

- ◆ Consider treating *Raheemah* as she would like her own daughter to be treated.
- ◆ She should have the right perspective about the whole situation, and realize that she is part of the family, along with her son *Ahmad* and her daughter-in-law *Raheemah*. However, *Ahmad* and *Raheemah* are the people in charge and she needs to let them take care of their responsibilities.
- ◆ The mother must realize that it is okay for *Raheemah* to handle things in different ways from what she is used to. She should be flexible and allow *Raheemah* enough room to explore and learn on her own rather than always ordering her around. By doing this, *Raheemah* will feel free to turn to the mother for advice whenever she needs it and will appreciate her help.
- ◆ The mother can always offer her help and let *Raheemah* know that she is more than happy to give a helping hand. However, she shouldn't impose her ideas on her daughter-in-law if she isn't asked for them.
- ◆ The mother should make an effort to make *Raheemah* feel comfortable in her own home. She should let her know that she's not offended if *Raheemah* needs to go to her room for a little rest or relaxation, or if she wants to go out for dinner with *Ahmad*. She could, for example, offer to *Raheemah* that she can take care of little *Haytham* while *Raheemah*

takes a nap or goes shopping or goes out with *Ahmad* once in a while.

♦ The mother has to keep in mind that she should be instrumental to her son's happiness with his wife. She should direct her efforts toward earning rewards from Allah through helping the family maintain the right atmosphere of compassion, love, and kindness. The mother should also use her time to pray, fast, read *Qur'an*, and learn more about getting close to Allah and being a better Muslim.

3) The Sister-in-Law Dilemma

Introduction: Problems with in-laws can be a major source of family conflict. In many situations, it negatively affects the husband-wife relationship, and, furthermore, it causes tension between them that affects their ability to positively parent their children. However, there is a lot of damage control that the husband and the wife can do, but they have to have the will for it as well as the proper Islamic knowledge. Many of these problems are caused by traditional cultural practices that are often contradictory to Islamic concepts.

1- Do you think there is a problem in the marriage relationship between *Ali* and *Waheeba*?
Yes, there absolutely is a problem

2- What do you think the reason for the problem is?
The problem is caused by *Ali*'s unwillingness to put effort into resolving and improving this situation and that leads to a lack of communication.

3- What would your advice to *Waheeba* be?
There are several different ways in which *Waheeba* can help improve her situation. The following are some suggestions:
a) *Waheeba* should try as hard as possible to diffuse any arguments with *Safa'* and not allow the arguments to escalate in the first place. She should try not to let trivial matters lead

to arguments. If *Waheeba* finds that her and *Safa'* have differing opinions on an issue that could potentially lead to an argument, she can make comments such as: "you may be right *Safa'*" or "that's one way of looking at it," etc. These kinds of comments can help stop the discussion from turning into a disagreement.

b) *Waheeba* can also make a point of taking that extra step to improve her relationship with *Safa'*. She should always remember that she is doing this with the intention of pleasing Allah first and foremost and in order to have a good family environment. *Waheeba* should be proactive and not reactive when dealing with *Safa'*. This means that she should not be turned away by *Safa'*'s interference in her life, but rather she should try to strengthen their relationship by making an effort to compliment *Safa'*, buying her little gifts, and helping her whenever possible.

Waheeba needs to be tactful when talking to *Ali* about her problems. She needs to bring up the issues at a good time, a time when she is not too emotional or angry. *Waheeba* also needs to choose her words carefully so that *Ali* does not feel that she is insulting his family or his sister and become defensive. Though this is challenging to do, *Waheeba* needs to be careful not to displace the anger she has for *Ali*'s family or sister onto *Ali*.

4- What would your advice to *Ali* be?
By asking *Waheeba* not to complain about his sister, *Ali* is conveying to her the message that no matter what his sister does, she is never at fault and, it is *Waheeba*'s responsibility to please *Safa'* under any condition. By acting this way, *Ali* is neither doing his sister nor his wife any favors. This will not solve the problem but, on the contrary, it will cause the situation to move from bad to worse. *Ali* has the responsibility of practicing some leadership in this matter and not let their relationship turn into a power struggle.

Ali needs to change his attitude regarding listening to his wife about her problem with his sister. It is his duty to listen to her, comfort her, and suggest some ways to improve the situation. Just by listening to *Waheeba* discuss her problems and by being understanding and empathetic, *Ali* will make her feel much better and she will consequently be more tolerant toward, and willing to deal with, other problems that might arise. If the friction between *Waheeba* and *Safa'* continues, and *Safa'* begins to go overboard by insulting *Waheeba* or greatly interfering to a point where it can no longer be overlooked or ignored by *Waheeba*, at this point, *Ali* needs to take action. *Ali* needs to talk with *Safa'* and bring to her attention that this is affecting his life negatively and that Islam advises us not to interfere with what does not concern us.

Ali needs to remember not to take sides. Whenever he feels that there is tension between *Waheeba* and *Safa'*, *Ali* should, in private with *Waheeba*, express his appreciation for her patience and willingness to accommodate different points of view. He could make such comments as: "May Allah accept your efforts," "*Masha* Allah, you're open-minded," or "I appreciate you being so accommodative."
(Note: *Ali* should do this in a manner that does not include any backbiting or undermining of his sister.)

Ali could also express his appreciation to *Waheeba* by frequently complimenting her, bringing her little gifts, and doing her favors.

Ali can also ease the personality clash between his sister and his wife by privately mentioning good things about each one of them to the other one. For example, when he is alone with *Waheeba* he can mention to her that *Safa'* thinks highly of her and when he is alone with *Safa'*, he can tell her the good things that *Waheeba* has said about her.

5- Do you know a situation like this?

6- Do you think anything could have been done to prevent such a problem from taking place?

Yes, there are several things that could help prevent this situation from occurring:

a) First, both spouses need to have the proper Islamic knowledge of how to balance the spouse's rights with the rights of the family.

b) Communication is key. *Ali* and *Waheeba* should always aspire to have an excellent channel of communication open, where they can comfortably discuss any issues that arise in a comprehensive and calm way.

4) If you don't eat it warm, you don't understand a thing!!

1- In your opinion, do you think the way *Hilal* and *Hassenah* treat each other represents a problem or not?

Of course it represents a problem. Spousal relationships should be based on mutual respect, *Mawadah,* and *Rahmah.* When two spouses argue and fight for no obvious reasons, this is not a good sign. It doesn't provide a good family atmosphere for the growth of a positive spousal relationship and the healthy development of the children.

2- Do you think little fights between spouses stimulate the marriage or is it bad for it?

Fights, in any way, shape, or form, whether little or big, have a bad effect on any marriage. It leaves ill feelings in the hearts of spouses and creates a gap between them. It is a myth that little fights stimulate marriage. The least damage that fights would cause in any marriage is feelings of resentment among spouses. However, it is very likely that the spouses may have different opinions concerning some minor or major issues. There is no harm in that, as long as it is dealt with properly, and each of them respects the other's opinion and doesn't undermine or insult her/him. Also, some couples like to tease each other, and there may be a situation where one of them is big on teasing while the other is not used to it. It is advised that they should have certain guidelines to make sure that teasing doesn't create problems or cause one of the spouses to feel hurt. The following guidelines are recommended:

♦ Don't insult or imply any personal deficiency even in a subtle message of teasing

♦ Stop teasing as soon as you see that it is not appreciated by the other spouse

♦ Be sensitive to how your spouse responds to your teasing. Observe verbal as well as non-verbal responses, such as your spouse becoming withdrawn, quiet, or giving you a wide-eyed surprised look.

While teasing under the above guidelines is okay, crossing the limits mentioned above may hurt feelings and create a distance between the spouses. In many cases, the spouse who is hurt either withdraws or waits for an opportunity to take revenge through an insulting teasing comment to the other spouse. This may become continuous and is, no doubt, destructive to the loving, caring relationship between the couple. It is better to let your spouse know that you don't feel comfortable with this teasing and ask him/her to stop it in a firm but gentle way. Some couples also make insulting teasing comments about a member of their spouses' family. This practice is not healthy and has a bad effect on the marital relationship; as such, it should be completely avoided.

3- What do you think is the reason for all of those fights?
In order to get to the bottom of the problem, it is important to think about why *Hilal* and *Hassenah* are fighting for no apparent reason. It could be that they are treating each other like they used to treat their buddies or friends, not realizing that the marriage relationship is different and needs more consideration and sensitivity in the way the couple interacts with each other.

4- How do you think both *Hilal* and *Hassenah* felt fighting all the time and in front of their guests?

I expect that both *Hilal* and *Hassenah* must have felt bad about fighting all the time. One of the bad consequences of fighting is that a power struggle between the two spouses ensues where each one of them is fighting to gain control over the situation. *Hilal* and *Hassenah* must also have felt embarrassed for fighting in front of their guests.

5- How do you think the guests felt about *Hilal* and *Hassenah*'s fighting while they were visiting them?
The guests must have felt embarrassed, insulted, uncomfortable, and out of place.

6- What is your advice to both *Hilal* and *Hassenah*?
Hilal and *Hassenah* need to take a serious look at their marriage and the way they are treating each other. They need to sit down together and come up with a plan in order to start correcting their attitudes and begin working together toward a strong relationship that will, *Insha'a Allah*, last for life. They also need to go through the process of *tazkeiatu annafs* to help them control the way they deal with each other, stop insulting one another, and treat each other with respect.

5) I feel like we are growing apart

1- Is this a common problem?
Yes it is a common problem, especially in the first few years of marriage.

2- Is this a serious problem?
We believe it is a serious problem because it affects the feelings of each one of them toward the other. Usually each spouse is left with the impression that the other spouse doesn't care about his/her feelings and needs. This becomes a vicious cycle that creates a huge gap between the couple.

3- What do you think the cause of the problem is?

The cause of this problem can be summarized in the following:

♦ Both *Tarek* and *Zahidah* consider their own needs to be the most important to them and don't consider the needs of the other spouse as legitimate or as important as their own needs.

♦ The expectations of *Tarek* from his wife and the expectations of *Zahidah* from her husband were never discussed in detail or mutually agreed upon. Each one of them has certain expectations from the other but has never communicated these expectations clearly to their partner.

4- *Tarek* and *Zahidah* made a promise to themselves before they got married. What can they do to fulfill this promise?

Most probably, *Tarek* and *Zahidah* have seen a model of "the two strangers living under the same roof" and they didn't like it, and that is why they made this promise before marriage. However, sometimes things are easier said than done. It is not enough just to theoretically believe in something. It takes effort, hard work, self-discipline, and a strong will to change oneself. But above all, it takes an open minded attitude. Both *Tarek* and *Zahidah* may agree on the principle that it is important to compromise, but when it is actually time to compromise and sacrifice one's preference, s/he doesn't feel like doing this, and thinks that it is not fair, and that her/his need is more important. They get into the attitude of "if he/she really loves me, he/she would do it for me"

Before we discuss what both of them can do together to fulfill their promise, we would like to remind the reader that all the ingredients of a successful marriage we mentioned in chapter four as well as throughout this book will certainly help make things easier.

Let us now see what both can do together to fulfill their promise:

♦ **Be indispensable**; Both *Tarek* and *Zahidah* may like to consider making themselves indispensable to each other. There is a great benefit for this. It cements and bonds the two spouses together at an emotional level, as the memories they have about the time they spend together are highlighted by a feeling of comfort, satisfaction, and joy. Each of them would feel that the best time they ever had is when they are around each other. If *Tarek* is away on a business trip, *Zahidah* would really miss him and would be eager for him to come back. If *Zahidah* is away visiting her parents, *Tarek* would be counting the days, eagerly awaiting her arrival.

♦ **Learn to compromise in a graceful way**; Compromise is a basic requirement for the success of any relationship. A spouse, who puts his/her partner's needs ahead of his/her own, is sending a strong message of love, consideration, and sincerity. No message could be more powerful than this, even gifts or a thousand "I love you" notes. On the same token, a return of the compromise by taking turns in putting the other spouses' desires first is an assuring message that the love is mutual. If the same spouse keeps giving in to her/his partner's need and, hence, keeps putting off his/her own needs, they will end up feeling rejected and uncared for. He/she will feel like all his/her partner cares about is the service he/she provides, not he/she personally. No matter how many times they hear, "I love you", they won't believe it; it will sound phony to them. At this point, he/she will begin to feel resentment and question whether he/she should compromise at all. He/she will also start taking a new stand on the way he/she deals with his/her spouse.

Whenever spouses compromise, they need to do it in a graceful way and with willingness and acceptance, otherwise, it doesn't carry a loving message.

♦ **Keep in touch**; It is very important that the two spouses keep in touch at an emotional level, such that each one of them is assured that her/his partner still strongly loves and cares for her/him. In a busy life such as that of our times, people are always living under pressure. *Tarek* and *Zahidah* need to get away from the every day routine, and spend a little time, just the two of them. They can arrange to leave the baby with a family member or a friend. Going for a walk twice a week, lunch or dinner in a restaurant once every couple of months, or a picnic at the park for an afternoon, will help them stay in touch. Such outings will give them an opportunity to listen to each other's concerns, exchange ideas, and brainstorm solutions to the issues occupying their minds. This requires willingness from both of them. Also, *Zahidah* should talk to *Tarek* about how she feels. This will help the relationship stay on the right track as long as it is done in a caring way and not a blaming way. *Tarek* and *Zahidah* should also consider reading a book together or following up on each other's *Qur'anic* memorization, even if it is just a couple of verses a week.

♦ **Keep the romance alive**; To enrich their relationship and stop it from turning into a dry mechanical one, *Zahidah* and *Tarek* should do their own little things to keep the romance alive. Writing notes of kind words and buying each other little gifts is one way to do it. Also doing something special for one another is a great idea; for example, *Zahidah* could prepare Tarek's favourite meal, and *Tarek* could prepare breakfast in bed for *Zahidah* every now and then.

♦ **Maximize efforts and time**; *Tarek* and *Zahidah* need to learn to be more efficient and organized. This can save them a lot of effort and allow the couple to have some free time. Preparing simple meals rather than complicated ones, and considering cooking enough for two to three days at once may be a good idea for their purposes.

♦ **Be patient and allow room for adjustment**; Both *Tarek* and *Zahidah* need to allow each other some room while adjusting to the new perspective of looking at things. They need to overlook any behavior that might look too withdrawn or resentful and give the other spouse enough time and room to adjust and accept the new situation.

5- Can you relate to this problem or know of a similar situation?

6- He only thinks of his parents

1- Do you think this is a common problem?
This problem is a serious one. It is causing continuous, ongoing friction between the two spouses and changing the home environment to a cold and tense one.

.

2- What do you think is the reason for the problem?
The problem is caused by *Hamdy*'s unwillingness and inability to balance the distribution of his resources (time, money) among his loved ones.

3- What would your advice to *Hamdy* be?
Hamdy needs to learn the real meaning of the Islamic concept of justice and then apply it in his life. Whether it is his parents or his wife and children, they all have rights over him. Justice is about balancing all of their rights. According to Islam, no one should ignore his parents and only take care of his spouse and children. At the same time, Islam teaches us not to ignore our spouse and children and only take care of our parents. The *Qur'anic* verse admonishes us to be fair in our dealings:

$$\text{"اعْدِلُواْ هُوَ أَقْرَبُ لِلتَّقْوَى"}$$

"..act equitably, that is nearer to piety"[230]
The fact that, in the distribution of inheritance, Allah *SWT* made sure that there are designated portions for various family members indicates that there are rights for everyone and that these rights should be observed. Not only did Allah *SWT* give certain shares to parents, but He also entitled other family members to specific shares.

In addition, the *Hadeeth* of the prophet *SAAW* also instructs us to give each one his/her due rights.

4- What would your advice to *Alia'* be?

---

[230] (Q5, V8)

Alia' needs to continue being patient while working on improving the situation. *Alia'* should realize that changing *Hamdy*'s perspective in this matter will probably take some time and effort. Here are a few suggestions that *Alia'* should consider:

a) *Alia'* needs to discuss this matter with her husband in depth rather than making passing comments about this issue. We suggest that . . .

   - She sets a time with *Hamdy* for discussion
   - She assures *Hamdy* that she fully agrees and supports him in looking after his parents.
   - She gets *Hamdy*'s feedback on what he thinks is the best way of taking care of the family as a whole including his parents, the children, and both of them so that everybody is looked after, no one is neglected, and justice is applied in a way that will please Allah *SWT*. She could refer back to the *hadeeth* that states to give everybody his rights[231].

   "فاعط كل ذي حق حقه"

   - She could suggest to *Hamdy* that, in order to base their actions on firm Islamic knowledge, they need to do research on this matter rather than asking the imam scattered questions about the rights of parents' on their children. The research should be about the Islamic perspective on how to balance fulfilling one's duties toward parents vs. fulfilling one's duties toward his/her spouse and children. For the purpose of the research, they could use authentic Islamic books and clarify their research findings, or any doubts they might have, through talking to the imam, knowledgeable members of the community, or sending their questions to a well-known imam or an Islamic research organization.

Alia' needs to be extra careful not to let any resentful feelings she might have toward *Hamdy* or his parents show through her comments or actions with her children in order to avoid the children having a negative image of their father or grandparents.

---

[231] Al Bukhari and At-Termezi

For example, *Alia'* shouldn't make comments such as, "Sorry kids, we can't afford sending you to swimming classes because your Dad sent all the money to your grandparents."

5- Is there anything which could have been done to avoid such a problem?
To avoid such a problem, both *Hamdy* and *Alia'* could have done their share.

As for *Hamdy*, first he should have checked and clarified the Islamic validity of his concept of how to look after his parents and be good to them while still fulfilling his duties toward his wife and children. *Hamdy* should have balanced the distribution of his time and money in order to be fair to both his parents needs and his wife and children's needs. Second, *Hamdy* should have included his wife and children in his efforts to take care of and express his love and gratitude toward his parents. For instance, by encouraging and helping his wife and children to write letters to their grandparents and sending them along with their family photos, *Hamdy* will also be helping the growth of a special, loving relationship between his wife and children and his parents. By considering visiting his parents with his family, instead of alone, *Hamdy* will help the bond between them grow. This might mean that *Hamdy* will have to space his visits out a little more. For example, instead of going to visit his parents once a year alone, *Hamdy* can try to go once every second year and take one of his children with him.

As for *Alia'*, she could have helped avoid this problem by being proactive. This means that once she sensed the presence of this problem, she should have sat with her husband and discussed this matter and took the necessary steps to improve this situation (the steps mentioned above) before the situation got worse.

7- My husband is rarely home

1- Do you think this is a common problem?
Yes, for sure this is a common problem as many families can relate to this situation.

2- What do you think is the reason for the problem?
Obviously the reason for the problem is *Na'eema's* lack of understanding of the reality of her family situation. It is clear that *Hasan* is away from home for valid, legitimate reasons. It is hard to keep a job in today's very competitive environment and the husband is the one responsible for earning the living for the family.

3- How would you solve this problem?
In order to solve this problem, *Hasan* and *Na'eema* need to have a common understanding of the reality of their situation. Both need to cooperate and contribute to their marriage's success. Both need to share in carrying the family responsibilities. While *Hasan* is working long hours to provide for the family, *Na'eema* needs to look after other family responsibilities and be supportive.

4- What would your advice to *Na'eema* be?
The following is our advice to *Na'eema*:
- Understand the reality of your family situation.
- Stop making negative comments about *Hasan* to anybody and everybody.
- Try to help save some of *Hasan's* time by taking care of as many family responsibilities as possible, such as grocery shopping, banking, taking care of the bills, etc.
- Regarding the community work, instead of blaming *Hasan* for his contribution, *Na'eema* needs to volunteer her own time and be part of community planning and activities. The more volunteers the community has, the less the burden is on every volunteer.

♦ Talk to the children about how caring and loving their dad is. Let them know that when he is not around he is working hard to make things better for the whole family and the Muslim community.

♦ In an effort to compensate for *Hasan*'s long working hours, *Na'eema* should take care of planning activities with the children. By doing all the legwork that consumes time, *Na'eema* will make it easier for *Hasan* to be involved in the family affairs and all can enjoy each other's company.

♦ By understanding that community volunteer work is a necessity for the survival of generations to come and will help establish and maintain a Muslim identity, *Na'eema* has the chance to earn rewards from her husband's involvement if she makes the right intention. Whenever her husband is outside helping take care of community matters, *Na'eema* should accept his absence, support him in every way she can, and make her intention clear that they are both partners in this volunteer work.

5- What would your advice to *Hasan* be?
The following is our advice to *Hasan*:

♦ *Hasan* should make an effort to clarify *Na'eema*'s understanding of the reality of their family's situation. Perhaps, he should put aside some time where the two of them can discuss openly how to make everybody happy. He should invite *Na'eema* to bring up any alternatives that she thinks they, as a family, should consider so he can spend more time with the family. The two should discuss all these suggestion together and agree on a certain course of action.

♦ *Hasan* should let *Na'eema* know how bad he feels when she constantly complains to others and ask her gently to stop this kind of behavior.

♦ *Hasan* should explain the importance of community work and why he has to be involved. He should remind her about the great reward that lies in community work. He should even encourage her to get involved and help her start volunteering.

- *Hasan* should talk to his wife about the importance of having a good, warm family atmosphere, where two parents are working together and not openly criticizing each other. He should point out the effect of this atmosphere on the healthy development of their children and on a good long-term spousal relationship.
- *Hasan* should make an effort to allocate some time to share certain activities with *Na'eema* that bring them closer and strengthen their bond. For example, they can agree about certain books she can read and then summarize her findings to him weekly. Also, they can try to take a family vacation where they can spend time doing activities together and bond, even if it is only for a week every year. This way, they are putting in extra effort to keep their personal relationship healthy and flourishing instead of blaming one another and becoming distant.

8- I can't enjoy a thing around him

1- Do you believe that this a serious problem?
Yes, we believe this problem is quite serious and in the long term, if not dealt with, may cause grave damage.

2- What do you think the reason for the problem is?
The problem is basically caused by *Sameer*'s wrong attitude and to a lesser extent, *Faten*'s inability to make him realize that his attitude is destructive.

3- How do you think *Faten* is feeling?
Faten probably feels overwhelmed, upset, helpless, and frustrated. She may be loosing confidence in herself because no matter how hard she tries, she is not able to please her husband. *Faten* may also feel isolated because she doesn't know who to turn to for help with her problem and isn't sure if anybody would understand her situation.

4- How important do you think good communication is in order to achieve a successful marriage?

Indeed good communication is an important and key factor in achieving a successful marriage as we indicated in detail in chapter four. Usually, when two people get married, they bring different backgrounds, different expectations, and different ways of dealing with issues to the marriage. Good communication ensures that spouses will be able to understand each other's points of view and get closer to one another. If the communication between the spouses is bad, the gap will increase between the two of them, and a misunderstanding is more likely to occurr. If this is left for long, ill feelings may develop toward each other and the gap will widen more and more. Bridging such a gap will be difficult; small problems will keep escalating and may lead to a disaster. This, in turn, will strain the relationship and could destroy the marriage. No doubt, good communication is a great asset for a successful marriage.

5- What would your advice to *Sameer* be?

We would like to remind *Sameer* of the following:

♦ Marriage in Islam is based on compassion and effective, loving communication (*Mawadah* and *Rahamah*). These two wonderful qualities should be the bases for all dealings among spouses and family members. *Sameer*'s high expectations of his wife should not be an excuse to order her around and pick on her. If he is trying to get her to do more good actions and good deeds and use her time more efficiently, he should do it in a gentle, loving, and gradual way. Pushing, criticizing, and undermining *Faten's* efforts is only going to discourage her more and more.

♦ People have different potentials and abilities. *Sameer* should not judge his wife's abilities based on his own abilities. The prophet *SAAW* said, "Whatever I ordered you to do, do as much as you can." If *Sameer* is interested in helping *Faten* use her time more efficiently, instead of picking on her and demeaning her efforts, he should give her a helping hand so she can learn through his actions.

- Pushing someone to do more than s/he could handle, does not work. On the contrary, it sets them back. *Sameer* needs to be realistic about his expectations from his wife, otherwise he will burden her and she will get resentful toward him. The prophet *SAAW* said,

"إن المنبت لا أرضاً قطع ولا ظهراً أبقى"

"The one who pushes himself beyond his limits, exhausts his means, doesn't reach his goals, and gets burnt out" [232]

- *Sameer* should keep a cheerful and easy-going attitude. He should try to overlook minor shortcomings and appreciate and encourage every little effort from his wife's side. This will encourage *Faten* to continue improving and try her best to do more. The prophet *SAAW* recommended that we have this attitude by saying, "Allah will have mercy on an easy-going cheerful servant of His when he buys, sells, and in all other dealings."

- *Sameer* should not interfere in all areas of *Faten*'s responsibilities such as house keeping affairs, kitchen matters, personal issues, etc. The prophet *SAAW* said, "One of the signs that the person has a solid belief is that he doesn't interfere in others' affairs." *Sameer* should give his wife some room to experiment and come up with her own ways of doing things. *Sameer* should train himself to accept his wife's way, as there is no rule for what is right and what is wrong in these matters. All these are minor issues and it is better to have a good spousal relationship than to do everything your way.

6- What would your advice to *Faten* be?

Faten is advised to keep practicing patience and make *dua'a* to Allah *SWT* to ease the situation. She also shouldn't give up on her husband or their relationship together. *Faten* should try to convey a clear message to her husband about how she feels when he treats her the way he does. She could talk to him about how she feels hurt and insulted, and ask him gently to try to treat her

---

[232] Al-Bazzar

differently. If comments in passing don't work, she should set aside a time to talk about this matter with him. Another idea is to write a letter to him explaining the situation from her point of view.

Faten should make it clear to her husband that she is keen about improving their relationship and their marriage based on her understanding of the *hadeeth* of the prophet *SAAW*,

"جهاد المرأة حسن التبعل"

"The *Jihad* (struggle) of a woman is in being a good wife"[233]

If *Faten* feels that she is not able to improve the situation because her husband is not responding, and she still feels bad about how he treats her, she should then seek counseling through a trusted, good Muslim who can help with this matter.

9- Where did my wife go?

1- Why do you think that *Hussain* got worried?
Hussain got worried about *Safia* because he didn't know where she was or what was going on with her. *Hussain* didn't know if *Safia* was safe or not and whether he should be doing anything to ensure her safety. He felt worried about her because he is responsible for her protection and safety.

2- Why do you think *Safia* was upset? Would you feel upset if you were in her situation?
Safia was upset because she felt that *Hussain* was being over protective and limiting her freedom and her movement. *Safia* was also concerned about how this would affect her ability to make friends. For example, if she has to call to check with *Hussain* before going somewhere and she can't reach him, what

---

[233] Alkafy volume 5 page 507

should she do then? *Safia* also felt frustrated as she would be embarrassed in front of her friends if she has to call her husband before she can make a decision.

We think many wives might feel upset as the first reaction when in *Safia's* situation.

3- Do you think *Hussain's* worry is justified?
We believe that *Hussain's* reaction was very normal. It is justified as long as he explains to his wife that his feelings of responsibility toward her safety is the source of his worries.

4- What is your advice to both *Safia* and *Hussain*?
Safia and *Hussain* got married just a little while ago. They are at the stage of getting to know each other at a deeper level. They are learning about each other's moods, worries, needs, concerns, and so on. It is important that they be sensitive toward each other and use the best manners while communicating their concerns and feelings to one another.

Hussain probably viewed *Safia's* spontaneous action of going into the home of a lady she had just met for the first time as irresponsible. He got worried that this would be her pattern of behavior. On the other hand, *Safia* viewed her husband's demand as controlling and she got worried that this would be his pattern of behavior. Since this incident occurred at the beginning of their marriage, this is understandable. When *Safia* and *Hussain* spend more time together as a married couple, each one of them will know more about his/her spouse's personality. *Safia* will most probably discover that *Hussain* is not as controlling as she thought, and *Hussain* will probably discover that *Safia* is not an irresponsible person. Both of them will gain more trust in each other, which will enable them to react in a more relaxed way toward each other in situations like this.

Meanwhile *Safia* and *Hussain* should discuss and agree about the general rules regarding this matter. Their rules should be based on the fact that Islam requests the wife to seek her husband's permission before she leaves the house. They should be accommodative and sensitive to each other's feelings throughout the process. For example, they could agree that she can go to common places such as the market, shopping mall, out for a walk in the neighborhood, taking the children to the park or the doctor's clinic without previous notification to her husband, but inform him just before she leaves home or leave him a message on his answering machine. *Safia* needs to call her husband when she is out from time to time and let him know where she is and that she is okay. They also have to agree among themselves about the rule for visiting close friends and family members.

10 - Family Stages: The Husband/Wife Relationship at Different Stages

Introduction

In this chapter, *insha'a Allah* we will discuss the various stages involved in forming a family after getting married in detail. We will accompany the reader on a wonderful journey starting with the day the newlyweds consummate the marriage and start living together and ending with the stage of the empty nest after all the children grow up and leave the family home to start their own lives. During this trip, we will stop at several stations to explore the beauty of each one of them as well as the associated challenges. These stations include, but are not limited to " The Sweet Critical **Two**", "Forming a Family, the Stage of Having Children" covering pregnancy with its beauties and pains, delivery, children taking over, the early years and their problems, going out with children, school years and teen problems, and then children growing up and leaving home to start their own lives. Let us now start our interesting journey and explore these wonderful stages in more detail.

The Sweet, Critical Two

What do we mean by the sweat, critical two? We mean the first two years of marriage. They are the sweetest two years in the life of marriage, if both spouses learn how to live them properly, yet, at the same time, they are the most critical years for the marriage's success.

They are sweet because everything is new, and both spouses are exploring a new life. Finally, they are living together as husband and wife. Finally, they are managing their own affairs without other people's interference, and it is completely up to them, *insha'a Allah*, to make a successful life for themselves living in a sacred bond. These exact reasons also make the first two years critical. Everything is new for them, and they may not know how to deal with certain situations in the proper way that will ensure the continuation of a healthy relationship.

These two years are sweet because both spouses are experiencing, for the first time in their lives, this closeness and lawful intimacy with its intense feelings, experiencing how important it is for each of them to try her/his best to please and satisfy the physical needs of the other partner. It is critical for the same reason, namely because this is a new experience and so many things could go wrong if both spouses are not careful in the way they approach this matter. Yes, it is critical and one way to avoid mistakes in this stage is by following the manners and etiquettes of spousal intimacy derived from the teachings of Prophet Mohammad *SAAW* and by being very careful and gentle toward each other's feelings.

The sweetness of these two years is very clear. Both spouses are excited to have a partner for life. They can feel for each other and experience new things together. This is very fulfilling, pleasing, and satisfying for both of them. Finally, they are now married and living together. These years are critical for both of them because they are now detached from the bigger family of each, with all the feelings that is associated with this separation such as missing siblings and parents, missing the way they did things as well as various emotional memories. This is especially obvious when the newlyweds move to another city after marriage.

They are sweet because of the change in social status and the increased feelings of independence. Yet they are critical because each spouse has to work hard to build this new relationship with the other spouse. They both have to adjust to the new environment and learn how to compromise at levels that are different from the compromises they are used to with their siblings and parents. They also have to train themselves to keep feeling good about the other spouse, even if there are differences that may arise from the different wants and needs of each.

They are sweat because now the newlyweds have their own home and on the way to forming their new nuclear family. Yet they are critical because it is time for those same newlyweds with all those overwhelming feelings to carry the new full responsibility of running a home with all its chores as well as the new social obligations.

These two years are sweet because it is the time for building the foundation of this new relationship. This foundation is very important for the health of their relationship until they part. They are excited to face such challenges. Yet, it is critical because building this foundation is not a simple or trivial matter. If anything goes wrong in their efforts to build this foundation, the results could have a long lasting effect on this relationship that may not impact their lives in the first few years, but may manifest itself in so many problems in the later years of marriage.

These years are so sweet because the love and compassion of each spouse toward the other is so intense and new, and the feelings are so nice and fresh. Yet they are critical because one of the spouses may react to these feelings in an exaggerated way, which may affect the other spouse negatively. Although these feelings may settle down later, and the conflict may be resolved, it may leave bad feelings in the later years if both spouses didn't handle the situation in the best possible way.

They are sweet, as we mentioned, because the wife now has her own home, her own nest. She is now the lady of the house. The whole domain is hers. Yet, because of the same reason, there are now new rules to follow, with her husband. These rules come with the territory. Now she has to adjust to the idea that her husband has a say about her being outside the house. She has to get his approval before visiting other families and friends, and he has to know her whereabouts all the time. This may be critical in the beginning and could be a source of friction and conflicts.

Forming a Family, the Stage of Having Children

Although some couples may be blessed with children in the first year of their marriage, most newlyweds nowadays wait for a few years before having children. It is important that spouses be there for each other during all stages of marriage. Each stage has new and different challenges, and spouses should adjust and try to be the best supporters of each other during these stages. Let us discuss the challenges during these stages, their impact on the spousal relationship, and the proven remedy to make sure the marital relationship is kept intact, strong, and healthy during these times:

Pregnancy and Delivery
There is no doubt that the pregnancy and delivery stage is very enjoyable, but, at the same time, is very tough, particularly on wives. In more than one location in the Qur'an, Allah SWT points out this fact to us. He says,

"وَوَصَّيْنَا الْإِنسَانَ بِوَالِدَيْهِ حَمَلَتْهُ أُمُّهُ وَهْنًا عَلَى وَهْنٍ وَفِصَالُهُ فِي عَامَيْنِ أَنِ اشْكُرْ لِي وَلِوَالِدَيْكَ إِلَيَّ الْمَصِيرُ"

" And We have enjoined upon man goodness toward his parents: his mother bore him by bearing strain upon strain, and his utter dependence on her lasted two years. Be grateful toward Me and your parents. With Me all journeys end"234

He also says,

وَوَصَّيْنَا الْإِنسَانَ بِوَالِدَيْهِ إِحْسَانًا حَمَلَتْهُ أُمُّهُ كُرْهًا وَوَضَعَتْهُ كُرْهًا وَحَمْلُهُ وَفِصَالُهُ ثَلَاثُونَ شَهْرًا حَتَّى إِذَا بَلَغَ أَشُدَّهُ وَبَلَغَ أَرْبَعِينَ سَنَةً قَالَ رَبِّ أَوْزِعْنِي أَنْ أَشْكُرَ نِعْمَتَكَ الَّتِي أَنْعَمْتَ عَلَيَّ وَعَلَى وَالِدَيَّ وَأَنْ أَعْمَلَ صَالِحًا تَرْضَاهُ وَأَصْلِحْ لِي فِي ذُرِّيَّتِي إِنِّي تُبْتُ إِلَيْكَ وَإِنِّي مِنَ الْمُسْلِمِينَ

---

234 (Q31, V14)

268

"We have enjoined upon man goodness toward his parents. In pain did his mother bear him and in pain did she give him birth: and her bearing him and his utter dependence on her took thirty months; until when he attains his maturity and reaches forty years, he says: My Lord! grant me that I may give thanks for Thy favour which Thou hast bestowed on me and on my parents, and that I may do good which pleases Thee and do good to me in respect of my offspring; surely I turn to Thee, and surely I am of those who submit."[235]

This fact is also emphasized by the prophet *SAAW* in the incident that is narrated by *Boraidah* after his father:

أن رجلاً كان في الطواف حاملاً أمّه يطوف بها فسأل النبي صلى الله عليه

وسلم هل أديت حقها ؟ قال : "لا .. ولا بزفرة واحدة"

"A man was making *Tawaf* around the *Ka'bah*, while he is carrying his mother to perform *Tawaf*. He asked the prophet *SAAW*, 'Did I repay and fulfill her due rights?'

The prophet *SAAW* said, 'No, not even one moment of the delivery time'"[236]

All of the above is a clear indication that pregnancy and delivery is not an easy matter. There are physical and psychological changes happening to the wife. Her emotions are being tested and she is going through a completely new experience, especially with the first pregnancy. Coupling this with the absence of the extended family for most Muslims living in North America, pregnant wives indeed go through a very tough time. In some cases they become very sensitive to the extent that the jokes and teasing that they may have accepted earlier from their husbands or close friends may not be acceptable now. As such, a husband has a great role to play during this stage. It is mainly a role of support, encouragement, and help. He should be gentler and kinder during these tough

---

[235] (Q46, V15)
[236] Al-Bazar

269

months leading to delivery. He must do extra chores at home. If his time doesn't permit him to do this, he should seek help by hiring somebody to take care of certain house chores to relieve his wife of part of the burden.

Taking good care of his wife's health is another important area for the husband to attend to during this stage. Ensuring regular visits to the family physician and/or gynecologist for check ups and follow-ups on the fetus' development and its general health is very important. Husbands who are caring and express concern about their wives' health situation provide much needed support at this stage and ensure the continuation of a healthy relationship.

Children Take Over
After the excitement of delivery and the arrival of the new baby, the challenges of coping with an entirely new lifestyle at home start. This may be taxing on the marital relationship if spouses are not emotionally and physically ready for this stage. Babies and young children have special needs that must be fulfilled immediately. These needs can't be postponed or delayed until spouses feel that the time is suitable for them. For example, in the first few months after the delivery of every new baby, lack of sleep is a main source of pressure on the family, particularly the mother. Cooperation from the husband in helping his spouse is a must during these demanding and exhausting times. Maybe once every couple of nights, the husband should help with feeding the baby the formula once during the night to give the wife a chance to catch up on her much needed sleep. In addition, he should attend to the babies needs occasionally during the day to give his wife a chance to get some rest. During this time, it is also recommended that the family reduce their social engagements to adapt to the new situation and concentrate more on helping each other take care of the tasks at hand. The family's priorities should also be reviewed and adjusted to fit the new situation. Another source of help would be to team up with other families and try to help each other in terms of reducing the burden on both families of certain chores such as shopping, etc. If one family can do the shopping for both

families once a week, doubtless this would reduce the amount of time spent on shopping per family. Teaming up with another family to help each other is also very useful later on when occasionally one family would leave the children with the other family for a day or so, while they finish other urgent business, go for an outing together, or spend some quality time as spouses without the interruption of the children's needs. Of course, both families must reciprocate the favors for this to work out.

At this stage, the stage of having children at a young age where they can't attend to their needs on their own, one common source of spousal friction and conflicts is going out as a family.

Here is a scenario that is, unfortunately, all too common in many households:

It was 6:38 pm and the clock seemed to be ticking faster than usual. Tick-Tock, Tick-Tock. I heard Ahmed call from downstairs, "*Arwa*, are you ready yet? We have to be out of here in 15 minutes, hurry up!" I thought I detected a hint of impatience in his voice. Ready! I was far from ready. I still had to dress the kids, dress myself, brush their hair, feed the baby, and then reload the baby bag with diapers and milk. I knew that unless some extraordinary miracle was to occur, there was no way that I could complete that large amount of work in that little amount of time. As if to top it all off (by it I'm referring to the stressful situation I was in) I suddenly heard the distinct wailing of my one and a half year old daughter, *Sama'a*. I ran over quickly, allowing her loud bellows to guide me, to investigate what was going on. I should have guessed it. The earsplitting bellows lead me straight to *Ashraf*'s room, my three year old son, who happens to be notorious for making his sister cry. I dashed into the room, the two of them seemed to be engaged in a pinching game together, and *Ashraf* was obviously winning this round.

"*Ahmed*," I yelled out, as I separated the two kids, comforted *Sama'a,* and simultaneously scolded *Ashraf*. "Can you come help

271

me? *Ashraf* still needs to be washed and dressed!" His loud sigh floated up to me from downstairs. As he walked up the stairs irritated, I heard him grumbling under his breath: "Great, we're going to be late yet again. Why can't you ever get the kids ready on time? And you're probably still in your pyjamas! Am I the only one that has any concept of time and punctuality in this house?"

And so it went, the story of our lives for several years was just that. *Ahmed* and I seemed to be late for every outing we've had since our kids were born and, getting the kids ready for an outing was often so exhausting that by the time we were finally ready to go I was in need of a nap. The clock ticked louder; the fifteen minutes passed. We were still nowhere close to ready.

Instead of going through this same episode every time the family is going out and ending up with bad feelings between the spouses that may strain their spousal relationship, families need to treat the situation differently. Here are some suggestions to help avoid or at least minimize such events as a source of conflict:

If you are going out to visit another family, and it is up to you to set the time, never promise the other family that you will be there by 6:30 sharp, for example. In a nice and humorous way, you can say, "You know that we have two little angels, and it takes time to get them ready, so expect us between six and seven *insha'a Allah*." As a husband, try to be part of the solution, not just to nag your wife all the time and complain that she didn't get ready on time. Try to help her be ready on time by doing the following:
- Dressing one of the children
- Trying to start early by reminding your spouse about your visit as early as possible to start preparing the children
- Trying to reduce other unimportant house chores for that day
- Putting a smile on your face and taking it easy. It is not the end of the world to arrive for a family visit a few minutes late. Don't spoil the outing for yourself and your children.

Remember the ingredients discussed in chapter four! It is here when you will need to use some of them, patience is definitely a great virtue in these situations, and your support is definitely needed.

The School Years

This is another stage of family life that has many joys, but at the same time, provides its share of pains. The joy of seeing your first child joining the kindergarten class of the neighborhood school and being excited to watch him board the school bus for the first time in his life; the joy of buying new school clothing for him/her; the joy of feeling that s/he is growing and moving from one stage to another; the joy of seeing him/her write his/her first letter of the alphabet, then write his/her first word; the joy of listening to him/her spelling that first word aloud; the joy of attending the first parent/teacher interview; the joy of going over the first report card; the joy of the first graduation party, where your child's eyes glow with light while s/he receives a medal or a certificate and your eyes fill with tears of happiness; these are the joys of this stage.

There is no doubt that parents enjoy plenty of happy moments and joyful times during their children's school years. However, there are also many challenges that they face and have to work hard to find solutions for, particularly for parents of children belonging to visible minority groups, and more so for Muslim parents. These challenges may be a source of pressure for the whole Muslim family. Indeed, those challenges could also strain the relationship between the spouses. One very common source of conflict between spouses in this stage is the amount of involvement of each spouse in the children's school activities and extra-curricular work. We have witnessed both extremes during our counseling sessions. On one hand, we have seen fathers who insist that their children's needs and upbringing are the mothers' responsibilities and don't help the mother at all, leaving her under tremendous pressure to take care of all the kids' needs, attend school activities, parent/teacher interviews, etc. On the other hand, we have also seen mothers who, because of lack of skills, can't help at all in this area and leave that responsibility entirely up to the father. He is the only contact with the school administration, he attends parent/teacher interviews, he buys the kids' school materials, etc. There is no doubt that both extremes are unacceptable in Islam. It is important to understand that the children's upbringing is a joint responsibility between both parents. This doesn't at all mean that the father has to spend the same amount of time with the child as the mother does. This can't be right, especially in the cases when the father is working full time during the day and the mother is a stay-at-home mom. It simply means that they both have to participate in the *tarbiyah* plan of their children and then divide the tasks accordingly. Both parents should have a clear vision for what they want for their children and try their best to achieve this vision through following the proper parenting methodology learned from the *Qur'an* and the teachings of Prophet Muhammad *SAAW*. See our book "Meeting the Challenge of Parenting in the West, An Islamic perspective." Following these techniques in dealing with the children, with their needs, and with their environments, will, without doubt, help in reducing the tension within the family and keeping the spousal relationship healthy and strong *insha'a Allah*.

The Teen Years
This is another stage of true struggle. When children grow up and become teenagers, there are many challenges for them and for their parents alike, particularly in the North American environment. On one hand, teens are going through tremendous change during their adolescent stage, physically, emotionally, psychologically, intellectually, and socially. On the other hand, they are heavily drawn to fitting in within the immediate popular teen culture. They place a very high importance on their peers' approval and acceptance. They don't want to feel different. However, at the same time, knowing the negative aspects of popular teen culture and their contradiction to Islamic values and ethics, parents are usually trying to protect their teens from falling completely into this trap. More often than not, parents don't use the proper *Tarbiyah* methodology to help their teens pass this stage safely. In addition to this, the absence of the fathers from the life of their

male teens is very common among Muslim families living in North America. These two factors, coupled, place an incredible amount of pressure on the family and could easily strain the marital relationship. Cooperation between both spouses and learning the proper Islamic techniques in dealing with this age group is key to the success of the *Tarbiyah* process.

To help spouses avoid the major problems of this stage that result from using ineffective and unproductive *tarbiyah* methods, it may be a good idea here to list the six signposts we presented in our book "Muslim Teens, Today's Worry, Tomorrow's Hope." Here they are:

- The early start
- Being an approachable friend to your teen
- A clear and common vision of *tarbiyah* between both parents,
- Active participation of both parents in the process of *tarbiyah*,
- Use of *Tarbiyah* methods that lead to a strong and confident personality for your teen.
- The elevation of your teen's level from Islamic knowledge to Islamic conviction[237]

To implement the above *tarbiyah* road map, spouses' cooperation and understanding is a must. They both have to work together and exercise a great deal of wisdom in implementing the aforementioned principles. Those who followed these techniques, *alhamdulellah* ended up with terrific results in terms of their teens' success in their life, and they also achieved their goals of building their teens' strong personalities. This success further enhanced the warm and healthy family atmosphere, and that had a great impact on reducing spousal conflicts and frictions and enhancing the marital bond. Success brings success and failure begets failure.

---

[237] Review the Muslim Teens book by the authors in detail for tips and techniques on how to parent teens successfully

Ingredients such as open mindedness, communication, sharing, respect, and patience are great assets during this stage. Spouses will no doubt need to use them regularly in dealing with their teens as well as in dealings among themselves. Also in this stage, spouses' cooperation in implementing the proper *Tarbiyah* methodology and supporting each other is highly decisive.

The Empty Nest: Children Leaving Home, Parents Left Alone

This is a very significant stage and could be very demanding on the marital relationship if spouses didn't invest properly into their relationship during the previous stages. At this stage, the children are grown up. They all now have a life of their own. They either are married and forming new families of their own, or have moved to other cities to pursue their careers. The nest is now empty. After years and years of a very busy life with their children, the two spouses are now on their own. They are once again alone together, with nobody else in their immediate life to take care of, to help, or to interact with. Now they have to communicate among themselves regularly and find comfort in their own relationship with nobody else around. That is why good communication skills and sharing become very helpful and important, particularly at these times. Wise spouses should never forget that one day they might be alone together with nobody around. As such, they have to prepare themselves for these times. They should never loose sight of this fact and should always make sure that their relationship at various stages of their marital life is contributing positively toward a more comfortable and pleasant time during the empty nest stage. This stage is particularly difficult and tough on spouses if it happens to coincide with the retirement of one or both of the spouses. After a very active and busy life, all of a sudden, they have lots of time on their hands and don't know what to do with this time.

Here is how a friend expressed her feelings regarding the empty nest; "I couldn't believe it when it happened. 27 years seemed to come to a sudden halt in one instant. The night of my youngest son's wedding, my husband and I went home alone. It was a strange feeling - something I hadn't felt in a very long time. There was a kind of emptiness associated with 2 people walking into a 4 bedroom house - 3 of which would never be permanently occupied again. I felt a tang of regret, how had I failed to see this coming? Why hadn't we prepared for this time of our life just as we'd prepared for any other? When we found out that we were expecting Mariam, our oldest daughter, we spent months planning her birth, buying her clothes, and setting up her bedroom. We researched the kid's schools long before they began attending, we planned for their junior high school, secondary school and college years, and, of course, we invested many months of preparation in their marriages. But this, we'd never prepared for this. I guess it just always seemed so far off in the distance. How many parents of 3 young children that you know of are occupied with preparing themselves for their empty nest years? If I remember correctly, all that was spinning around in my head at that time was how to potty train Mounir, how to help Adam get over his peculiar fear of soap and whether or not I should allow Mariam to join the school choir.

It's funny how humans have a way of losing sight of the bigger picture and getting all caught up in the nitty gritty details of the time. Or perhaps it's sad. Over the many busy years, my husband and I allowed everything to take priority over our marriage and now we would pay the price. It hurt to sit down at the kitchen table with him and scramble for something to talk about. I would often see him looking over to the stairs as if he expected one of the children to come running down and break the awkward silence. Even though a family goes through many transformations over the years, it starts with 2 and ends with 2, so invest in each other generously."

Here is some practical advice to ensure that *insha'a Allah* the marital bond in this stage will continue to be healthy, strong, and enjoyable for both spouses, and will not suffer any set backs:
- ◆ Communicate, communicate, and communicate with your spouse during various stages of your marital life. Sharpen

your communications skills and use them regularly together. Aspire always to be of the collaborative type of communicators. Your goal should be a shared understanding. The format you use would be one of consensus building. The tone of your voice should always be friendly, positive, and productive. Your attitude is to treat differences with respect and to minimize any sayings that may hurt your spouse.

♦ Share, share, and share. Share the bond with your spouse in almost everything during the various stages of life. Don't wait until you are in this stage to start thinking about sharing. Be proactive, anticipate the future, and invest in the present to ensure a warm, healthy, and wonderful relationship at a time when both of you are in real need of real, affectionate companionship.

♦ Ensure that you have your special time to spend with your spouse during other stages. Make sure you take vacations together and enjoy each other's companionship during this special time. Don't get caught up in attending to house chores and taking care of the children without having time to rejuvenate and revive your energy.

♦ Make sure you live a positive and active life style. Be part of your Muslim community activities and gatherings. Continue to be involved in educational study circles and religious lessons in your center. Be part of useful community projects together if possible.

♦ Make sure to travel together attending several Islamic national or regional conventions. Planning for these trips together and the experience of being with other Muslims in great numbers provide lots of fun and support.

Don't forget your self-purification. In addition to the regular activities described in Chapter 7, *Umrah* trips are a wonderful source of joy and spiritual uplifting.

11- Further Tips

♦ **Never go to bed with an unsettled argument; learn to have differences without letting them affect your relationship**

"الاختلاف في الرأي لا يفسد للود قضية"

♦ **Express opinions in a calm and polite way. Do not shout or yell.** Learn to keep your cool even at the most tense moments and learn to be kind to each other.

"وَلاَ تَنسَوُاْ الْفَضْلَ بَيْنَكُمْ"238

♦ **Don't idealize each other. Accept small mistakes as long as they don't form bad behavioral patterns**

"كل ابن آدم خطاء وخير الخطائين التوابون"239

♦ **Consider each other's feelings and satisfy each other's needs; never make jokes about your spouse or her/his family if these jokes are not appreciated.**

♦ **Respect each other's needs even when you don't understand them.** Try to fulfill them as long as they are not against Islamic injunctions.

♦ **Help each other be better people**
   o Get over needs and wishes that hold you down
   o Increase your knowledge and help each other practice what you learn
   o Get over bad habits such as negative expressions of anger, bad tempers, excessive eating, laziness, over-sensitivity, etc.

---

238 (Q2, 237)
239 At- Termezi and Al-Hakem

- **Appreciate each other; learn to express your appreciation to your spouse for almost everything s/he does.** For example . . .
  o This meal is so delicious, May Allah bless your hands
  o You look beautiful in this dress
  o This is neat on you
  o Your comment about having a positive outlook on life and not despairing from what is going on during yesterday's community meeting was very encouraging and had a great effect on the attendants and the general mood. *Alhamdulellah,* we achieved the purpose of the meeting, and we now have groups working together rather than just complaining. *Jazaka Allah Khairan.*

- **Learn to communicate your feelings to your spouse.** Let him/her know what you feel, whether it is feeling hurt or happy, but do it in a respectful and calm way with the proper intentions to avoid hurting your spouse, not with the goal of venting your anger and getting back at him/her.

- **Expect less; give more.**

- **Learn to forgive each other immediately.** Don't let any bad feelings pile up.

- **Although teasing has its place in the marital relationship, make sure you stop if it is not appreciated.** Never mock your spouse or ridicule her/his ideas.

- **A sense of humour is a wonderful asset.** Make sure to not only utilize it properly, but also respond to it in the best possible way when it is utilized by your spouse.

- **Don't complain about problems; try to find solutions.** Take steps, and then get your spouse involved.

♦ **Show courtesy toward each other, even in very little things. It does make a difference.**

♦ **Always think of the family as a WE business.** Forget about ME and YOU. Try to always work as a team. If you succeed, you will succeed together, and if you fail, the entire family will be affected. You will both be affected by any problems. I place this tip in the number one position because I have never seen it fail. Any couple who gains a "we" perspective eventually experiences great success in marriage. On the other hand, marriages start to shrivel when it becomes a matter of two "I's."

♦ **Things are always easier said than done.** The challenge is to really practice what you preach. You can only do this if you regularly engage in a process of self-search and soul cleansing.

♦ **Make sure that the subtle signals you are giving to your spouse don't contradict the verbal agreements and numerous discussions you have had together about various issues.** An area where this gap often occurs is between the theoretical understanding of the status of women in Islam by some husbands and the subtle signals they repeatedly give to their wives that indicate completely the opposite. For example,

   o A husband agrees during discussions with his wife on numerous occasions that it is very important for the wife to seek knowledge and increase her level of spirituality. Whenever the wife asks him to take care of the children, so she can attend the sisters' study circles or the *Imam's* sessions in the Mosque, the husband always finds an excuse, and she always ends up not attending these lessons and consequently not furthering her Islamic knowledge.

In this case, the subtle signal that the husband gives his wife is that he is not serious about her religious education, which completely contradicts what he tries to convince his wife that he believes and aims for most of the time.

o A husband regularly talks about the importance of women being part of the Islamic activities and out-reach programs within the community, but at the same time insists on requesting his wife to prepare fancy dishes that require lots of time to prepare and leave her exhausted at the end of the day. She can't fulfill any *Dawa* role with her neighbors or attend to any community needs because her time is being totally consumed in the preparation of her husband's dishes. The subtle signal given by the husband here is in complete disagreement with what he claims to believe in. Such behavior creates nothing but resentment, on the wife's part, and mistrust toward her husband.

A wife could also give her husband mixed messages, such as in the example below:

o A wife may tell her husband, during discussions, that she is happy with their financial situation and doesn't need more material possessions. However, she complains on the phone to her friends that she can not buy the new TV set she wants or go out with them for lunch at a their favorite restaurant. She does this often and seems very affected by this issue. This completely contradicts what she has told her husband in terms of how satisfied she is with their lifestyle.

♦ **Be willing to change any baseless habits you may have.** You have to take the first step.

"إِنَّ اللّهَ لاَ يُغَيِّرُ مَا بِقَوْمٍ حَتَّى يُغَيِّرُواْ مَا بِأَنْفُسِهِمْ"

"Surely Allah does not change the condition of a people until they change their own condition"[240]

♦ **Make sure you don't base your judgment or behavior on culture and traditions.** Always try to have Islamic values as your ultimate reference on every issue. Cultural values could be one of three categories. The first category is values agreeing with our Islamic values. These we have to treasure and use. The second category is neutral values. These we have to test with the new environment. If they are suitable, then we should use them. If they are not suitable, we should not insist on using them just because they are part of our culture. The third category is anti-Islamic values, and these we must be fully avoided.

♦ **Don't shy away from touchy topics.** In a marital relationship, everything should be discussed; nothing should be hidden. The trick is to discuss issues in the proper way with the proper attitude. Here are some suggestions to ensure successful discussions:
  o Select the right time for the discussion, a time that is suitable for both of you
  o Be objective in your discussion, and listen to what the other spouse says
  o Try to find the points of agreement rather than emphasizing the points that differ
  o Be calm and control your emotions
  o Never use foul language or unacceptable expressions that you may regret later
  o Be solution-oriented. Don't exaggerate previous conflict situations.
  o Always try to look to the future. Only look back at the past to avoid repeating its mistakes and to learn from previous experiences
  o Try to always limit the discussion so that it is between yourself and your spouse. Don't allow

---

[240] (Q13, V11)

others to interfere without your permission. If it is absolutely necessary to include another party, make sure that the input of this party is limited, is very specific to the issue being discussed, and is based on your invitation.

♦ **Turn up your listening sensitivity. In the midst of a conflict, there is absolutely nothing that improves the situation as dramatically as listening.** We understand that when you are fuming about some intense issue, the last thing you want to do is listen, but when you open yourself up to what your spouse is saying, resolution has begun. It works like magic. When you are listened to, you aren't nearly so eager to win at the other person's expense. To be listened to makes you want to listen.

♦ **Make a point of praising something about your spouse at least once a day.** It was said: "Pleasant words are like a honeycomb, sweet to the soul and health to the bones."

Arabic Terminology

In most Islamic books, there are Arabic terms that are frequently used throughout the books. These words seem to constitute basic vocabulary that needs to be available to the reader. In the following glossary of Arabic terms, we attempt to provide most of the terms used in this book with their definitions.

Glossary of Arabic Terms

Term	Definition
Ahadeeth	The collection of the sayings of Prophet Muhammad *SAAW*
Al Fawahish	Shameful deeds
Ansar	Supporters, usually refering to the Muslims of the city of *Madinah* who supported the prophet *SAAW*
Aqeedah	Islamic creed
Athkar	Plural of *Thikr,* which refers to the remembrance of Allah through words, meditation, and reflection
Da'wah	Call or mission. It usually refers to calling others to follow Allah's way.
Deen	A way of life. It is usually used for the religion of Islam.
Derham	An old currency used by Arabs made of silver or copper. It has a lesser value than a *Dinar.*
Dinar	An old valuable golden currency used by Arabs.
Dua'a	Supplication
Eid	The Muslim celebration after the month of Ramadan and/or during the pilgrimage

Fajr	Dawn. It usually applies to the first obligatory prayer of the day, whose time extends from dawn until sunrise.
Fetnah	Temptation
Fiqh	The ability to understand and derive rules and regulations from existing texts and evidence for practical Islamic applications and regulations related to the immediate environment
Gelbab	A loose, one-piece dress that cover the whole body
Golab Jamen	A famous sweet dish common in the Indian subcontinent
Hadeeth	Reports of the prophet's sayings, actions, and approval
Hadramout	A region along the south coast of the Arabian Peninsula
Halal	Allowed or permitted according to Islam
Halaqa	Circle. Usually refers to a study circle
Haram	Forbidden or prohibited according to Islam
Hijab	Muslim women's proper dress. It covers everything except the face and hands. It could take any form as long as it meets the requirements of being non-transparent and loose so it doesn't describe the body detail
Ihsan	The process of perfecting your deeds. According to the *hadeeth* of the prophet *SAAW*, it is to worship Allah as if you see Him, and if you don't see Him, He sees you.
Ihssun	To provide immunity. In the marriage context, it refers to the process of ensuring that people are protected through marriage from resorting to illicit means to fulfill their sexual desires
Insha'a Allah	God willing

Isha	The fifth Islamic prayer of the day. Usually it is an hour and a half after sunset, depending on the geographical location.
Istekhara	To seek advice from Allah via a specific prayer to guide you to make the right decision regarding any issue
Itekaf	Seclusion. Usually it refers to the act of staying in the mosque for a longer time than the time of the prayers with the purpose of worship. Although it can be done at any time, it is practiced more by Muslims during the month of *Ramadan.*
Jannah	Paradise
Kabab	A famous meat dish common in the Middle East
Khimar	A large, loose one-piece scarf that covers a lady's head as well as her shoulders and may reach down to her waist
Mawadah	One of the two most important foundations on which marriage in Islam is based. It emphasizes a deeper sense of love, wonderful communication, and kind treatment. The other elements is *Rahmah,* which implies kindness, compassion, and leniency.
Mo'ahadah	To enter into an agreement, to sign a contract, or to make a pledge.
Mo'aqabah	The process of punishing yourself for committing mistakes that should have been avoided
Mohasabah	The process of reviewing, assessing, and evaluating your deeds regularly to ensure that they are as close to Allah's orders as possible
Mojahadah	The process of striving hard to be your best in everything you do

Moraqabah	The process of observing your duties toward Allah and of feeling that He is with you at all times
Motaqeen	Those who observe their duties toward Allah
Nafl	Extra. Usually it refers to an extra act of worship over the obligatory and the *Sunnan* that a Muslim may volunteer to do on his own to get closer to Allah
Nawafel	Plural of *Nafl*
Niqab	Cover over the face of a lady.
Qawamah	A degree of responsibility and authority that Allah gave to men to take full care of women's maintenance and protection and to spend from their possessions on women. It implies no superiority or advantage before the law. The man's role of leadership in relation to his family does not mean that husbands hold a dictatorship over their wives. Although this degree of *Qawamah* gives men the authority to make the final decision in matters related to family, it also entrusts them with the responsibility to consult their wives and to provide protection and maintenance to the family in the best possible way.
Rahmah	Kindness, compassion, and leniency
Ramadan	The ninth month of the Islamic calendar. Muslim are supposed to fast from dawn to sunset during this month.
Sakan	A place of dwelling. In the marriage context, it implies the inclination of spouses to each other and the mutual comfort they should provide to each other on the physical as well as the emotional level

Salaf	The generation of the early Muslims who came after the generation of the companions of the prophet *SAAW* and the generation that followed them
Sana'a	A city in the southwest of the Arabian Peninsula, now the capital of Yemen.
Seerah	The biography of the life of Prophet Muhammad *SAAW*
Shaqae'q	Equivalent to each other
Shaytan	The devil
Sunnah	Way, teaching, or guidance. In the Islamic context, it always refers to the guidance provided by Prophet Muhammad *SAAW to Mulsims.*
Sunnan	Plural of *Sunnah*
Surat/Surah	*Qur'anic* chapter
Tafseer	The explanation or the interpretation of The *Qur'an*
Tarbiyah	The art of dealing with human nature with guidance and providing the right direction in order to better people
Tawaf	To go in circles around the *Ka'bah*
Tawfeeq	Success
Tazkeiah	The process of purification. Usually it is used for soul purification via extra acts of worship and remembrance of Allah
Tazkiatu Annafs	The process of the purification of the soul
Thikr	Remembering Allah and mentioning Him
Ummah	Community
Waleemah	The meal served to guests on the occasion of marriage. It is a *Sunnah* to slaughter a sheep or a lamb on such an occasion and use its meat to prepare food for the guests.
Zakah	The meaning of the word is growth. The religious terminology is "obligatory charity"

References

- U.S. Census Bureau < http://www.census.gov/>
- National Center for Health Statistics < http://www.cdc.gov/nchs/ >
- Americans for Divorce Reform < http://www.divorcereform.org/ >
- *Rudolf Dreikurs M.D.* The Challenge of Marriage. New York: Hawthorn Books, Inc.
- Centers for Disease Control and Prevention,
- Institute for Equality in Marriage,
- American Association for Single People,
- Ameristat,
- Public Agenda
- http://www.aacap.org/publications/factsfam/divorce.htm
- Statistical Records of Women Worldwide (L.Schmittroth, 2nd ed.[New York: Gale Research Inc. 1995])
- *Najma M. Adam.* "Supporting Battered Women" Islamic Horizons. March/April, 2003.
- *Dr. Neil Clark Warren.* "Work it out, the triumphant marriage" Focus on the Family. October, 1995.
- American Academy of Child and Adolescent Psychiatry publication on Children and divorce, 1998
- *Paul Szabo.* "The Child Poverty Solution" Report to Canadian House of Commons. March, 1999.
- *Dianna Hales.* "What no marriage can do without" Readers Digest. August, 1993.
- *H. M. Yousof.* The Selection of a Spouse in Islam. *Arabic.* Dar Al-E'tesam, 1979.
- *Dr. Jamal Badawi* Polygamy in Islamic Law.
- *M. A. Hamed.* How to please your wife. *Arabic. 2nd ed.* Dar Almanar Al-Hadeethah, 1991.
- *Dr. Yousof El Qaradawy.* Contemporary *FATWAS.*
- *Sh. Sayed Sabeq. Fiqhussunah.*

- *Suzan Heitler.* The Power of Two: Secrets to a Strong Loving Marriage. New Harbinger Publications Inc., 1997.
- *Muhammad al-Jibaly.* The Quest for Love and Mercy: Regulations for Marriage and Weddings in Islam. Al-Kitab & As-Sunnah Publishing.
- *Muhammad al-Jibaly.* The Fragile Vessels: Rights and Obligations Between the Spouses in Islam. Al-Kitab & As-Sunnah Publishing.
- *Muhammad al-Jibaly.* Closer than a Garment: Marital Intimacy According to the Pure *Sunnah.* Al-Kitab & As-Sunnah Publishing.
- *Ahmad H. Sakr Ph. D.* Matrimonial Education in Islam. Foundation for Islamic Knowledge.
- Institute of social research. Monitoring the future study. University of Michigan, 1998.
- The Canadian Press, October 23rd, 2002
- The Ottawa Citizen October 23rd, 2002
- http://www.archives.state.al.us/populate/usa.html
- *Al Qaradawy, Yusuf.* The Status of Women in Islam. Trans. *Mohammed Gemea'ah.* Cairo: Islamic Home Publishing & Distribution, 1997.
- *Dr. Ekram and Mohamed Rida Beshir.* Meeting the Challenge of Parenting in the West: An Islamic Perspective. *2nd edition.* Beltsville, Maryland: amana publications, 2000.
- *Dr Ekram and Mohamed Rida Beshir.* Muslim Teens, Today's Worry, Tomorrow's Hope. Beltsville, Maryland: amana publications, 2001
- *Badawi, Jamal.* Gender Equity in Islam: Basic Principles. Plainfield, Indiana: American Trust Publications, 1995.
- *Khattab, Huda.* The Muslim Woman's Hand Book. London: *Ta-Ha* Publishers, 1993.
- Lemu, B. *Aisha* and *Fatima* Heeran. Woman in Islam. Leicester, United Kingdom: The Islamic Foundation, 1978.
- *Nazlee, Sajda.* Feminism and Muslim Women. ed. *Huda Khattab.* London: *Ta-Ha* Publishers, 1996.

- *Sheriff, Sarah.* Women's Rights in Islam. 1989. London: Ta-Ha Publishers, 1996.
- *Hammudah Abd al 'Ati.* Islam in Focus. *3rd revised ed.* amana publications, 1998.
- Random House. The American College Dictionary. New York, 1964.